Me, Gorbacnev and the Tourists

The story of who *really* took down the Iron Curtain

PHIL CALDWELL

Published by Goldcrest Books International Ltd
www.goldcrestbooks.com
publish@goldcrestbooks.com

ISBN: 978-1-913719-65-4
eISBN: 978-1-913719-66-1

This book is dedicated to my three daughters, Laura, Mary-Jean and Rosie, in the hope that they may live in a world of friendship and peace; to my wonderful German teacher and mentor, Ken Wood, sadly no longer with us but never forgotten; to those millions worldwide who lost their jobs in the tourism industry in the pandemic of 2020 to 2022....

.... and to all those living in a state of oppression, with the sincere wish that they may soon see their basic rights and freedoms restored.

Outline map of the Iron Curtain countries in 1988,
showing places featured in the story.

Key: GDR = German Democratic Republic
✕✕✕ = Denotes the Iron Curtain, with Iron Curtain
countries to the right of this line

Maps not to scale.

Outline map showing route of Trans-Siberian Railway
and places featured in the story.

Contents

From Stettin in the Baltic to Trieste in the Adriatic,
an iron curtain has descended across the continent.

Winston Churchill, March 5th**, 1946**

PROLOGUE

September 2020

It's becoming something of a daily ritual. I take up position in front of the TV and spend the next couple of hours flitting between news channels, mainly the BBC and Al Jazeera, and occasionally Sky, despite its rather over-the-top, triumphalist jingle; and even more occasionally, Euronews. My mission is to find some news – any news – that isn't about lockdown, doesn't feature graphs showing infection rates careering inexorably upwards for the second time this year, and isn't about the impasse in the Brexit negotiations with Monsieur Barnier in Brussels.

This is proving to be difficult. With the greatest patriotic respect to the Beeb, I have to admit that Al Jazeera's reach on the geopolitical scale has edged them into pole position on the remote control, and I feel my knowledge of the world hitting new heights. The people of Chile are going to the polls to vote on a new constitution and the opposition candidate has won the general election in the Seychelles. These will be good conversation topics, in the unlikely event that I bump into anyone from either of these two countries in my quiet corner of suburban Leicester. An Asian giant hornet's nest has been successfully vacuumed out of a tree in the U.S., close to the Canadian border, and I conjecture whether Trump might look to pin that on China as he seeks fresh strategies to retain the top job in his country's brutal election.

This lingering before the telly is, in part, a procrastination tactic. Since my inbound travel business went into immediate meltdown after the UK and Europe pulled up the drawbridge and stopped what was shaping up to be the best ever season in its tracks, I've been trying to keep myself busy with a succession of projects: basic Bahasa on Duolingo; a TEFL course; bringing my inadequate culinary skills up a notch or two; and a serious overhaul of my sorely neglected garden. The highlight of this last project was dismantling a large, twelve-year-old compost heap and discovering that a family of rats had taken up residence there.

I know I should find the next big scheme but am suffering from a lack of motivation, and the light-bulb moments that got me through the last six months seem to have lost their filaments. Lethargy has set in.

It's Al Jazeera who comes to the rescue, and somewhere in the recesses of my stagnating mind a light bulb starts to flicker into life. Two situations, each playing out far from the other, evoke memories of two seismic events that took place in Europe in 1989, one of which I was present at.

'German Embassy'... 'Dictator heckled': could there be a story in this?

In the Thai capital and other cities across the country, the young have taken to the streets to demand the resignation of the prime minister and his government, and – quite incredibly given the historic veneration of the institution – reform of the monarchy. With the king spending most of his time in Germany, the protestors have gathered at the German Embassy in Bangkok and I'm reminded of when

I walked, thirty-one years earlier and in a different era, amongst people who were, in a sense, also protesting. They too were outside a German embassy, this time in Prague, sitting and lying on the pavements and roads. They were not standing defiantly like the Thai protesters but sheltering under makeshift tents with their meagre belongings, pinning all their hopes on a chance of freedom and of writing their own epoch-making chapter in the history books of Europe.

Away from Thailand and closer to home, the Al Jazeera newsfeed reports that 'Belarussian security forces use stun grenades and tear gas against anti-government protesters in Minsk', highlighting a further escalation in the stand-off between huge crowds – frequently consisting of women and the elderly – and the object of their anger, President Alexander Lukashenko and his black-clad, often violent security forces, following the president's claim to have won a landslide victory in the country's August 9th election.

In both countries, vast armies of the disgruntled voice their dissatisfaction with the status quo; vast, leaderless armies insistent on change, insistent on new, more open regimes and greater freedoms.

On August 17th Lukashenko gave a typically bullish speech at a tractor factory in Minsk. To his clear astonishment, the assembled workers heckled him.

Back in that different era, thirty-one years ago, that same expression of disbelief was captured by the cameras on the face of a president as the gathered onlookers, until so recently cowed by years of fear and oppression, vented their collective spleen at the diminutive dictator addressing them from a balcony in Bucharest. The Romanian revolution was underway.

Chapter One

A BOYHOOD GLIMPSE BEHIND THE CURTAIN

My love affair with the German language began in 1973 during an Easter school trip to the Bernese Oberland region of Switzerland. I was thirteen and, as I recall, it was the only overseas excursion the school undertook in my seven years there. It may well have been an experiment the school decided not to repeat after the inhabitants of the sleepy village of Wilderswil witnessed nightly snowball fights between us and a party of French combatants from a neighbouring hotel, noisy skirmishes which grew increasingly confrontational as the week wore on. Or it could have been because a significant number of the group were clearly more interested in a competition to see who could amass the most Feldschlösschen (and other brands) beer mats, through targeted under-age raiding of local hostelries, than they were in discovering what really happened to Sherlock Holmes and Moriarty at the nearby Reichenbach Falls. Whatever the cause, there were no further forays onto European soil, a decision which our parents – in the economically challenging seventies – almost certainly greeted with some relief.

By the time our overnight train from Calais pulled into Basel, I had learnt by heart all the phrases in the 'Useful Vocabulary' section of the handbook our teachers had prepared for our trip, and had taken to reciting them loudly in front of my fellow travellers. There was something satisfying in pronouncing the crisp, guttural sounds of a language which – possibly through far too much exposure to war films – almost demanded to be barked rather than enunciated in a normal voice. And one of our chaperones, Mr Norris, only added fuel to my fervour for this nascent skill by commenting that my German accent was near-perfect.

The seeds had been sown, but it would be eighteen more months before I was allowed to be formally exposed to the wonders of German grammar and syntax. French was *de rigeur* from first form on while German was deemed to be an altogether more demanding proposition, so was not introduced into the curriculum until fourth form. The common denominator was the teacher.

Mr Wood had taught us French in first form, so we had some idea of what to expect. As homesick eleven-year-olds coming to terms with the grim realities of boarding school life, our early misery was made that bit more profound by Mr Wood's classroom methods. His preferred intimidatory tactic was to ask some hapless pupil to answer a question he had posed and then, to encourage a correct response, place the sharp point of a mathematical compass on the boy's cranium. He then held our bulky hardback course book, *Parlez-vous français?*, an inch or so above the compass. Modern-day language teachers often advocate an icebreaker activity to begin the lesson. This was not so much an icebreaker as a potential skullbreaker. The sensation of the cold steel compass tip resting on the skull was usually enough to guarantee added focus on answering the question correctly. Mr Wood subscribed to the age-old teachers' mantra: 'start off by being a bastard, then ease off when you've got the bastards' respect'. The problem was that Mr Wood didn't get around to the 'easing off' part for several years, even though he had our unconditional respect from the first time the course book hovered menacingly over our terrified heads.

Despite – or possibly because of – his unconventional ways of extracting information from students, Mr Wood was a first-rate teacher. From the moment he walked into our first German lesson and sketched the outline of a male figure on the blackboard, sternly announcing '*Er ist der Vater*', the language used in his classes was German, and only German. Our stifled titters on hearing the word '*Vater*', in which the 'v' is pronounced like an 'f' and the 'a' like 'ar', were countered with the much-feared stony glare, pregnant with an implied threat of retribution. This was the first and last time we expressed anything resembling mirth at the pronunciation of words which would normally, on first hearing, arouse teenage hilarity.

Mr Wood was also a very accomplished sportsman and coach, excelling in tennis and fleet-footed as a winger on the football pitch. His athleticism was matched by his striking appearance: blond and with never a hair out of place, he had won the heart of my mother on my first day at Bootham School. She and I had hauled my impeccably packed trunk up to the back door of Junior House, where he checked in a procession of scared boys and their anxious mothers, already in a state of near grief at leaving their babies to whatever fate was destined for them. From that day on, right up to the present day, the name 'Mr Wood' causes my mother to raise a hand to her chest, inhale sharply and let her eyes drift upwards in an 'if only' expression. She claims to have gone weak at the knees in that first encounter, which probably helped her overcome those mounting feelings of grief.

In the summer of 1976, with two years of German under my belt and an enthusiasm for the language that was growing unabated, I found myself in Germany for the first time. It was the return leg of an exchange visit my mother had set up with an old friend of hers, Hilary Vogel. Hilary was married to a German called Arno (who worked as a ship's pilot) and lived with their three children, Alison, Carsten and Dirk, in the small town of Altenholz, a suburb of Kiel in the northern province of Schleswig-Holstein. Carsten had spent a couple of weeks at my home in Northumberland before the two of us travelled by train to Harwich via London and took the overnight ferry to Hamburg, where Hilary and Dirk met us and drove us to the family seat.

This was my second attempt at an exchange. The first attempt had happened the previous summer, when my family had hosted a German boy called Matthias, after making an arrangement with the school. The two weeks he spent with us were an unmitigated disaster: Matthias turned out to be a junior regional tennis champion and insisted on playing tennis with me from early morning for as long as daylight allowed, making his discontent known whenever I suggested we might pause for lunch, tea or simply to do something else. It didn't help that I never succeeded in recording more than two games in any set we played, and he frequently chastised me for my lack of competitiveness and, well, plain ability. His meteoric rise to local stardom had completely gone to his young head, and my family and I, ever keen to please and be good hosts, spent the fortnight in abject misery.

After Matthias returned to Germany we were stunned to receive a letter from his father, a headmaster, stating how enthusiastic his son had been about his stay and how much he and his family were looking forward to welcoming me into their home later in the summer. Fortunately, my parents didn't take much persuading to pen a suitably diplomatic letter containing a suitably plausible excuse as to why I was no longer available to travel to Germany that summer, and a painful rematch was thankfully avoided.

*

My debut day in West Germany had been July 24th and now, a week later on the 31st, I stood with Mr Wood on a platform at Lübeck station, waiting for the 9.23 train to Rostock. I was under strict instructions that, naturally, only German would be spoken between the two of us for the duration of our trip into East Germany. A couple of days earlier Mr Wood had written to me (in German, naturally) from his base in Steinfurt with his final orders:

Dear Philip!
I hope you are well and learning a lot! I can now give you the following information about our trip to the GDR.[1]
We'll go there on Saturday 31st, spend a night in Rostock and travel back to Lübeck on Sunday. We'll meet at Lübeck station, so look for me in the ticket hall. I will wait for you there, and will have purchased our tickets. Everything else I've got already.
Our train times are as follows:
Leave Lübeck 9.23
Arrive Rostock 11.44
And on Sunday:
Leave Rostock 9.25 or 16.12
Arrive Lübeck 11.53 or 18.55

---

1. *German Democratic Republic ('DDR' in German: 'Deutsche Demokratische Republik').*

We can either travel back early or late on Sunday,
depending on what works best for your host family.
Don't forget your passport!!
Till Saturday, best regards,
Ken Wood

Several factors had combined to bring us to this point; teacher and pupil standing together on a north German station platform, ready to board a train to an East German city neither of us had known anything about a few weeks earlier. Firstly, we both happened to be in West Germany at the same time, reasonably close to each other's locations. Secondly, there was the draw, the thrill, of a journey into the unknown, a first chance for both of us to see what life was like in the 'Soviet Bloc' and how this other half lived. And then there was the book: '*Sansibar oder der letzte Grund*' (Zanzibar or the Final Reason). Written in 1957 by the novelist Alfred Andersch and one of our A-level German text books, '*Sansibar*' is the story of a young boy, a Jewish girl, a ship's captain, a communist activist and a local priest who all, in their own different ways, resist Nazi oppression, some by attempting to flee pre-war Germany completely.

Their stories play out in the Baltic seaside town of Rerik, some forty or so kilometres west of the city of Rostock. Our mission was to go to Rerik and identify some of the landmarks mentioned in the book, not least the town's red towers and a pub called The Wismar Arms (*Die Wappen von Wismar*). The mission would be brief, as we had scheduled just one night in Rostock, with the return journey to Lübeck the following day.

My first visit to Germany was such a momentous occasion that I'd taken the fortunate decision to document my entire stay, even though I wasn't generally in the habit of keeping a diary. The narrative for July 31st and August 1st reads as follows:

Saturday 31st July

Had to get up at 6.30, and then was driven to Kiel station by Mrs Vogel, and my talking[2] seemed to be going quite well for that time of the morning – in fact, it was to be my best day of talk so far, especially when I was with Mr Wood, probably because most of the time there was only the two of us. At Lübeck I met Mr Wood and had to show my passport, the journey from Kiel lasting about an hour, and we awaited the arrival of the train to Rostock, which turned out to be very crowded, and eventually we squeezed into a compartment with four East Germans – two elderly women, an elderly man, married to one of the elderly women, and a middle-aged woman. I could understand them all (although the single old woman said nothing), except the jokes of the old man, as he had a bit of an accent.

German stations seem good, platforms side by side and one cannot really get confused, although the trains could be better. Anyhow, the East Germans were all very amiable and seemed happy enough, but they knew what to do at the frontier – not to smile or laugh when the soldiers were examining our papers. And that was interesting: at Herrnburg the soldiers boarded our train and stayed on until Bad Kleinen. And at the border, security was strict: the great wire fence, No-Man's Land, the towers, soldiers and binoculars, and the dogs in the cages. We were told that the dogs were released and allowed to run free under the train, without muzzles, and on our return journey we discovered this to be true, thus holding the train up for

---

2. *i.e. my talking in German*

forty-five minutes both times. They certainly believe in safety precautions.

We had to deal with three guards, and the first two were incredible – shouting everything in military style, they were so ignorant, and we got them confused. We had to sign and write out various documents, and one of the soldiers, fat with spots, gave me a suspicious look, as I declared that I had nothing really besides a passport to prove my identity. Their uniforms were superb, very smart, and although they appeared rather fearsome with their dogmatic disciplinarianism I had to smile, an unwise thing to do apparently – the soldiers never smiled or joked. Fortunately Mr Wood did all the talking, as was usually the case; as the East Germans said, his German was fabulous, although they thought at first we were Dutch.

We could also change money on the train, and we had visas stamped in our passports. We were not searched and things passed very smoothly and it was extremely interesting; on this trip I found the military side the most interesting aspect. During the two-hour journey to Rostock, we chatted with the people in the compartment about our reasons for visiting, about life in East Germany and about who we were – all very interesting. The East Germans are allowed thirty days out of the country per year, and seemed to be reasonably contented with the state of their lives, and seemed to be trying to defend it, but they kept no secrets about the efficiency of the soldiers.

The countryside was a great contrast to the West. The houses were mainly unpainted and some of the small country communities seemed to be very poor and ramshackle. The emphasis in the north was definitely on agriculture. Rostock was slightly special, however. After a very pleasantly spent two hours on the train, we pulled into a crowded Rostock station and decided that first we had to find our hotel. Rostock was most interesting, and a mixture of old and new. As at the border, there were signs advertising friendship with the USSR[3] everywhere – I eventually photographed one. Soldiers were all over the place, but what was interesting was the clothing of the citizens – very colourful and, in fashion, more advanced than West Germany and not unlike Britain, with bags, etc.

Everything was very clean, although there were a few youths hanging around, and this I had been told never happened. I must admit, however, that there were very few, but the place did seem to have a reasonably relaxed atmosphere about it. About one mile from the station, perhaps a bit less, we passed an orchestra playing 'Viva Espana' in a typical holiday atmosphere (for Rostock is a resort in many ways) and then entered our luxury hotel, a massive white building called the Hotel Warnow, quite near to the river. I took the lift to the top floor: room number 810 was my room, with a balcony, two beds with continental quilts, a telephone, radio (inoperative – broken wires), alarm clock (also inoperative), brochures, desks, chairs, bathroom with shower and bath, washbasin and a surplus of towels. The balcony commanded a view over South Rostock, a large city. I shuddered to think of the cost for my mother and father, as the hotel was pretty grandiose.

But perhaps not – the meals were cheap, as we found out when we had dinner in the restaurant, also very smart, but the prices were extraordinarily good, and for excellent food also, although the first course always failed to cover the plate and service was slightly slow. That evening we had to queue for half an hour outside for a table. The thing about

3. *Union of Soviet Socialist Republics.*

East Germany is that there are always queues, wherever one looks, perhaps because of the shortage of jobs – unemployment is not a word in the East German dictionary. Unfortunately, all the shops were closed during our stay as everything apart from usually expensive items like record players, etc, are very cheap, a lot cheaper than in the West, but then again the people are poorer.

After lunch we had a most confusing time, finding the times of buses and trains to Neubukow and Rerik, and being given false information all the time and also interviewing taxi drivers over prices and distances. We went back and forth from station to bus station, and eventually worked out that the only possibility was to get up at five-thirty the next morning and catch the 6.25 train to Neubukow. Then we returned to the hotel with a list of times, and as we were entering the hotel we noticed a 'Rent-A-Car' notice on the door, enquired, and that evening found out that our attempt had failed because we wanted to hire (and it was very cheap) on a Sunday, and the garage man was away on a Saturday, and thus could not clean the cars!! Despite pleas that this didn't matter, we failed.

After a rest in the lounge and looking at newspapers, we began a short tour of Rostock (our area) on foot with Mr Wood's recently bought map. Very attractive and, as cars are so expensive, the broad streets were quite empty of traffic; the cars are all the same, either Polish Fiats, Moskvitches and another type which I can't remember. The motorbikes are all Russian or East European. But the pedestrian precincts were very attractive and I took the odd photograph. We had a cup of coffee in the Ratshauskeller, very cheap again, but the coffee was full of beans which we had to let settle, and that after we had ordered bean-free coffee because they had told us there was no bean-coffee.

Anyway, we continued our tour and entered a church. The communists give no help to the churches but do not forbid them, and the one we visited was particularly magnificent with old gravestones on the floor. We also toured a poorer area of the city, but in general, the place was most appealing, with trams everywhere. We then returned to the hotel for supper – on this day I always had fish for my first course. Sunday lunch – I had meat. After queuing, we got in and ordered our usual beer, quite good really and not too strong. I often ordered two. Mr Wood had spent Friday night in Lübeck, and was going to spend Sunday night in Lübeck too. He was staying near Münster with the chief forester. Mr Vogel says it is always good to marry a forester's daughter. This forester had two sons only. And Mr Wood intended to continue writing his book with the aid of some other people.

In East Germany, we often found we had to change money, and we always found we needed more. I gave him fifty marks and told him to send the hotel bill, etc. to Mum and Dad. After supper, we had a short tour of Rostock by night, and we passed a discotheque playing English music. We discovered many interesting buildings, and the nice thing was it was perfectly safe to walk around the city by night. There was obviously a ship in port, as there were many sailors. Mr Wood told me much about the system of government in the country and life in general, all of which was very interesting. It would not, in fact, be hard for me to get a job, or live, in the DDR, as there is a labour shortage. The signs of friendship with Russia are virtually ignored by the people, although there is a story that when a man was tried for pulling the emergency brake in a tram, in defence he said that the tram was going too fast for him to be able to read the sign, and therefore he had to stop it!

After our walk, we decided we needed to have an early night, but the problem was how to wake up at 5.30. As the alarm clock was broken, and no one would answer when I telephoned service, I went down to reception and asked to be woken at 5.30 by telephone. On the way back I had some fun in the lift when it started to go downwards, but it eventually worked. I didn't sleep too well that night.

Sunday, 1st August

Woken by telephone, though I could not hear what was being said. The day appeared changeable and after Mr Wood and I had collected our 'packed breakfasts' we set off in pouring rain towards the station, and fortunately we saw a tram which was going towards the station and boarded it without paying, thus getting a free ride to the main station. There, we had a certain amount of trouble in finding which the correct train was and on which platform we should be. We eventually found places beside a very smartly dressed Russian soldier (short, thick neck, like many Russian men), and the train to Neubukow was surprisingly full, with many children obviously returning from camp in Rostock. Some people did indeed appear rather poor and peasant-like; a bit French-looking in their clothing.

The countryside was interesting, mainly corn fields and woods, and some towns appeared reasonably well-off but unpainted, all very rural. Our packed lunches were foul, and I ate the egg and banana before shoving the rest inside a Neubukow wastebin. The journey was an hour long, and just before Neubukow Mr Wood went to sleep and I had to wake him. At Neubukow we had to wait for a bus and hoped that we could also order a taxi to take us from Rerik back to Neubukow. This seemed unlikely in a place like Neubukow, but just after we had spied a taxi parking place a taxi came around the corner towards us and we booked it from Rerik for between 11.45 and 12.00.

Then we caught a very modern bus, quite out of place in these surroundings, and after about twenty minutes very suddenly came upon Rerik, to the surprise of both of us. In the coach we had tried to remember quotes from the book, and work out which route Gregor[4] had taken to Rerik – he obviously came over a hill – but everything was relatively flat here. 'Ostseebadort Rerik' (The Baltic Resort of Rerik) seemed quite modern in places, and there was a town plan and shop by the bus stop-cum-petrol station, which was closed. If something like this was closed, the East Germans could only wait until it opened the next day. Later, we discovered that the usual queues formed in Rerik: at the little shop, the children's cinema, and other shops. But we had at least three hours to explore Rerik, and we started by walking towards the great red church in the centre, with one great red tower, but other red towers were not in sight, nor, after exploration, was a 'Wappen von Wismar' or a harbour, only a small harbour ('Haff') for small sailing boats.

We walked around, speculated over where the centre of Rerik could be, and noticed that the peninsular just beyond Rerik was totally taken over by Russian troops and admittance to that zone was impossible. We could only look across to the houses of the Russian zone and reckon that the harbour and inn could perhaps have been in that area. We, in the course of the morning, spoke with some inhabitants of Rerik; a middle-aged lady was very helpful but did not know a lot about past history. She directed us to a priest and a museum but said there was another church, so later we looked around the area of Kirchestrasse (Church

---

4. *Gregor is the communist activist in the novel.*

Road) but found nothing. We also spoke with old men, whom Mr Wood reckoned would have had very hard lives: the Russians had come and robbed them. The priest, after morning service, was occupied busily with other people and the 'Heimatmuseum' (Local History Museum) was open only on Tuesdays! So the history of Rerik remained a secret.

By the time we left we were sure that everything had been invented by Andersch. Mr Wood doubted that he had ever been there. I thought perhaps that he had seen the one red tower of the church and taken it from there. It was true, there used to be a small harbour at Rerik, but now on the beach there were only baskets and a few enthusiastic bathers braving the indifferent weather. I was nevertheless quite warm, and the sea breeze was very soothing. We needed something to soothe our feelings of obvious disappointment. As we walked around this very attractive little town, groups of children were walking towards the Youth Band[5] building, and we also saw a party of Japanese. Mr Wood bought postcards, sausage with stale bread (the bread in East Germany is of a very low standard) and a bottle of Rostock-brewed lemonade.

I had photographed Russian tanks as they rolled through the streets of Rerik; perhaps rather an unwise thing to do, but the military side of the visit did fascinate me. On the way back, when we passed a convoy of Russian tanks in the taxi, the taxi driver made no comment about them, despite the fact that we had to carefully squeeze past them. He knew they were coming, however, as a taxi preceding them was waving a red flag. On the postcard map that Mr Wood bought, it only showed a man swimming in the Russian-occupied zone, with no mention of the existence of Russians

---

5. *Almost certainly a reference to the 'Jugendverband', the only official youth association in the GDR.*

on the peninsula. I photographed here and there, across the 'Haff' to the Russian zone, for example.

The people in these parts pronounce Rerik with an accent on the 'e' – very Scottish, and in fact the accent in general has a rather Scottish tone about it. After our tour, which I have described briefly (anything accidentally omitted shall be included later), we rested as we were tired. The taxi driver arrived – a cheerful, simple sort of fellow, large with a slow, quite deep voice, but very pleasant, and another person who thought that we were Dutch. The journey cost 17m 80 pf for almost twelve kilometres. He had heard of places in England, such as Bradford, which Mr Wood was able to tell him about, and there was also a discussion about beer, although I said nothing for the whole journey. My German was not as good today as my peak day yesterday, and I had a headache from about one o'clock onwards.

In Neubukow, also with its signs advertising Russian friendship, as had Rerik, we boarded the train on platform one; there were two platforms, but it only looked like one. On the train journey back Mr Wood was obviously sleepy, and when we reached Rostock we walked once more to the hotel and immediately got a table for a hard-earned dinner. After dinner, we relaxed for a while and then made our way to the station, but before that something very interesting happened.

As I left the hotel I put my bag down outside the hotel and walked straight across the road, tramlines and all, and stepped over two (I think) small walls partitioning the road. Then I photographed part of the massive building[6] and walked back exactly the same way. I had a very, very slight suspicion that this was not quite the done thing, but

6. *i.e. our hotel.*

it was only when I had crossed back and saw a policeman in grey uniform walking towards me and trying to attract my attention that I knew I had done something wrong – and I realised exactly what. I'd been jaywalking, and hadn't used a pedestrian crossing. But there was absolutely no traffic and the nearest pedestrian crossing was miles away!

The policeman greeted me, introduced himself, and asked me what I thought I was doing. I told him I was English and thought it was time to call Mr Wood who – I explained on the way over to him – was my German teacher. As I said I didn't understand very well, he asked Mr Wood to repeat to me in English what he had slowly said in German about which rules I had broken, and Mr Wood began to tell me in English what I had done wrong, but I stopped him because I had understood everything.

I was positive he had asked me for one mark, and a few moments later when he asked for three marks, I told him he had said one mark, which he denied. Mr Wood therefore handed over the three marks which the policeman eagerly accepted, and then he wrote me out a ticket, a 'Verwarnung',[7] which I took, knowing it would be the best souvenir of this trip to East Germany. Tonight, as I write this (Wednesday), Mr Vogel has returned from a night piloting expedition on an East German ship, 'The Rerik'!, and on this journey the ship captain apologised most humbly for the policeman and what he had done. He said he had probably done it because he thought I was a 'Saxon' (!).[8]

But it was a bit of drama as we took leave of the city of Rostock, the architecture of which we had been most impressed with. But we still had some East German money which we thought we could not change back on the train and

---

7. *A caution.*
8. *A reference to regional rivalries!*

hence bought some huge mugs of not very pleasant-tasting coke before going to the station and boarding the train. We eventually found ourselves alone in a compartment meant only for women and small children, after a party of Dutch had left. Mr Wood had bought a few East German books to use up money and also had a book which he had bought in Lübeck but kept dropping off to sleep as we steamed on towards more excitement at Bad Kleinen, where the soldiers boarded and stayed on to Herrnburg, at the frontier.

One soldier entered and checked our passports – it was a very lenient examination. We were very surprised when another very stern, youngish soldier, tall with glasses, came in and demanded to see our passports again, which we told him had already been examined. But apparently, we had not filled in something the day before that we should have, so more forms to fill in, and then he asked us if we had anything to declare, before he began his cross-examination – about Mr Wood's profession, mission in East Germany, life in general, about the book he had bought in Kiel, where and why he had bought it, and various other things, as well as asking us what 'wir sitzen zusammen'[9] was in English.

It was a proper cross-examination, a rather tense one, but always amusing as there was perhaps a funny side to it, particularly if one is perfectly innocent. We were glad he saw our 'Sansibar' books.[10] He even looked under the seats. Some of the soldiers I recognised from last time. We also found out that one could, after all, change money on the train, but as Mr Wood only had a few pfennigs left, it was not really worth it.

At the frontier, there was a delay as the dog did its

---

9. *We are sitting together.*
10. *because, being anti-fascist, the novel would have been approved of in the GDR.*

job,[11] and the soldier almost lost it under the train, and we watched a soldier with binoculars march up and down on top of the bridge. Then once again over the formidable frontier into the West, leaving the Iron Curtain behind, one could immediately see the difference in housing. We had ten minutes at Lübeck to find my platform – Lübeck from the train certainly appeared impressive – but my train was late anyway. I took leave of Mr Wood, boarded the train and left for Kiel, and did nothing in the hour-long journey.

At Kiel station, I was met by Carsten and immediately started telling him and the family everything. I still had a headache when I returned to the house, partially relieved, but Mr Vogel saw it as a chance to celebrate and I had three scotch and lemonades. He kept saying that I almost ended up in prison, and the atmosphere was very jovial that evening. I told them all about my experiences, although my German had already begun to crack up a bit with tiredness. Still, it had been a fantastic weekend and a great experience. I went straight to sleep and slept uninterrupted until after ten o'clock the next morning.

––––––––––

That morning, after my long, recuperatory sleep – no doubt made more profound by Mr Vogel's generosity in his role as host – I awoke to a large envelope from home containing the usual newsy letter from Mum, a relatively rare and shorter epistle from Dad, some even rarer scribblings from my brother Mike, and a wad of newspaper cuttings from the sports pages of the *Daily Telegraph*. Dad's letter enthusiastically described England's dramatic comeback against the West Indies in the Fourth Test at Headingley, as too did the newspaper cuttings, with both recording that despite a spirited batting display

––––––––––

11. *i.e. searching under the train for possible escapees.*

by Tony Greig, England had fallen short by fifty-five runs after a second innings, lower order collapse. These were the days of Steele, Willey, Greig, Woolmer, Underwood and Knott, of Bob Willis's unaesthetic yet highly effective run-up and, for the West Indies, the mesmerising pace of Roberts, Holding, Daniel and Holder. And no helmets then, just guile, lightning-quick reflexes and sheer guts.

As I grew up, away from home, this had become a tradition, and my excitement at receiving news from my northeastern homeland was heightened all the more on finding *The Journal*'s verdict on the Magpies' latest showing (or the stats from my birth county Somerset's performances in the County Championship or Sunday League) neatly folded and inserted between the pages of Mum's weekly letter. This morning's letter was no exception but, judging by the good luck wishes and exhortations not to take my camera into the GDR, was intended to arrive before I embarked on my journey east. This delay may in fact have been a good thing as, amongst the *Telegraph*'s clippings on England's narrow defeat, Mum had rather unhelpfully included a more sinister media report:

BORDER GUARDS SHOOT TOURIST

A West German tourist, shot by East German border guards when he crossed into Communist territory, is recovering in hospital, a Bonn government spokesman said yesterday.

The condition of Herr Willi Bubbers, 49, was given by an East German foreign ministry official when Bonn's envoy to East Berlin protested over the incident. Herr Bubbers, from Hamburg, was on a camping holiday and was shot several times after entering East German territory.

Chapter Two

BACK IN THE GDR

On July 13th, 1981, the front page headlines in the *Neues Deutschland*[12] newspaper, with its rousing slogan 'Proletariats of all nations, unite!', are of nationwide, round-the-clock efforts to bring in a boom harvest. These are supplemented by regional progress updates and news on the 'forces of peace' in cities such as Munich and Lisbon protesting against NATO's nuclear ambitions. The paper, proclaiming itself to be the mouthpiece of the ruling German Socialist Unity Party, features photos of grain mountains and cheerful farmers top left, easily catching the eye of would-be readers ready to cough up fifteen pfennigs for the privilege of accessing its content.

Contributions in the inside pages include statements on:

- how the national policy of equal rights for all has led to a highly educated female population;

- celebrations in the Mongolian capital Ulan Bator on that country's sixtieth anniversary of its People's Revolution;

---

12. *New Germany.*

- how the collaboration between workers and
farmers in cooperatives around a town called
Wurzen is boosting both the GDR economy and
the farmers' own standard of living.

The sports reports start on the penultimate page of the
paper, page seven, and lead on how, back home, Birmingham
is witnessing the supremacy of GDR heptathletes in an
athletics meeting being held in the city.

Sitting in the Club Room on the fourteenth floor of House 7
at the 'Dr Theodor Neubauer' teacher training college in the
East German city of Erfurt, and taking time out between
classes, I am absorbing word of these triumphs and jotting
down useful vocabulary I come across in the articles. I've been
trying to stick to a promise I made to myself some years earlier
to learn at least ten new words or phrases each day I spend in
the German-speaking world. My green 'Vokabelheft' exercise
book is one of my most important possessions. It now bulges
with lists added under the alphabetical headings for A, B, E
and V, as my capacity to learn the number of words starting
with those letters had outstripped the space I had originally
allocated for them in the little green book – and because such
a high proportion of German words start with those letters.

I was ten days into a summer school course entitled
'Social Life in the GDR', having some months previously had
my straw drawn by the British Council when they selected
which fortunate applicants had been successful in their bid
to experience life on the other side of Europe's East–West
divide. This was after my University, Leeds, had sanctioned
my request for a short, sharp immersion overseas instead of
the usual full gap year that language students were supposed
to take. Such self-inflicted abstention from boozy nights
abroad and free grant money probably seemed odd to those
hell-bent on extending their student days for as long as

possible. Some invisible inner force was intent on propelling me into the big, wide world as quickly as possible, however, and because I'd spent a full year working in Germany after school, and would be spending three months earlier that summer in Italy to satisfy the Italian side of my language degree course, I was granted an exemption.

As well as the ongoing objective of amassing as many useful words and idioms as possible in the green book, this was a golden opportunity to scratch well below the surface of the country I had first discovered five years earlier. There was nagging trepidation, memories of border protocols and unscrupulous policemen, and the Cold War – while not at the heights it had reached in the sixties – was showing no signs of an imminent truce. The antipathy for the capitalist, imperialist West, alongside the ever-present, enduring veneration of the Soviet Union, was clear enough from the pages of *Neues Deutschland.* But personal, unbiased judgements had to be made, and new insights were needed into why this state of affairs persisted; after all, not everything I had seen in Rostock and Rerik had been bad, or shocking. On the contrary, we'd mostly been met with warmth and encountered people we were able to converse with easily (Mr Wood more so than me). We'd also been surprised to find higher than expected living standards.

The first ten days in Erfurt had been hard going, but revelatory. The course content was delivered in two-hour blocks and included Saturday morning sessions, so fatigue set in early amongst some participants, in part because evening activities almost always took place, or culminated, in the bar in the Club Room on the fourteenth floor. The lectures themselves covered a wide spectrum of topics, but were rather too weighted in favour of extolling the virtues of the GDR's education system, unsurprising given our location in a teacher training college. Topics included socialist ideas on talent, the theory behind collectives, a brief history of the post-war years, the significance of art and folk traditions and festivals, and the welfare system. There were normally opportunities to pose questions to the lecturer at the end of each session, but with little or no scope for whole class debate.

As the days and lectures came and went, we started to get a picture of the fundamental principles upon which the nation had been founded thirty-two years earlier, on October 7th, 1949, and how the Marxist–Leninist vision of a worker-owned state had been implemented in the ensuing decades. As part of the Soviet area of occupation in Europe after 1945, East Germany had taken Germany's crushing defeat in World War Two (referred to in the GDR as the 'Day of Freedom from Fascism') as a cue to restructure and develop its economy and society along lines espoused by, and practised in, the Soviet Union. The key emphasis was on the contribution of each member of society towards the overall good of the nation, as opposed to pursuing self-enrichment. In return, the state would guarantee work, health care, a good education, and protection of individual rights. Foreign policy was directly aligned with the Soviet Union's and geared to forging ever closer ties with socialist and sympathetic governments across the world. Capitalism and imperialism were rejected, with history books highlighting the ruinous failures of these 'immoral creeds', while lauding the victories of popular struggles against oppression.

*

At this point, a few paragraphs from the GDR's constitution might help to give a very broad-stroke delineation of what the nation professed to stand for:

Article 1, paragraph 1: The German Democratic Republic is a socialist state of workers and farmers. It is the political organisation of working people in city and countryside under the leadership of the working class and its Marxist–Leninist party.

Article 2, paragraph 1: All political power in the GDR is exercised by the workers in city and countryside. All the efforts of the socialist society and its state have the human being as their main focus. The most important task of the developed socialist society is the continued raising of the material and cultural living standards of the people, based on the rapid speed in the development of socialist production, an increase in efficiency, in scientific-technical progress and in the growth of productivity.

Article 4: All power serves the well-being of the people. It ensures a peaceful life, protects the socialist society and guarantees the socialist way of life and the free development of its citizens, protects their dignity and guarantees the rights enshrined in this Constitution.

Article 5, paragraph 1: The citizens of the GDR exercise their political power through democratically elected people's representatives.

Article 6, paragraph 1: In keeping with the interests of its people and international obligations, the GDR has eradicated German militarism and nazism on its territory. Its foreign policy pursues socialism and peace, and security and understanding between peoples.

Article 6, paragraph 2: The GDR is allied eternally and irrevocably to the Soviet Union. This close, fraternal alliance guarantees the people of the GDR further advancement along the path of socialism and peace. The GDR is an inseparable part of the community of socialist nations. True to the principles of socialist internationalism, it contributes to its strength, nurtures and develops friendship, mutual cooperation with and support of all nations in the socialist community.

Article 6, paragraph 4: The GDR supports security and cooperation in Europe, global peace stability and general disarmament.

Article 9, paragraph 1: The economy of the GDR is based on socialist ownership of the means of production. It is developed in accordance with the economic laws of socialism, based on socialist conditions of production and the determination to realise and achieve socialist economic integration.

Article 9, paragraph 2: The economy of the GDR serves to strengthen the socialist order, to continually improve the material and cultural needs of its citizens, the development of their personalities and their socialist societal relationships.

Article 9, paragraph 3: In the GDR, the principle of a directed, planned economy, and all other areas of society holds sway. The economy of the GDR is a socialist planned economy. The central state leadership and planning of fundamental matters of societal development are linked to the individual responsibility of local organs of government and workplaces, as well as to the initiatives of the workers.

Article 21, paragraph 1: Every citizen of the GDR has the right to take part in comprehensively shaping the political, economic, social and cultural life of the socialist community and the socialist state. The fundamental principle is: 'Work together, plan together, govern together!'

Article 27, paragraph 1: Every citizen of the GDR has the right to voice his opinion on the principles of this Constitution freely and publicly. This right cannot be diminished by any relationships within service or the workplace. No one shall be disadvantaged if he exerts this right.

Article 27, paragraph 2: Freedom of the press, of radio and of television is guaranteed.

Article 30, paragraph 1: The personality and freedom of every citizen of the GDR are inviolable rights.

Although these, and the ensuing articles, right up to the final proclamation in Article 106, might seem fairly turgid stuff, for any left-leaning course participant in Erfurt that July they were the foundations of the utopia they had come to see. And the lecturers – some irrepressibly dull, others engaging and occasionally witty – generally did a solid job of erecting attractive edifices on those foundations. Their audience was drawn, though not intentionally, from across the political spectrum, and we heard a few days into our stay that the local media had run a piece, just before our arrival, on how each of us had been handpicked by our national communist parties to be immersed in how it was really done in a proper socialist state.

*

In an international group consisting mainly of Brits, Norwegians, Finns, Italians and French, it was the French contingent that furnished the most vociferous support for the system. One afternoon, I sat on the train opposite a married couple, Jean-Pierre and Francine, returning from one of our many trips into Erfurt's pleasant surroundings. With the very genuine intention from my first day to keep an open mind, I let them both ooze conviction about the supremacy of this brand of society over any other they had encountered:

'The country was born in terrible conditions! Do we ever stop to think that the economic disparity between East and West Germany is entirely logical? West Germany had the support of the Americans to rebuild after the war. The East had to pay reparations too, but only had the Soviets, in a similarly bad way after the appalling destruction there, to help them out. So is it any wonder that the bond between the two countries is so strong? In 1958 the people of the GDR were still dependent on ration cards, while their neighbours in the West were well on the way to recovery! And where in the western world does a government grant its people completely free health care and a guaranteed job after a guaranteed programme of training?'

Such were the compelling arguments of an emotional Jean-Pierre and Francine, and even if I *had* been interested in adopting a contrary position in order to offer some good honest polemic, and to give the French a bloody nose, it was difficult to deny that these specific cornerstones of the system did have a certain appeal. It was an appeal that had particular relevance to me given I would soon be joining the ranks of 'the great unwashed' leaving university, and trying to make some practical and, better still, commercial use of a Modern Languages degree. And on just one aspect of the welfare offering, it was a long time before western societies came to entertain the idea of the one-year maternity break that East Germany was already giving its new mothers in 1981.

In education too, the notions that everyone had access to exactly the same system, irrespective of family means; that young people were taught – as the most fundamental principle – that the interests of the individual went hand in hand with those of society; and that there was little point in groups falling out with each other when they all shared the same common goal of strengthening society ... these were all highly seductive concepts. Equally seductive was the idea that the better trained you were in a variety of disciplines, the more likely you were to be able to render a meaningful contribution. Every child was given a place at Kindergarten. At school you were set to learn a lot of useful life skills, what we might today call 'portable'. The catch was that in a geographical sense, you were not able to carry your skills as far as you might wish.

Marx held that the development of the individual was closely aligned to the development of the forces of production; everyone had to learn how to operate the machines used in industrial or agricultural processes. Hence, and unlike in the West, work placements and exposure to work practices were lengthy affairs, and schools often joined up with nearby factories to provide this all-important, hands-on training.

In the early eighties, the GDR was working towards the transition from socialism to communism, from a system in which each got his slice according to his contribution and capabilities to a system in which the slice distributed was based on need. It was out with any form of individual ownership and in with the collective effort, all with increasing top-down control to make this happen. It was a system in which any residual class differences would be eradicated: equality of income and equality of outcome. In a sense, justifying the adoption of a socialist model, growing out of the ruins of Berlin and Dresden, and testament to the failure of the imperialist state, had been the easy bit. Elevating selected historical events to support the cause, and using these to implant core principles in young minds, had not been too taxing either. But even our lecturers were aware that the next steps would be an altogether different proposition. However, the 10th Congress of the ruling SED party in mid-April that year, acclaiming the virtues of the education system, had set the next Five-Year Plan in motion and everything would, they were sure, turn out well.

*

That day, when my Gallic colleagues were in full flow as the train chugged through the peaceful, bucolic landscape around Erfurt, we'd been to a Pioneer Summer Camp at Wilhelmstal to witness how the GDR kept its children entertained during the summer holidays. It was an uplifting occasion, full of warmth and fun, with fears of a display of forced joy and happiness quickly allayed. The children, aged between around eight and thirteen, lined up to sing us in, neatly and proudly decked out in their gleaming white shirts and blouses, navy blue skirts and trousers, and red or light blue neckerchiefs. Some of the girls in more responsible positions, wearing dark blue blouses and grey or black skirts, showed us around the camp and introduced us to the other children busily going about their activities.

I found it hard to remember when I had last been among such a pleasant, well-behaved, respectful and genuinely engaged group of children. We talked together, laughed and shared stories about young life in our countries, completely unconstrained as we delved into all corners of the camp.

They sang, danced, played games and drew pictures for us, some of which I kept and still have as mementoes of the day. I spent a wonderful half hour or so chatting to one of the girls, maybe around ten years old, about life at home and at camp, and about pop music. I hadn't heard of any of the artists she mentioned, and when I told her I liked to listen to Genesis, not expecting it would mean anything to her, she replied that she knew of the band but didn't like them because they came from a capitalist country.

She filled a sheet of A1 paper with drawings of flowers, trees, clouds, children playing with a ball, a skateboard and two tents. In one tent, named 'W Pieck',[13] sat a girl with a brown bob haircut and shoes removed, with these placed in orderly fashion next to the tent. In the other tent, the 'Karl Marx' tent, a pair of feet and legs protruded from under the canvas. Next to the tent was a red signboard, emblazoned with flowers and leaves, with the words 'Practise Solidarity!' at its top in bold capitals. A clothesline was suspended between the apexes of the two tents, with a yellow T-shirt hanging from it and bearing the single word 'Football'.

*

Back in the Club Room on the fourteenth floor of House 7, 32 Peoples' Friendship Street, we enjoyed our usual nightly intake of the local brew with our 'cultural chaperones' Jürgen, Christina, Kerstin and friends, and agreed that our trip to the Pioneer Camp had been time well spent and one of the highlights of our immersion so far. The course was peppered with afternoon outings to a variety of fascinating places and sites, any one of which, for their historic interest or architectural beauty alone, would have been well worth

---

13. *Wilhelm Pieck, president of the GDR from 1949 to 1960.*

dedicating a few hours of our time to. Crucially for our hosts, these outings also bolstered the course narrative. But we knew and accepted that that was part of the deal, that we were there to drink in the entirety of what was laid out before us. For us, it was a major bonus that we had an opportunity to access places which we had learnt about in our various studies back home, but would probably have never been able to visit under normal circumstances.

Having done history A-level, and spent long hours writing essays on Martin Luther's extraordinary audacity in kick-starting the Protestant Reformation in Europe, I felt it was something of a pilgrimage when we made our way up to the Wartburg, the castle where the great man had hidden in 1521 when a warrant for his arrest was issued. This was after the Diet of Worms, at which Luther had refused to recant his views on the Catholic Church, its doctrines and, as he alleged, its abuses. With no mention of the seismic consequences for religion and the political structure of Europe that Luther unleashed, the furthest our brochure on the 'Wartburg Town of Eisenach' went towards acknowledging his presence there was to state the following: 'Martin Luther lived for some time at the Castle, where he translated the New Testament and in doing so contributed decisively to establishing the German language as it is spoken and written today.' It did not matter, as I had seen the place which had played such a prominent role in the upheavals in religion and politics in that century and beyond, a place which had featured in my assignments on the Church's selling of indulgences and Luther's Doctrine of Justification. With the latter promoting the idea that faith in God, not good deeds, was the key to salvation, it is understandable that the GDR authorities were keen to keep the bulk of Luther's work and his achievements under wraps.

While sympathising with many of their grievances, Luther railed against the peasants and Thomas Müntzer, leader of the 1525 revolt centred on the town of Mühlhausen, and condemned the widespread burning of religious houses and attacks on the nobility. The revolt was crushed, Müntzer was executed, and the heroics of the peasants were expounded in a sixty-page booklet given to us before we wandered through the town's ancient, cobbled streets. One of the delights of discovering the small towns and villages of Thuringia was the sensation of stepping back in time and witnessing the Germany of old, a peaceful, time-warped Germany of half-timbered dwellings with fractured, little, or no plaster at all on their walls, in stark contrast to the prim and manicured homes across the border in their pastels, yellows, blues and pinks.

Our lecturers, always keen to be seen as offering some semblance of balance, gave the lack of investment in restoring old buildings a black mark, albeit a fairly insignificant and thoroughly understandable one when set against the remarkable achievements of the nation. With the essential requirement to move further away from individual ownership to the panacea of collectivisation, who could rationally expect it to be otherwise? Another admission was that the history books skipped from 1525 to the French Revolution and then to the 1848 year of uprisings in Europe, and that filling in the gaps was proving problematic. Such a selective approach was presumably made more logical by the fact that there were only so many notable popular revolts during that period, against a backdrop of imperialism on a massive scale. In order to avoid a curriculum almost entirely dominated by a systematic dismantling of all that imperialism, which might have raised even young eyebrows, it therefore made sense to focus on events in the recent past rather than on the older stuff. And so that is what happened.

*

Setting aside the battle of Collectivisation versus Private
Ownership, we just felt privileged to be able to experience
this relatively untouched Germany, and to visit towns such
as Weimar where Goethe – who was eating into quite a
chunk of my university time – had spent most of his life.
We went on rambles through the quiet glades and seemingly
forgotten hamlets of the Thüringer Forest, along roads
blissfully undisturbed by traffic, save for the odd tractor
from a bygone age, to Friedrichroda and the Georgental, the
eerie Dragon Gorge and through Gotha's mediaeval streets.

We wound down one evening to the strains of Liszt and
Bach in the ornate palace of Schloss Molsdorf, a far cry
from the sighs of ghosts at what remained of Buchenwald
concentration camp. We were warmly welcomed into
kindergartens; at factories training the next crop of raw,
eager recruits; at collective farms to meet farmers all working
towards their common goal; and to a workers' hospital, clean
as a new pin, with all the latest medical technology – and
without a patient in sight.

On other evenings we were taken to the cinema (where
we watched 'Levin's Mill', a film highlighting the moral
unacceptability of anti-semitism), or to a local theatre, or
treated to a slideshow in preparation for the following day's
excursion. We had to make our own entertainment too
and, as I pointed out in my summary report to the British
Council, in the hope of preparing future participants far
better than I had been, each of us was expected to sing a
typical song from his or her homeland during our soirées
in the Club Room. With our chaperones mindful of the fact
that the word 'cultural' was very prominent in their job
descriptions, as was promoting international friendship,
they egged us on to humiliate ourselves in front of our new-
found friends. Bob, one of the few other Brits, and I were

sufficiently distressed by the prospect that we adopted a 'safety in numbers' mentality and regularly joined forces to belt out 'We all live in a yellow submarine' and 'On Ilkley Moor bar tat', and hoped that we had served our nation well.

Bonds grew with the chaperones, the Club Room evenings became increasingly relaxed, and boundaries were gradually tested and pushed. We were aware of the constraints the chaperones were under, but as time passed these were overridden by common threads which grew into strings, and then ropes: we were all students, and we were all on the cusp of experiencing the realities and demands of the adult world in our own societies. Jürgen was a DJ and managed to get his hands on and bring our kind of music up to the Club Room, where we drank and danced together long into the nights.

Trust and confidence in each other became so strong that a sort of mock, yet good-humoured, scrutiny developed. Not a lecture passed without our tutors referring to the 'allseitig entwickelte Persönlichkeit', the culmination of all institutional and societal strivings. The concept roughly translates to 'the fully rounded and developed personality', in other words, a person who can offer the maximum to society through possessing a broad range of moral, ethical, ideological and technological attributes. The phrase was so overused in class as to become the object of near ridicule, and we condemned any behavioural aberrations on the part of Jürgen and his helpers as evidence of their definitely not cutting the mustard and straying from the path.

One early frequent visitor to the fourteenth floor, who had clearly never been on the path from the start, was a college technician called Mathias. A big, blond, heavy-drinking bear of a chap, Mathias, through his friendship with Jürgen, would manage to infiltrate the Club Room most evenings and instigate some quite unusual drinking games, punctuated by bouts of joke-telling. His favourite, and probably top of the league of slightly risky jokes at the time, was: 'Who is the biggest boozer in the GDR? – Erich Honecker,[14] because you see him hanging around in every pub.' This was a reference to the practice in most hospitality and other venues to suspend a large picture of the leader in a prominent position on a wall. As his alcohol intake grew, Mathias would often launch into a tirade against the powers that be and bemoan his dismal life, including the barriers to his freedom to do what he wanted, say what he wanted and go where he wanted. We all liked Mathias, his open heart, warmth, larger-than-life persona and generosity in buying the drinks, but had an uneasy feeling that things might not end well. One evening, there was no more Mathias (and with this, an enforced diminution in the amount we drank), and I took his disappearance as a cue to write in my report to the British Council:

'I think it is worth stressing the importance of making contact with other students and people in the town, as it is in this way that many new and some quite fascinating revelations are made. However, it is also advisable to be a bit discreet when following up any contacts made inside the college. There was one rather awkward and unpleasant incident when one of the technicians (who was earmarked as being not one of the state's greatest supporters) was warned against any further contact with us.'

On our final evening together, Jürgen somehow managed to smuggle Mathias into our farewell gathering in the Club Room, which was both a relief to us and an opportunity to say our goodbyes. As we drank toasts to each other, to our futures and to our reunions, Mathias wept openly. Our plans to build on blossoming friendships made in those three

---

14. *Erich Honecker led the GDR from 1971 to 1989.*

weeks, the sort of plans which are so often made after short acquaintances but so seldom realised, could only ever be one-sided and never shared by our hosts. Our talk of us all meeting up in Paris the following year was inconsiderate, nor would it happen. In our exuberant camaraderie, we had inadvertently but foolishly made the pangs caused by impending separation far more acute for Mathias than they were for us. Whether in Paris, Helsinki or London, Mathias could not so would not be there with us. This hurt us, but it hurt him much more.

*

Some evenings earlier, the whole course had been summoned to a presentation by, and discussion with, a 'star' guest from the Ministry of Foreign Affairs. Mr Warnewski, if I remember correctly, had recently returned from his posting in The Hague as the GDR's Ambassador to the Netherlands.

We all sat dutifully and listened to our speaker wax lyrical over the GDR's human rights record, its opposition to the arms race, and its dismay at West Germany's insistence that the GDR was only transitory; and to his repeated references to the peace programme of Leonid Brezhnev,[15] a shining light in a world where capitalist countries were hell-bent on increasing tensions and expanding their spheres of influence.

It was probably after the fifth or sixth mention of Brezhnev and his peace programme that I decided that all this was going too far and that someone had to say something, so I started preparing my counterattack for the ensuing discussion. Up to that point, end-of-class discussions with our lecturers Dr. Bolz, Dr. Bär and their colleagues had been fairly uneventful and uncontroversial affairs, with relatively safe ground

---

15. *Leonid Brezhnev was General Secretary of the Communist Party of the USSR – i.e. in charge of the country – from 1964 to 1982.*

being kept to and a general feeling that we should not ruffle too many feathers. After all, Messrs Bolz and Bär had both gone out of their way to make us feel comfortable in our new surroundings, were well-organised and very cordial, though they shied away from expanding on the subject matter of their lectures outside the classes and seminars. Shooting them down in flames during the early days might, it was felt, lead to an uncomfortable remaining sojourn; and we didn't want any adverse comeback on our sponsors (in my case, the British Council) who, after all, were subbing this once-in-a-lifetime freebie opportunity and might have taken it amiss if Erfurt had struck them off the list for the rest of time.

But there were limits, and I felt that a limit had been reached tonight. With my mind made up, and a growing sense of 'Cometh the hour, cometh the man', I sketched out my question for the discussion on my notepad, triple-checking the grammar, deliberating over whether the vocabulary I planned to use would convey the appropriate balance of gravity and factual accuracy. And the potential fallout had to be weighed up against the thrill of this fleeting moment of rebellion. What was the worst that could happen? Might I be taken under escort to Erfurt Hauptbahnhof and banished from the nation in perpetuity? I had no sense of what penalties could be incurred by foreigners who upset important people in the GDR nor, more critically, how the assembled ranks of my fellow students in the room would react to the host boat being rocked.

By the time Mr W's sermon had finished and the time allotted for discussion was signalled, my feet were feeling at best lukewarm, if not entirely cold. I decided that the sensible tactic was to let others lead with a few questions and hope that my feet would warm up, rather than pitching in with them both right at the start. After around five minutes of fairly feeble, non-confrontational enquiries to Mr W, who sat on a raised platform before us flanked by other ministry officials and Drs. Bolz and Bär, I raised a tremulous arm from the relative safety of the fifth row, hoping deep down that it wouldn't be noticed. But it was, and my time had come.

'How can you talk about the peace programme of Leonid Brezhnev, when in the course of the last thirteen years the Soviet Union has, on two separate occasions, invaded neighbouring countries?'

For a few seconds, a total, crushing silence enveloped the room, a silence which echoed disbelief at such a crude and blatant attempt to derail the mood of *entente cordiale* which had characterised the hours spent passively soaking up the mantras repeated by our lecturers. Then came a sort of muted uproar, a release of tension from which it was impossible to discern whether the crowd was with me or wanted my head. Only the tutting and headshaking of Jean-Pierre and Francine in the row behind me gave a clue to what that faction thought – that for them this was why the guillotine had been invented.

At least my self-inflicted mental torture was over. I had got my question out, made my bold and probably extremely foolhardy protest, and that would, barring reprisals, be that. I just had to sit back and await the predictable stock retort in defence of Soviet actions, and whatever followed in the coming days. Or so I thought.

Mr Warnewski, after letting his audience restore itself to order, fixed me in a stern, no-nonsense gaze and said:

'Which two occasions are you referring to?'

I had really not expected to have to spell it out, though perhaps I should have. In that moment, a challenge to the dogma of a high-ranking party official took on the mantle of an all-out assault, not only on my hosts in the GDR, who had treated me with kindness and respect, but on the whole terrifying might of the USSR. In being forced to give substance to my criticism, I was digging myself a lot deeper into this than I felt comfortable with, and the consequences were anything but certain. The room gave a sharp intake of breath.

'Well, Czechoslovakia and Afghanistan,' I replied, in a tone suggesting that the question had been entirely superfluous, a tone which could only make an increasingly dangerous diplomatic incident lurch even further out of control.

There was a resigned, benevolent sort of nod from Mr W, some muttering and shuffling of papers amongst the panel, and subdued mumblings from those members of the audience who were not by now gazing at the floor to signal that my ill-conceived onslaught on the entire Warsaw Pact had nothing to do with them.

'I thought this question would come up,' he said with a certain assuredness, a voice of stability and calm in an increasingly desperate situation.

This was something of a victory: the fact that he had apparently expected the question, even though it came, of course, from an uninformed British student, gave it a certain validity, and I felt the sensation of a warmish glow welling up inside me as the turn of events seemed to produce an outbreak of respect for me from most, if not all of my peers. There then followed a ten-minute exposition from Mr W, bolstered by supportive interjections from his ministry colleagues, on how the Russians had actually been invited into Afghanistan to uphold the 1978 Soviet–Afghan Friendship Treaty, but with very little on why Dubček had been ousted in Czechoslovakia in 1968.

No matter, I was not going to press the point further.

*

During the last two days of our time at the summer school there were radio and TV interviews to give, and a verbal report to be submitted to our course organisers by a representative from each country. For some reason, possibly because of my 'head above the parapet' performance in single-handedly dismantling the pretensions of Soviet foreign policy, the small cohort of British students put me forward to deliver the verbal report, convincing me that I was their man.

In spite of my no doubt unwelcome intervention on that heady evening, Dr Bär and Dr Bolz had continued to be nice to me, and a bond had grown between us. As energy dissipated amongst the course participants, many had started to drop out of, or completely skip, excursions and evening functions, and numbers had dwindled. The prospect of spending an afternoon learning about apprenticeships at a nearby factory had been the last straw for many, who had absconded in favour of sampling the local ice cream at the Nordstrand[16] or wandering around the town, which was resplendent with roses and other floral delights as it was every July for the city's flower festival. Driven by a combination of wanting to do the right thing and not incurring the displeasure of the British Council, I doggedly turned out for every course activity, no matter how dire it sounded.

Dr Bolz made mention of this in one of our final classes, and for a moment I wondered whether I too had become, in his eyes, the *allseitig entwickelte Persönlichkeit*, that rounded, complete individual who was the cornerstone of GDR society. For my part, I gave a deservedly upbeat and positive appraisal of the course, suggesting that future years might focus less on education and more, for example, on the judiciary, the

---

16. *A lakeside recreation area on the edge of Erfurt.*

police (who apparently earned less than normal workers, which might have accounted for a tendency to find ways to supplement their income) and on music. There had been a lot on folk traditions, and Heine's[17] assertion that 'Today is a result of yesterday' – that the future is to be found in the past – had led to a profusion of local and national festivals and customs. In Thuringia, young girls would collect 'Easter Water', believed to have magical powers, and carry it in silence into the forest, and Easter, Whitsun and Christmas were all seen as key times in the annual rhythm of rural life.

We had heard about the Church, completely separated from the atheist state but tolerated as long as it supported the shared goals of promoting peace and helping mankind. We had been surprised to learn that there was not just one political party but five; each one was signed up to and funded by a different sector of working society, but all were identically tasked with building peace and national prosperity, with none standing in opposition to the others. We heard too that the GDR sat at number ten in the league table of the world's industrialised nations. And that the size of your living space was not important, it was family values and the relationship between the parents, and setting a good example for the kids, and not speaking ill of your work colleagues in front of them, that mattered.

So there was some scope for improvement in course content, I reported, and room for the lecturers to be a little less acerbic and a little more inquisitive about our ways in the West, but all in all we'd been given a pretty thorough induction and, crucially, been afforded opportunities for independent research by not being distanced from the population at large.

---

17. *Heinrich Heine (1797-1856), German poet and writer and admired by Karl Marx, not least for his satirical polemic against Germany's governing classes.*

Our hosts had been hospitable throughout, and I praised their efforts to make us feel at home and help us with practical advice in what was an unusual environment for us. I deliberately skirted round the subject of food, however, but felt that the future few destined to be chosen by the British Council would benefit by knowing that:

'...the food, although very good, did not exactly provide a balanced diet. Basic vitamins were lacking, and since purchasing (low-quality) fruit involved queuing for some considerable time, the resulting deficiency in rest and healthy nutrition forced several to resort to vitamin tablets as a way of keeping going.'

*

Unwilling to let us go without experiencing the state's hub, pride and joy, the Ministry of Education invited me and three other Brits up to East Berlin for a couple of all-expenses-paid (except drinks and food) days to round off our stay. We decided that this was a vote of confidence in our standards of behaviour and adherence to the programme in Erfurt, and weren't sure whether to feel proud of this or not. They put us up at the Hotel Unter den Linden, situated unsurprisingly on the famous Unter den Linden Boulevard and within a stone's throw of the imposing, neoclassical, Brandenburg Gate.

There was a high-ranking government delegation from Sri Lanka in town, so a lot of closed-off main arteries, and the Spartakiade[18] was in full flow. The flower of the country's youth marched, competed and celebrated in colourful exuberance around the Fernsehturm,[19] the dominant landmark with its bulbous top which rose above the city. We

18. The Central Youth Games, held every two years, either in Berlin or Leipzig, between 1966 and 1989.
19. The TV tower.

were given free rein to go where we pleased, hindered only by the black marketeers, intent on helping us convert our Deutschmarks to Ostmarks, effectively worthless outside the GDR, at increasingly enticing rates of exchange.

This preoccupation with getting hands on hard currency surfaced again when, on our one evening in East Berlin, we ventured into a discotheque further down Unter den Linden and sat at a table with some friendly older ladies, who were probably only in their early thirties. Things were going well, and after a couple of hours of frenzied dancing, we felt sure that we were doing our bit towards promoting friendship between peoples, successfully bridging any ideological divisions. With our meagre stocks of Ostmarks dwindling fast, our female companions decided the time had come to propose that we retire to their respective apartments where they would tap into our supplies of Deutschmarks in exchange for further, more intimate companionship. It was at this point we realised that cultural bonding came at a price, so made our excuses and left for the safety and questionable comfort of our hotel.

East Berlin was tranquil, lacking the bustle of western cities, and we saw a lot of rabbits. On the second and final day we decided to try to get up as close as we could to the Wall. Following our map, we ended up walking tentatively down an eerily empty street which led to a church. Believing the Wall to be somewhere near this church, we entered its large churchyard to investigate further. After a few minutes we saw it, looming threateningly just beyond the church, a jumble of bulldozed gravestones scattered in small piles along its base. It was as though its erection had been so rapid and urgent as to override even the most fundamental, time-honoured respect and decorum offered to the dead. It was a truly shocking sight, a symbol not just of political division, but of how that division had been deemed so essential as to sever family and community ties, as well as the ties between the living and their departed loved ones.

*

Years later, as the Wall was first haphazardly and then systematically dismantled, following the tumultuous events of November 1989, I thought back to Dr Bär and Dr Bolz and wondered what was going through their minds as the state and system they had so enthusiastically and genuinely supported came to its ignominious end. For I was in no doubt of their sincerity, and wondered whether they would be able to find a way to come to terms with the reality that lay ahead of them. I remembered Dr Bolz's words that capitalism could of itself be a positive force, but not when linked inextricably to imperialism, militarism and exploitation, and I thought this probably provided the best shred of hope for him and his worldview as he faced up to life in a different ideological regime – provided, of course, that we in the West behaved ourselves.

I hope that he, and all those who took such good care of us in Erfurt that summer, fared well.

Chapter Three

A DANUBIAN SUMMER

The River Danube starts its 2,845-kilometre journey in Germany's Black Forest, famous for its eponymous gateau and cuckoo clocks, close to the town of Donaueschingen, where the inhabitants have been in dispute with those of nearby Furtwangen for many years over where the river's true source lies. From there, it either flows through or forms part of the borders of ten different countries, before emptying out into the Black Sea in separate channels at its delta.

Regular attendees of pub quizzes will probably know that this is a world record, with the Nile, passing through nine countries, being edged into second place. The Danube does, however, occupy a second place itself, this time in the league table of Europe's longest rivers, losing out (by 845 kilometres) to the Volga further east. Other notable claims to fame are that it once formed a frontier of the Roman Empire, and that it now runs through no fewer than four capital cities: Belgrade, Budapest, Bratislava and Vienna.

In 1992, the Danube joined forces with the Main and the Rhine to form a 3,500-kilometre waterway from North to

Black Seas, with much of its length navigable and used as a valuable trading route. Like the Rhine, the Danube has long provided summer cruising possibilities for day trippers and those with more time on their hands. Some of its stretches, like the steep-sided, vine-clad Wachau Valley in Austria; the serene, verdant Danube Bend north of Budapest; or the dramatic Iron Gates further downstream on the Romanian-Serbian border, offer some of the most picturesque river cruising in Europe, along a course extending from Germany, through the heart of central and eastern Europe, and on to the Balkans.

The river is also the subject of probably the most famous waltz ever written. In 1866, the Austrian composer Johann Strauss (the Second) wrote 'On The Beautiful Blue Danube' in an attempt to lift the country's deflated spirits after its defeat by Prussia in the Seven Weeks' War that same year. The song has virtually become Austria's second national anthem, and its fusion of gliding and staccato notes customarily features in Vienna's annual New Year's Eve concert.

The Danube may be beautiful in parts, but its colour is certainly not blue, unless light and sky conspire favourably to make it so.

If quizzers are given a chance to notch up some bonus points for naming all ten countries the river flows through (or forms a border of), they would list Germany, Austria, Slovakia, Hungary, Croatia, Serbia, Romania, Bulgaria, Moldova and Ukraine, thereby winning the extra points, and no doubt a good measure of respect from their competitors.

*

If the same question had been posed in 1982, the tally of countries touched or dissected by the river was less impressive, and might not have been worthy of inclusion in the geography or general knowledge section at all. Nevertheless, at eight, the tally was still creditable. This contraction is explained by Moldova and Ukraine both then being part of the Soviet Union, while Croatia and Serbia were in what was still Yugoslavia. And for the record, though it does not affect the numbers, Slovakia formed the southeastern portion of Czechoslovakia.

*

The lounge at the departure gate for the BA flight to Vienna was almost full. I squeezed myself between two ladies, their copious bags of duty-free purchases overhanging the void from their laps, onto one of the few remaining seats, and surveyed my fellow passengers, wondering which of them were mine. The two ladies hemming me in appeared to be in the right age category, and I briefly considered asking them whether they were part of the SAGA Holidays group, before deciding against it. There was no need, at this early stage, to draw attention to who I was, and what a critical role I would be playing in the next four days of their lives.

My instructions from head office in Folkestone had not – surprisingly, I thought – included rounding up my group in some obvious part of Gatwick airport to check them in, brief them, calm any pre-flight nerves and answer any questions about their forthcoming holiday and cruise. This was something of a relief, as I'd never been to Austria before, let alone to Vienna, nor had I ever worked on a cruise ship. In fact, I'd never escorted a tour of any sort anywhere before and was feeling decidedly uneasy about the whole prospect. So anonymity, at least for a couple more hours, seemed the wisest course of action; it would guarantee an undisturbed and enquiry-free flight and allow me some much-needed time to swot up on the delights of Vienna, and on what lay beyond.

*

A couple of months earlier, while putting every waking hour into trying desperately to achieve a respectable degree back at Leeds University, I'd noticed a hand-written card pinned to the German department's noticeboard. The card was advertising the position of 'Cruise Representative on Danube Cruises for SAGA Holidays' (with 'for the over 60s' in small letters). The advertisement was very short on detail, not least on which qualities and qualifications would be required for candidates to have any chance of attaining this lofty status, save for a good level of spoken German. There was no mention of a need for experience working with the elderly, nor first aid skills; not even a short stint as a bingo caller. With the clock of opportunity having ticked round to shortly before midnight, and options for my university afterlife wearing worryingly thin, this was a chance that I felt had to be grabbed. I suspect many of the other final-year German undergraduates, whose futures were looking similarly forlorn, would have thought the same. Like me, they would have seen this unassuming invitation as a rare beacon of light, of hope, shining out from the grim cork backdrop of exam timetables.

So I was more than surprised to be summoned to interview in a small room in the department two weeks later. The chief inquisitor was a graduate of the German department called Paul Bowden who, very shrewdly, had hit upon the idea of recruiting for zero outlay from his former alma mater, where he knew he'd be sure to find the right language skills amongst a cohort of hopefuls who would already be penniless through having exhausted their student grants some time ago. In all likelihood, these penniless hopefuls would be facing further imminent penury, running out of options fast, and therefore ready to jump at a chance to earn woefully little money. Paul's number two on the day was introduced as Bobby Moore. It was he who posed the more taxing questions. The interview was notable for a complete absence of testing spoken German, which was disappointing as I felt that my relative fluency would have been my strongest suit in a situation where absolutely nothing else I offered qualified me to look after large groups of elderly people.

Paul and Bobby, however, had evidently spotted something which made me stand out from the hungry and desperate pack, and a couple of days later a letter arrived from Folkestone informing me that my application had been successful, and that I'd be jetting out to Vienna on June 26th to start my almost three-month contract escorting SAGA parties down and up the Danube between Vienna and Belgrade. I was elated, relieved and also somewhat surprised: some of Bobby Moore's questions had been truly brutal, had tripped me up and left me floundering. Paul would one day reveal to me that his co-interrogator had no connection whatsoever to SAGA Holidays, but was an old friend from his Leeds days who was still in the city and working as a bus driver – and that his name was not Bobby Moore.

That I would have to miss my graduation ceremony, assuming I became a graduate, was of negligible consequence when set against the upside benefit of securing gainful employment so unexpectedly soon, albeit for a short time. There would be no need to throw myself on the mercy of the state, at least not for the time being. And to be paid to speak German and venture back into Eastern Europe for a sizeable chunk of summer seemed a far more enticing proposition than donning gown and mortarboard and parading in front of my parents, colleagues and the university photographer for a single August afternoon. Sacrificing a transient moment of glory for what might possibly turn out to be a heaven-sent assignment, in spite of the extremely modest remuneration, seemed like it could be a very wise move.

*

Paul met the thirty or so of us at Vienna airport and guided us to our waiting *Austrobus* coach. As things transpired, I'd fallen into conversation during the flight with a couple sitting on my row and eventually revealed my identity to them. It became clear that they were due to become my charges in a few hours' time, and I realised it would have looked odd later to not have taken this inescapable opportunity to introduce myself. Luckily the talk was of grandchildren and previous foreign holidays, and I wasn't called upon to expand on the finer details of their forthcoming itinerary; nor did they ask me about all those groups they probably assumed I'd escorted in the past, which of course I hadn't.

My unveiling came on the coach transfer to the hotel, as we left the sprawling petrochemical plant at Schwechat behind us and penetrated the city's outer suburbs at some speed. Paul pointed me out and I stood up from my front seat and swivelled round, giving a rather forced and nervy smile, clinging to the headrest to prevent me being catapulted backwards through the front window should the driver make an abrupt halt. I was now being officially launched, and there was no going back. It was a moment of empowerment, the first time in my life that responsibility on this scale had been bestowed upon me, and it actually felt good.

From that moment on, any pangs of anxiety came second to the overwhelming sense of having been released into life's next episode, and that I would make a success of this. Those few seconds at the front of the coach proved to be a defining moment between my past and my future.

Twenty minutes later, we arrived at the Hotel Atlas on Lerchenfelderstrasse and, after issuing instructions to have bags outside doors for collection by eight-fifteen the next morning for a nine o'clock departure for the city sightseeing tour, we checked the group in and retired to the bar for my briefing over a wienerschnitzel, mashed potato and sauerkraut dinner. Hoping that we would be left in peace and quiet, Paul had pointedly suggested that everyone might like to avail themselves of this one and only chance to explore Vienna independently that evening, a tactic which worked as we were left undisturbed to consume several Ottakringer beers which, I noted for the benefit of my guests in future weeks, came in glasses costing 12, 18 or 24 schillings.

Absorbing these relatively minor practical details could, I decided, be a useful way of developing a reputation for local omniscience, although that could backfire if expectations got too high. As an official city guide, Brigitte, conducted the city sightseeing tour on Sunday mornings, I would never have a chance to lecture my charges on the history of the rococo style at Schönbrunn Palace. But I could at least impart the unwelcome news to the ladies that the privilege of relieving themselves there would cost them five schillings, whilst their husbands only had to part with one.

The following Sunday, I was jolted from my comfort zone of only needing to convey seemingly trivial but often essential information when Brigitte failed to show up, and it fell to me to educate an outwardly sympathetic group on the city's impressive array of baroque, renaissance and pseudo-gothic gems, as our coach crawled agonisingly slowly around the Ringstrasse.[20] The driver had evidently been conditioned over several years to pause for a protracted length of time in front of the vast complexes of the Hofburg, but there was only so much I could say about the Spanish Riding School, which was all I could recall about the imperial palace from Brigitte's tour the previous week. Lesson learnt, when the coach stopped to allow legs to be stretched I nipped into a

---

20. *Vienna's stunning inner ring road, over five kilometres long, and home to many of the city's most famous and spectacular buildings.*

souvenir shop on Kärntnerstrasse to buy a guidebook, while my clients proceeded at a leisurely pace on to Stephansplatz. I then swiftly memorised the key facts about St Stephen's Cathedral and caught most of them up in time to explain confidently that it was gothic, although the dome on the North Tower was in fact renaissance, and that its twenty-ton bell, known as the 'Pummerin' – so called because of the hollow, booming sound it made when it was rung – had originally been crafted from canons captured from the Turks in 1711.

For the rest of that particular Sunday morning tour, aided entirely by secret reading of my new guidebook in the front seat, I was able to demonstrate something more than a fragile grasp of Vienna's history, across the ages and right up to the near-present. As we stood in front of the Upper Belvedere palace, I announced that the Austrian State Treaty had been signed here on May 15th, 1955, bringing to a close the Allied post-war occupation of the city, an occasion which would have been well within the living memory of my audience, and hoped this would find some resonance with them.

*

Back on the previous Sunday's tour, as we entered District 2 and Leopoldstadt – which Brigitte explained had been given to the city's Jewish population in 1622, where it remained until 1938 – and moved on past the Prater Wheel, my watch told me it wouldn't be long until we arrived at the Reichsbrücke, in time for our embarkation at 11.30. To the southwest, we caught glimpses of the Vienna Woods and before us, across the Danube Canal, the almost dystopian aspect of UNO City, as we left all of Vienna's opulent splendour behind and headed towards the river. Soon it would be time to take leave of Paul, who'd decided to stay on for the sightseeing tour, and assume full, unfettered control.

The plan went like this. Each Sunday I would board the ship with my group of new arrivals, who had flown to Vienna from London the evening before. The group would cruise down to Cernavodă in Romania, arriving there the following Saturday afternoon. Some would fly back to London from Bucharest, others would spend an extra week in Sinaia, a resort in the southern Carpathian Mountains, before returning home. Meanwhile, another group would fly from London to Bucharest, and either spend the first week in Sinaia before the upstream cruise or take the 'cruise only' option, leaving Cernavodă on Saturday evening and arriving in Vienna the following Saturday afternoon.

My part in all this was to escort one group from Vienna as far as Belgrade; say my goodbyes to the group and leave the ship there; wait in Belgrade for the arrival of the upstream cruise; and then journey back with those passengers to Vienna, escorting them to Vienna airport for their homeward flight on Saturday afternoon. Then, I would meet the next group at the airport an hour or so later; stay overnight with them at the Atlas in Vienna; enjoy Brigitte's sightseeing tour on Sunday morning; board the ship for the noon departure downstream; and start the cycle anew.

The plan, but more particularly SAGA's budgets, didn't allow for a representative to be on board with the group between Belgrade and Cernavodă (and vice-versa), although those customers availing themselves of an extra week in the Romanian mountains were looked after there by a girl called Sharon Smith. I never met Sharon but often corresponded with her during the summer, typically on matters such as lost luggage and problems in changing back surplus local currency, and to warn each other about any members of our respective groups who had proved troublesome, including precisely what they had done to deserve such a classification.

So the focal points of my week would be Saturday nights spent on land in Vienna, Sunday and Thursday nights moored in Budapest, and Tuesday nights spent in Belgrade, awaiting the arrival of my upstream cruise party.

Though I never physically entered Romanian territory, the country would turn out to be a constant, often disturbing presence as I shuttled up and down the Danube during that summer of 1982.

The state of Romania in 1982

An analysis of why some of recent history's nastiest dictators managed to stay in power for so long would probably cite as common denominators the ability to get their tenures off to a good start, at least in the eyes of their citizens, and the obvious one of finding ways to instill ever higher degrees of fear into most of the population as they sought to tighten their grip on the reins. This often involved harnessing nationalist sentiment against an unwelcome occupier, or a segment of the population, or against a would-be intruder. Robert Mugabe was allowed to continue trading on his credit for liberating the country from the yolk of empire and white rule long after his country became one of the world's economic basket cases. Commonly, the good start was based on improving the lot of the masses. Saddam Hussein was lauded as being the force behind investing the proceeds of increasing oil revenues into transforming Iraq's welfare, education, public health and agriculture during the seventies, before he formally assumed complete control of the country in 1979. And Hitler tapped into the post-Versailles sentiment of humiliation, sharpened by the deprivations of economic depression, and found scapegoats, and funds for popularity-boosting infrastructure projects, to make an already amenable populace even more pliant.

Nicolae Ceauşescu was, in terms of his early ingratiation with his people, cut from a similar cloth. By December 1967, as both General Secretary of the Romanian Communist Party and head of state, he held total sway. As examples of how communism combined with nationalism should work, Ceauşescu was an admirer of what Mao was doing in China and Kim Il Sun in North Korea. But despite Romania being labelled as the most communist of all the Eastern European states, Ceauşescu pursued a policy of keeping the Soviet Union at arm's length and leaning increasingly towards the West; this was the bedrock of his early popularity at home and, unsurprisingly, among western governments.

This eschewing of Soviet attempts to incorporate Romania into its sphere of influence had begun when Ceauşescu's predecessor, Gheorghiu Dej, saw Moscow's intentions to earmark Romania as an agricultural nation generating produce for the common socialist good as a threat to his own authority. Consequently, he decided to plough a very different furrow, launching full steam into a programme of industrialisation, a policy continued and intensified under Ceauşescu. Romania had oil and badly needed a greatly enhanced refining capability in order to capitalise on its potential as a major world oil producer. Large loans were obtained from western banks to finance Ceauşescu's dream of making his nation a global industrial power, a dream fuelled by years of high oil prices in the seventies, but one which foundered when his refineries were dogged by delay after delay. By the time they were put into service, in the early eighties, the oil price had slumped and Romania was left with a massive debt to settle. The year

1982 was one of reckoning. The country was plunged into severe austerity and took to exporting almost everything of consumer value, especially food.

This resulted in widespread shortages of vital goods, serious enough on their own, but when set against the backdrop of the regime's broader actions to batten down the hatches they contributed to making life in Romania increasingly harsh. Ceauşescu's repressive measures against his people became more and more extreme. As Romania had geared itself up for the expansion of its industrial base, so too had it sought to ensure there would be sufficient labour to populate the factories. Decree 770, outlawing contraception and abortion, had been introduced to help the cause. By exercising the right to free speech and any possible criticism of the authorities, the perpetrator risked an unwelcome encounter with the 'Securitate', the leader's much-feared and universally loathed not-so-secret police, who did their brutal and largely effective best to convince their hapless countrymen that too much knowledge was indeed a bad thing. And as well as painting himself abroad as the sort of defiant nationalist who refused to submit to constant browbeatings by the Soviets, Ceauşescu's agenda at home included a relentless persecution of the Hungarians in Transylvania, in the central, north and western regions of his country. The xenophobia card – so often played by despots seeking approval from their subjects – was waved ostentatiously, almost with righteous indignation and pride.

Earlier, in June of 1978, Ceauşescu and his equally disagreeable wife, Elena, had been treated to the pomp of a state visit to the United Kingdom, where the government hoped he would part with around £300 million in exchange for some airliners to augment the fleet of Romania's national carrier TAROM. That, and his solid rebuttal of Russian endeavours to drag his country into their sphere of influence, had – it was felt by the previous Wilson government – earned him the reward of being welcomed as the first communist head of state ever to visit London. The red carpet was rolled out at Victoria Station, where the Queen and Prince Philip greeted the presidential couple, and the customary dinner took place at Buckingham Palace, where the Ceauşescus were accommodated for their stay. At some point, the Queen evidently decided that they were not exactly her cup of tea, as she is alleged to have hidden behind a bush when, while walking her dogs in the palace garden, she saw the pair approaching. That the planes were never paid for, together with Ceauşescu's subsequent hellish treatment of his people, caused the visit to go down in British history as one of our more embarrassing and less productive attempts at international diplomacy.

'Over to you now, Phil.'

Paul shook my hand as he took his leave from us on the quayside below the Reichsbrücke, giving me the sort of look which suggested that, having spent the previous few days on board ship with the group on the upstream cruise before meeting me in Vienna, he was more than happy to be heading to the airport to board his homeward flight; a look that also succeeded in imparting a feeling of confidence in my ability to rise to the challenges ahead, and that there was no possible prospect of my letting him or the company down. And that this would start with ensuring that the haphazardly arranged rows of surprisingly small suitcases, recently plucked by the driver from the innards of our coach, would somehow be transported onto the ship, safely and in their entirety.

By eight o'clock that first evening, the MV *Carpati* had made it into northern Hungary, and Almut, the ship's cruise director, had alerted me that the basilica at Esztergom would shortly be in view. This was the cue to prompt my customers to rouse themselves from their post-dinner torpor, temporarily interrupt the early exchanges in their whist games, or bookmark their paperbacks, and make their way on deck to witness its giant, almost alien, neoclassical grandeur. As this was one of the few genuine architectural highlights of the day, Almut, in her brusque, no-nonsense Germanic tone, was adamant that I should insist on full participation, not least as it also provided a rare opportunity that day for her to make pronouncements on the history of something. So far, the sparse offerings had included the onion-spired church at Hainburg and Bratislava's hulking rectangular castle, contrasting starkly with the sleek lines of the Bridge of the Slovak National Uprising below it, known by the locals as the 'New Bridge'. Other than that, her only utterance had been on the ecological diversity of the 'Donauauen', a vast wetland area full of unusual fauna and flora crying out for protection from the development it was being threatened with. But the almost total absence of commentary hadn't mattered. We'd pulled away from the Reichsbrücke just after midday, to the strains of 'On The Beautiful Blue Danube' crackling through the ship's tannoy, and my relatively content band of SAGA holidaymakers had been treated to repeated blasts of the song at periodic intervals during a lazy, uneventful afternoon on deck.

Almut was high in the pecking order on board and was one of three cruise directors I would work with that summer. At the pinnacle of the ship's hierarchy was of course the captain, and just as it was the captain's job to run the ship, it was the cruise director's job to run the passengers. The

Carpati, and her sister ship *Oltenita*, were chartered by the Austrian company Lüftner, who in turn sold off blocks of cabins to a small number of tour operators, each of which, like SAGA, employed a representative on board to look after its customers. The resulting composition was a mixture of Austrians, Germans, Swiss, Brits, Swedes and a handful of families of French railway employees. Each national grouping rarely had anything to do the others, except when disputes arose over seating arrangements in the lounge, which they frequently did. We representatives had to navigate the diverse channels of caring for the needs and interests of both our clients and our respective paymasters, and of staying on the right side of the cruise director and, if possible, each other too.

Then there were the girls and boys who did the real leg work, grafting away long hours in the kitchen and engine room, and the waitresses, bar staff, a hairdresser and a doctor. These and the captain all had one thing in common. They were all Romanian. And the vessels themselves, built at a shipyard in the Romanian Danubian city of Giurgiu in 1961, were likewise the property of the state in which they had been created. To reinforce the point that they regarded themselves, and wanted to be regarded, as holding dominion on board, the Romanians employed a separate cruise director who was charged with the 'cultural wellbeing' of the passengers. In reality, the brief was to keep a watchful eye on the Romanian crew (including the captain), discourage any more fraternising with the passengers and us representatives than was absolutely necessary in the course of duty, and ensure that any foreign currency spent on board and handled by the staff was completely accounted for.

To that end, any economic activity that might have tempted any of the crew – especially the bar staff – to cream off some fraction of the proceeds, was painstakingly scrutinised, often late after the last stragglers had departed the bar. Each bottle of spirits would be measured and its fluid levels logged under the watchful gaze of the Romanian cruise director, in case any of its content had been siphoned off for illicit resale. This was the nightly rigmarole, a charade which prolonged the bar staff's working day by a good couple of hours. Their, and our, chief scourge was a tall, slim, sinister young man called Alex, who always wore a black shirt and white suit, and who spoke with a rather menacing, slurred, immensely irritating transatlantic drawl when he chastised those of us who were unfortunate enough to incur his displeasure. In his dealings with those around him, Alex would have it his way or no way. But worse than this, he also embodied all the classic traits of a system loyalist, ready at the slightest pretext to bring the careers of his fellow countrymen and women to an abrupt and usually undeserved end.

To the good fortune of us reps and everyone working on board, Alex was not an ever-present figure on either ship that summer, and the other Romanian cruise directors who enjoyed that lofty position were all female and far more geared towards cooperation than confrontation. They were also less zealous in toeing the party line to the same extreme degrees.

Within hours of being on board, I'd come to realise that some sort of bonding with the bar staff was an inevitable consequence of the lounge bar's central hub status. Apart from a small reading room on the upper deck, there were no other covered spaces where passengers could sit outside restaurant hours, and even the lounge bar's capacity was inadequate on a rainy day. Any post-dinner entertainment – essentially, only the resident Roma band and anything we reps took it upon ourselves to organise – took place here, as did the initial welcome meeting, at which I would run through everything from the land excursion programme to where and how to exchange currency in the days to come.

On my first afternoon, I'd instructed the barman to reserve ten tables for my six o'clock meeting, to place four glasses and a bottle of a sort of Romanian pink champagne on each table, and to prepare enough shots of the official welcome drink, a concoction of plum brandy and vermouth. The resulting potion settled to form a thick, dark brown liquid with a bitter, vaguely herbal taste, and was often labelled 'paint-stripper' or 'poison' by those brave enough to sample it.

At least, that is what I thought I'd asked for. When I arrived at the bar at a quarter to six to check on arrangements, there were just three tables and a total of nine glasses awaiting my group, and all the other tables in the room were occupied. Catastrophe beckoned. Fortunately, at my moment of greatest need, Almut, who by her physical presence alone signalled to all in her way that she was not to be trifled with, strode in, saw my plight and proceeded to banish a group of terrified Swedish pensioners to some other unspecified public place of their choosing on the ship, of which there were very few. Sufficient space now created, Almut issued renewed orders on the correct number and distribution of glasses to the barman who, over the course of the next fifteen minutes, delivered what was required with an unmistakable air of reluctance. But disaster had been averted in the nick of time, and I had learnt valuable lessons.

The first of these was that the chances of forming bonds would be greatly enhanced if I could find a way to communicate properly, and the best way to do that was to get to grips with the Romanian language. At the top of the vocabulary list, after 'please' and 'thank you', should be essential plural nouns such as tables, bottles and glasses, then numbers, telling the time, the verb 'to like' and how to make it negative. The second lesson was realising that just because the bar staff, or any of the staff on board, found themselves in the enviable position of being able to work outside their stricken homeland and to spend time with westerners whose company or proximity could bring opportunities for self-enrichment, that didn't mean that they were any more motivated to provide a decent level of service. As poor service, and the sort of calamity that had almost just happened, would reflect badly on me, I had to find ways to ensure that in future the right number of glasses were on the right number of tables at the right time.

Learning enough Romanian to have a basic conversation, and get done what I needed to get done, turned out to be reasonably straightforward as there were so many similarities with Italian, still reverberating around my head after all the relentless preparation for my oral exam at Leeds a short time earlier. So this was a fortuitous start. I struck up reciprocal teacher-pupil alliances with a succession of barmen and cruise directors over the following weeks, with equal amounts of English imparted as Romanian absorbed, so both parties benefitted, and friendships were forged.

Attempts at persuading me to exchange my 'hard' currency floats of sterling and schillings into practically worthless Romanian lei, on the basis that my clients would be able to make good use of these once they reached the latter stages of the cruise and extension in Sinaia, gradually petered out. This was because the bar staff and crew, who were all at it, got the message that I refused to be sucked into the ship's black market, even if the exchange rate moved more and more in my favour with every hopeful approach. It was good that our relationships would be built on something other than financial gain, and that motivation could be achieved by other means.

That said, there was a reason why getting hard currency was even more important to my new friends than to the average citizen of every Eastern European nation, who knew full well that dollars and Deutschmarks were the surest way to obtain favours, or rare or quality goods, something above and beyond the limited and *ersatz* products available for mass consumption in the bleak shops. Once every two weeks our ship would be in Vienna, the gateway to the West, and if they chose to be tempted, to freedom. I discovered that many of the crew had established networks in the city or the wider country, possibly relatives who had made it there some years earlier, or just friends of friends. As confidences grew so did the enquiries into whether I knew such and such a suburban corner of the city, a promised place of refuge or meeting point. Whatever the scenario, the new life would require proper money, especially if the defector planned to try his or her luck without support in place, as many did.

To literally jump ship in this way was, technically, reasonably straightforward, given that a short window of shore leave on Saturday evenings was permitted, although those claiming to want to take a quick stroll along the quayside were obliged to leave anything resembling a personal belonging on board. But while this was technically easy, on an emotional level it was a very different matter. The only reason the crew, including the cruise director and captain, were allowed to work on the ship at all was because, in the vast majority of cases, they were married and had children. So, by disappearing into the Viennese night they were not only cutting family ties but also almost certainly creating problems with the authorities for their abandoned dependents back home. Yes, there may be some way that they would be reunited in the future, but this was by no means guaranteed and if it happened, it would not happen for some considerable time.

Almost every Sunday that summer the noon departure time from the Reichsbrücke would come, and the word would go round that we were a man, or woman, or several men and women, down. Romanian cruise directors might find, to their horror, that they would now be spending more of their time on the business side of the bar, and conducting the laborious nocturnal bottle audits themselves, rather than sleepily overseeing the process. On one Sunday in late August, the exodus reached a new, higher level of gravity when it became clear that the captain of the *Carpati* himself had decided that the lure of the anticipated better future, of milk and honey, had proved too much, and we were left leaderless, rudderless. Arrangements were apparently in hand to fly a replacement up from Bucharest and until he arrived, we were going nowhere.

*

On a normal Sunday, we would reach Budapest by late evening. The light faded as we drifted through the steep, wooded Danube Bend, an occasional fortification topping the unbroken swathe of green sloping up and away from the river. The lights on the right bank signalled that we were passing Szentendre, where by daylight we would have been able to make out the red-tiled roofs of the quaint artisan workshops full of curious visitors who had ventured the short distance north from the capital. Breaching the city limits, we sailed beneath Arpad Bridge, then past the recreational oasis of Margaret Island, on below its eponymous bridge towards the ponderous, complicated Chain Bridge, the spectacular neo-gothic symmetry of the Parliament, with its crown-like dome, now revealing itself on our left. High up to the right, the reptilian roof of the Matthias Church, its multicoloured zigzags prominent against the backdrop of night, competed for our attention. I'd heard and read about Budapest's splendour, but nothing had prepared me for the first time it greeted me, and I never grew tired that whole summer of those moments when our modest vessel slipped shyly into the illuminated metropolis. Hungary's capital more than lived up to its accolade of 'Pearl of the Danube'.

To say that both *Carpati* and *Oltenita* ranked among the less ostentatious occupants of the mooring berths between the Chain and Erszebet bridges was an understatement. With berthing space in short supply and high demand, our arrival time meant that there was rarely a space available with direct quayside access, and our diminutive cruiser had to lash up to one, or often more, of our larger rivals, which seemed more like small ocean liners in comparison. These included the *Theodor Körner* of the First Danube Steamship Company, and the Soviet Danube Navigation's *Dnepr* and *Volga*. Our passage from ship to shore could therefore only take place by walking through the more illustrious neighbours that blocked our passage; getting permission from the Russians to bring our cargo of westerners into such close quarters with their own citizens usually took considerable bargaining and a lot of patience.

The inconvenience of delay and lack of direct shore access was compounded by the sight of the bright, roomy, swish interiors proudly on show as my customers stepped warily from one ship to the next. Those billeted in the bowels of the ship, in *Carpati* and *Oltenita's* C deck cabins, with their bunk beds and absence of toilet facilities, glanced enviously at the amenities offered by the competition as they were hurried through, the Russian tourists held back at a safe distance. It was normally shortly afterwards that there were the first mutterings of discontent, or louder protestations, and claims that the brochure had not said anything about bunk beds. Life in a C deck cabin could indeed be challenging and more than a little claustrophobic and, if your cabin was located close to the engine room, a cause of serious sleep deprivation, as we reps often experienced. With the noisiest cabins only used for paying passengers as a last resort and when the ship was full to capacity, the reps were given what was left over after all the cabins were allocated among the new intake of guests. This often meant doing time next to the engine room, with a mechanical and nauseatingly rhythmical thudding and fuel vapours permeating the flimsy cabin walls when the ship was moving during the night hours.

When space was critically tight, or one of the tour operators had overbooked its allocation of cabins, we would find ourselves four reps to one C deck cabin. And as I was the only male rep, that created certain obvious practical difficulties when it came to getting dressed and undressed. Once, after someone's calamitous understatement of passenger arrival numbers, Almut herself was ejected from her own A deck residence and headed south to hunker down with three of us, bringing the entire contents of her original dwelling with her. But a problem shared turned out to be a problem quartered, and this enforced cohabitation and sense of being thrown together for a greater good erased any tribalism there might have been between us. Getting your own cabin on A deck was preferable, but there was no denying that we had a lot of fun exchanging anecdotes about troublesome clients and even more troublesome Romanian cruise directors, as the din from the adjacent engine room did its best to drown out our nocturnal conversation.

Hungary's fringe benefits

To the crew, setting foot on Hungarian concrete for a few short hours each week was like a breath of different, better socialist air; not fresh enough to warrant defecting to, but altogether lighter and more liberal with a moderate hint of a joie de vivre which was alien yet pleasant to them. As we trekked on our weekly pilgrimage along the quayside and streets to the grassy open spaces of Margaret Island – where, often in the searing heat of the Budapest midsummer, we would spend two or so happy, frantic hours playing football together – the crew curiously eyed the little roadside stalls laden with fresh fruit and the shops selling stuff that looked worth consuming. They must have asked themselves where they had gone wrong and where their neighbours had gone, or were going, right.

Despite Hungary having been a communist state since 1919, and the existence of the Hungarian People's Republic since 1949, after Churchill and Stalin's presumably straightforward decision in Moscow in 1944 to place it within the Soviet realm, the people, and more especially the workers of Hungary, had never entirely bought into socialist economic principles. Maybe the centuries-long joint venture of forming an empire with Austria had made a wholesale shift to the new ways and post-World War I revolutionary fervour too much to stomach. Whatever the underlying causes, there had always been a tendency to push back, often in subtle ways, against the rigid tenets imposed top-down by the ruling Hungarian Socialist Workers' Party. And this was even before the bloody suppression of the uprising of 1956, a nationwide revolt against economic stagnation, oppression and Soviet control of the country's affairs.

No other Eastern European people had voiced their

discontent so loudly and blatantly, nor would they again until 1989. But even before 1956 there had been defiance, just on a much more limited, mainly economic scale: hoarding of goods and produce, selling off of homegrown fruit and veg, but with most of this sufficiently below the radar for it to be tolerated. The government was ever conscious of needing to strike the right ideological balance between being seen to support socialism and their Russian allies and recognising that the Magyars, the tribes who had arrived and made camp in what is now Hungary more than a millennium earlier, were imbued with a spirit of independence, borne out of their linguistically and racially insular position in Europe. How could they most adeptly cosy up to their political masters to the east on the one hand, but keep them at arm's length and allow a softer form of socialism, one which gave a tacit nod to latent entrepreneurial ambitions, on the other?

The answer was to drip-feed privileges and to tinker with the economy around its edges; be seen to be maintaining the central pillars of the socialist state but keep the workers happy by deviating from the classic, Soviet model by providing something a bit more liberal. After the 1956 revolt, collective farms all over the country had broken themselves up anyway, so a new system had to be found to bring their members back onside. Households were allowed to have private plots of land, and in the sixties more general freedoms were extended; it became easier to travel to the West, and western goods started to be imported. The activities of the secret police became less intrusive, though by no means absent from people's lives altogether. In 1966 an initiative known as the 'New Economic Mechanism' heralded official acceptance of less centralisation and an embryonic form of market economy. Local authorities had it in their power and discretion to award a limited number of licences for private enterprises, though nothing that might threaten to undermine the state's own. The year 1982 was a landmark one in the watering down process. From January 1st that year, Hungarians could legally own property and run businesses, their new rights extending to virtually every area of economic activity bar mining and financial services.

This flowering of opportunity was in full swing by summer of that year, as Hungary loosened the shackles – not completely, but tentatively and unmistakably. The rituals of the old system were still there, and still to be followed, but there was a sense that genuine change was afoot and that this time it would not be crushed, nor even reversed. The following year the Soviet leader Yuri Andropov, during a visit to Budapest, complimented Hungary's General Secretary Kadar on the effectiveness of his reforms and said he might look to emulate them back home. This constituted a seal of approval and sanction rolled into one, from the very top, and – even though the economy stuttered during the eighties – evidence that momentum was now unstoppable.

The restaurants and bars may have been buzzing, the local girls sporting genuine variety and inventiveness in their choice of clothes, with a profusion of fresh fruit available for a modest outlay of Hungarian forints, but I still had to go through the same demeaning Monday morning act: handing over a long red and white box of Marlboro cigarettes to the customs officer who came to check and stamp our passports at 8 o'clock, or thereabouts, depending on how many other ships he'd had to collect his bounty from first. These will have been sold on, for the most part, to his fellow citizens, for to get through such a volume of cigarettes each week would have been a superhuman feat, even for a suicidally heavy smoker. So, at the top of my Saturday evening shopping list in Vienna, and on my expenses submission, there was always this guarantee of trouble-free admission to Hungary, and of none of my guests having to face a nervy and completely unnecessary inquisition.

An uneventful passport control would also ensure that the city sightseeing tour got off to a punctual start at the scheduled 8.45 departure time. The SAGA brochure waxed lyrical, justifiably so, on the multitude and array of Buda and Pest's historical gems, which we had just three hours to savour. The Budapest city tour was always a highlight of our itinerary. Hungary, and its history and culture, was rarely heard about back home. It did not feature heavily in school curricula, unless you'd chosen to do A-level history, and even then it would only have been referred to in passing as having been repeatedly devastated by Ottoman hordes as they rampaged westwards during the sixteenth century. I did do A-level history, was fascinated by that period, so also knew about the thrashing the Hungarians had taken at The Battle of Mohacs in 1526 and the Turks' progress to the gates of Vienna in 1529; but that was about it. In the early eighties, long before the advent of cheap flights, the nations and cities of Eastern Europe were well off the beaten track of the average western tourist, though the first real stirrings of interest would come soon. There was still a sense of adventure, of pioneering, and of privilege, in discovering what lay behind the Iron Curtain. Intrigue met with amazement as our *Volanbusz* chugged from one unique monument to the next on those revelatory Monday mornings in Budapest, and there was always a sort of muted euphoria both during and after our all-too-brief circuit.

Heroes' Square was the first stop, which usually lasted a bit too long. This is in no way meant as a criticism of that magnificent part of the Pest side of the city, with its arching dual colonnades framing the nation's most notable sons against the backdrop of City Park and the eclectic assemblage of buildings that make up Vajdahunyad Castle. The square is a place of grandiose proportions, with its polished flagstones and its wildly contrasting shapes somehow fitting perfectly into its whole aspect. As its centerpiece, Archangel Gabriel sits triumphant atop her white column high above the square, with her wings heavenward and her seven, proud horseman warriors at her feet. And close by, the two massive neoclassical art museums make a determined, equally valid bid to own the space.

The problem was that Heroes' Square is a tour guide's dream, as so many of the key players in Hungary's earlier history are represented in Zala's fine statues there, so it was a golden, obvious and very visual opportunity to run through most of that earlier history in one go. And guides, especially those working in the Eastern Europe of the eighties, can be prone to letting history prevail above everything else of local interest – provided, of course, in those days, that it was 'safe' history. Here in Heroes' Square, from the founding of the nation in AD 896 by Arpad, through the crowning of Stephen as the country's first king in 1000, into the glittering renaissance reign of Matthias Corvinus in the fifteenth century, and further on still, there was safe history in spadeloads.

Moreover, it takes time to list the main feats and achievements of fourteen statues, especially when the guide has only a tenuous mastery of the language in which he or she is extolling the virtues of all fourteen, and elderly – in fact, any – audiences can grow weary, which is what often happened, particularly on hot days. On most of the tours during late June and early July, our coach was allocated the same lady who, I guess, must have been in her early seventies. She was called Agi and clearly knew her stuff, but her command of English was at best questionable, and generated politely puzzled looks as her charges struggled to interpret her frequently incoherent commentary. There was the added irritation of not a word being uttered about the 1956 uprising, nor Hungary's role in World War II, despite the fact that these were probably *the* two events most of her listeners wanted to hear about, and possibly knew some detail of already. Not even as we passed by bullet-ridden after shrapnel-pockmarked façade was there any effort made to explain who had been fighting whom, and why. Even up at the Citadella, high above the river on the city's Buda side and bearing the scars of war, where the Germans and their Hungarian allies had made a final desperate stand against the Russians in 1945, there were no explanations offered.

The resulting feedback was usually along the lines of 'we love Budapest, but haven't learnt much about it', so one of the other cruise directors, Barrie Lloyd, a straight-talking Welshman who I got on with very well, and I decided that remedial action needed to be taken. For the good of our passengers, and of our employers' and our own reputations, but also for the good of Agi herself, who we felt couldn't be comfortable going through the distress of trying to make herself understood for the duration of a three-hour shift. The next time she arrived to conduct the tour, and after initial protestations which softened after Barrie pressed a small wad of bank notes into her palm, she agreed to spend the morning sipping coffee and eating cake in one of the city's many pleasant cafés, while I took over the microphone. This was highly illegal and would rely upon a lot of luck and discretion, not least on the part of Agi, banished to wherever she could enjoy her hastily rearranged morning as inconspicuously as possible. We hoped her loyalty to us would be more than just temporary. And as it would have been unwise to leave the coach driver out of our small-scale wealth distribution programme, he too was suitably recompensed for the loss of his regular partner, and seemed more than happy to be complicit in Agi's sidelining.

The tour went smoothly. At the main sights, I gathered my group as far away as possible from public gaze, and just hoped that I looked vaguely Hungarian. Amid the endless, unintelligible accounts of historical events, Agi had slipped in a couple of quirky facts which usually succeeded in eliciting something resembling low-level chuckling on the coach, and I had these in my armoury to bring out at the appropriate points in the tour. One related to a minor, rather inconspicuous bridge in Pest which the locals called the 'salami' bridge after the government was allegedly unable to pay the German constructors in hard currency so paid them in one of the nation's most famous food products instead. Another good one, though like many of the best tour guide stories unlikely to have even a grain of truth about it, was that when Hungary trounced England 7–1 at the Nepstadion in 1954 the celebrations of the 92,000-strong crowd were sufficiently raucous and wild as to register a small earthquake on the Richter scale. In anticipation of our coup, I had gleaned what facts I could on the '56 uprising and where the bloodiest exchanges had taken place, and managed to work these into my presentation from inside the secure environment of the coach where, with the driver onside, the ears were uniformly friendly. I tilted the balance in favour of more time up at the Castle area, where my customers could wander up the cobbled streets to the Matthias Church to take in the view of the Parliament, down the hill and across the river from the Fisherman's Bastion, while I could contemplate a reasonably good job well done – so far – over some refreshment at my favourite Café Corona, this time for twenty minutes longer than usual.

With no further appearance from our original leader for the next three weeks, and a sequence of altogether more comprehensible guides in her wake, Barrie and I were confident that this particular operational issue had been resolved. There were some pangs of conscience that our actions might have brought about a premature, though – on the basis of what I had witnessed – overdue end to someone's career, but we consoled ourselves by reminding each other that we had done the right thing, and had made some small contribution towards Agi's pension as well.

Then, one Monday morning in early August, to our horror, there she was, waiting at the bottom of the coach steps, ready as before to carry out her duties. Her wry, rather awkward smile as I approached announced that she could make herself disappear in a matter of seconds if the right measures were taken. With the deal done and her release clause activated without any fuss, Barrie then emerged from the ship to break the news that there was enough space on our SAGA coach for the handful of German tourists on board that week to join us, and I found myself conducting my first bilingual tour. Conscious of potential historical sensitivities, I went to great lengths to make tactful adjustments to the content as I went along. Despite 'tactful' occasionally bordering on 'clumsy', the tour passed off without serious incident, and nobody complained.

As things turned out, it was fortunate that I had a couple of outings as an unofficial Budapest guide. Towards the end of my tour of duty, there was an unhappy occurrence when a Lord and Lady C found themselves accommodated on C deck, insisting that they would never deliberately have chosen to spend their nights in such cramped, ill-equipped and gloomy quarters. Even though the solution of a free upgrade was swiftly offered, and accepted, our illustrious guests decided to milk the situation for all they could, and one of the suggestions for compensation they devised was that I book a taxi at SAGA's expense and escort them on a private guided tour of the city, with full commentary provided on all the sights of note. I duly obliged, did, I think, a reasonable job, thanks to my illicitly acquired experience, and mercifully no further concessions were requested by the couple during the remainder of their time on board.

*

Monday mornings were also notable for being the mornings after some long nights before. One of life's greatest truths is that holidaymakers, irrespective of age and myself included, have a shared tendency to treat the first night of their vacation as though it were their last on earth. Entire holiday budgets can be shattered, or at least severely dented, in a few hours of over-indulgence and general hedonism, as the shackles of daily routine are cast off and the long-awaited bout of escapism gets underway. Sunday nights on the *Carpati* were no exception, despite the only formal entertainment on offer being our four-piece band with their woefully limited repertoire of a handful of songs, most of which nobody knew. When Hölderlin, the acclaimed German philosopher and romantic poet, labelled the Danube 'river of melody', he would not have had this sort of thing in mind. To be fair, the four tried hard to please, and the resulting windfall from tips probably meant they were the wealthiest Romanians on board, so their efforts paid off handsomely.

My orders from HQ were not to leave the bar until the last of my guests had returned to their cabins. I had approached my summer mission under the misapprehension that elderly people were normally tucked up in bed by ten, so would not be calling on my services after that time. I quickly learnt that this assumption was wide of the mark, and that first night revelry was something that afflicted people of all ages and types, especially ladies who'd recently been widowed. It wasn't uncommon for me to drag what was left of me to my refuge at three in the morning, after the bar staff too had insisted that enough was enough, having let a sequence of partners try in vain to teach me to waltz, foxtrot and quickstep, with the odd cha-cha-cha thrown in for good measure. That meant just three hours of sleep before rising at six for breakfast duty, passport control and then the city sightseeing tour. It also meant that a high proportion of my guests missed the last hour or so of the tour because they were fast asleep, not just because they'd given up trying to decipher what Agi was saying, but because they'd seriously overdone it the night before.

After a couple of cruises trying to find my dance feet, and indeed whether I had any, I decided that broadening the entertainment offering could achieve two valuable objectives. Firstly, it would provide some variety to my guests, and secondly, and crucially, it would avoid me having to spend hours each night feigning enthusiasm for dances I didn't feel very enthusiastic about, nor perform very well. Being cajoled into risking yet another crude imitation of the rumba for the fourth or fifth time in an evening was taking an early toll. After some negotiation with both cruise directors, and convincing them that happy customers were more likely to become thirsty customers, we were granted an area of the lounge bar where we could, on specified evenings, remove ourselves to. Leaving our fellow passengers to continue to soak up the tortured strains emanating from the band's violins, my guests and I got to diversify into the camaraderie and hilarity of games and the occasional quiz.

And not a quiz went by without my posing the tantalising question: 'What do the letters S A G A stand for?'

The answers were many and varied, usually moderately rude, and rarely correct. Reading aloud some of the gamer attempts, together with a selection of my own embellishments gleaned from past groups, before revealing the real meaning, was always a high point of the evening. These included:

Send All Grannies Away

Senile And Geriatric Association

...and even

Sex And Games Abroad

This last one attracted disbelieving screeches of delight from the ladies and chortles and guffaws from their menfolk. When I'd calmed everyone down to announce that what the acronym *actually* stood for was *Social Amenities Golden Age* ('because we at SAGA consider you to be enjoying your golden age'), bawdy howls were replaced by a sort of communal cooing sound and general murmurings of 'well I never', 'who would've thought?' and 'well I never knew that!'

When it came to the games, each group had the same firm favourite, the ultimate test of spousal awareness. This featured the unedifying spectacle of a wife crawling blindfolded along a parade of six seated husbands, each with trousers rolled up to the knees, trying to identify her man by feeling the bumps and contours of twelve lower legs. After several minutes of groping and patting calves and rubbing shins, which sometimes seemed gratuitously prolonged, the blindfold was removed after the wife had made her choice, frequently the wrong one. My own personal favourite, and an opportunity for some mild sadism, involved tying couples together by their wrists with two pieces of string, one piece crossing the other, with each member of the pair then having to extricate him or herself without untying their own or their partner's string at the wrist. The solution was to slip a hand through a loop made in the knot around the partner's wrist, but no one ever succeeded in working that out, and the resulting bizarre bodily contortions, as each pair grew more and more desperate to free themselves, caused raucous laughter from the onlookers, many of whom were other passengers and curious bar staff who'd come to see what all the noise was about.

The beauty of this game was that I could let the pairs roll around on the floor, entwining themselves in each other and performing physical feats well beyond what would normally be possible for people of that vintage, all the while running the clock down to bedtime. And this in the knowledge that everyone would go to bed very happy, that bar takings would be healthy and that I'd avoided having to dance. A good ruse was to schedule games for Thursdays and tie up as many couples as possible. That way, most of them would be exhausted from their exertions and ready for bed by eleven, meaning Barrie and I could make an incursion into Budapest to explore a few of his chosen watering holes.

Barrie was a veteran of the Danube, so knew his way round the city's nocturnal hotspots. A short walk down the quay took us to a ship-cum-disco called 'Hajó Disco' ('Hajó' being the Hungarian for 'boat'), and that was normally our last port of call after a beer or two at the Black Cat Club. If excursion sales had been good that week and we were feeling flush, we would add a fiery goulash at the palatial Gundel in the City Park or in the wonderfully poky Hundred Years restaurant, a welcome break from the monotony of the indifferent but acceptable fare served on board.

At a time when mixing was still discouraged, the Hajó was a place where East and West contrived to come together and was always packed full with a blend of young and old, ships' crews and occupants and affluent-looking local girls seeking to make new, temporary friends. The atmosphere was heady and intoxicating, a release from our confinement, and it was a relief to be able to dance freely and without fear of disabling an elderly customer by stepping on her toes.

One night, when Barrie was not on my cruise and I had no wingman, I jumped into a passing taxi and asked the driver to take me to a place I'd heard about, deep in the Buda Hills, that more upscale tract of the city where the geothermal springs had been tapped into centuries earlier by the Turks to supply their healing waters to communal baths still extant today; to Kiraly, to Rudas, to where Hotel Gellert now stands, and to many others.

It was a venue which catered more to the population of young summer incomers from other Eastern European countries, was dimly lit, cavernous and without the frills and relative opulent cosiness of the Hajó. For some reason, probably because I was hot off the ship's dance floor and had decided not to get changed so as to get the maximum benefit from what was left of the night, I was wearing a jacket and tie, which was completely inappropriate to the dark and dingy surroundings and a walk on the wild side. I might just as well have had 'westerner' tattooed on my forehead; I felt distinctly out of place. But to do Budapest justice, boundaries had to be pushed beyond the inner-city safety of what I'd come to know, so once inside there was no thought of going back. And as I soon discovered, a bottle of the local brew cost less than a quarter of the western brands commanding inflated prices in my usual haunts, which also meant that most of the partygoers were blind drunk and completely uninhibited.

It turned out to be an unforgettable evening, but not altogether for the right reasons. After an hour or so I had made casual acquaintances from all corners of the Eastern Bloc, as well as Africa (socialist African countries such as Congo, Mozambique and Angola sent their young to study in Hungary and elsewhere in Eastern Europe) and had chatted for some time to two local girls at the bar. A couple of muscular, T-shirt-clad lads seemed to be shadowing them, and looking at me rather menacingly. The girls told me that the two had said they were English, so buoyed by the prospect of some compatriot banter and hopefully a reduction in the threat level, I tried to engage them in conversation. This was preceded by offers of handshakes, which were rejected. None of my polite enquiries into which part of our kingdom they came from or how long they had been in Hungary, etc, were answered, and it became clear to me – and the two girls – that the two young men were certainly not English. At that point, with the glares becoming ever more intense, an unmistakable instruction that I should leave the girls immediately, I wished all four a pleasant rest-of-evening and tactfully withdrew.

Apart from the time my father invited a visiting work colleague to our house in Northumberland in the early seventies, the closest I'd previously come to having contact with anyone from Poland had been nine months earlier at Leeds, where I was a member of the University Polish Society. At the end of the autumn term, I'd spent a few hours with a small band of similarly motivated students, who shared my growing interest in what was happening in the Gdańsk shipyards and the emergence of the Solidarity movement, making up parcels full of food and gifts to send to beleaguered shipyard workers' families in the Baltic city. Lech Wałęsa was the name on everyone's lips, as the world watched to see whether the Polish government of Wojciech Jaruzelski would accede to Wałęsa's recently formed union's demands for economic reforms, free elections and better working conditions. It was the first real challenge to the

authority of the Polish state, indeed to any of the Eastern
European governments, since the Prague revolt of 1968. In
the event, Solidarity was declared illegal and martial law
imposed in late 1981, but the die had been cast.

Now, contact with Poland was about to be resumed, and
in dramatic fashion. Since leaving the two girls and their
minders at the bar half an hour earlier, I'd found sanctuary
at the opposite side of the room and struck up conversation
with a Canadian guy called Les, with the two of us forming
a tightly knit, English-speaking island a few steps from the
dance floor. Les was well over six feet, broad-shouldered and
with long, mousy, tousled hair partially obscuring the kind
of pecs that any weightlifter would have been proud of.

Suddenly, I felt a firm tap on my shoulder and swung
round to see one of the muscular, T-shirted youths from the
bar with a furious, sneering expression on his sweat-coated
face. He moved the tip of his nose to within millimetres of
mine: 'Me no eeenglish, me no eeenglish, Polska, Polska!' he
screamed, before gripping the knot of my tie in one fist and
the tail of it in the other and pulling the knot upwards and
as tight as he could. Before I had a chance to remonstrate
or do anything to interrupt my garrotting, Les grabbed my
assailant and hurled him into the gyrating, seething mass
of humanity on the dance floor. He then proceeded to beat
him to within an inch of his life, as dancers ran for cover
in all directions. There was blood everywhere, well before
the bouncers intervened. Les, and what was left of the
Pole, were manhandled away towards the main entrance.
Moments later the lights came on to signal that the evening
had come to a premature end, and everyone traipsed out,
forlorn at having their fun truncated so abruptly and still in
shock from the spectacle that had played out in front of them
minutes earlier.

Back in my cabin, and for some time afterwards, I mulled over the evening's events. I felt a nagging sense of being indirectly responsible for terminating a good night out for hundreds of people, the sort of wild, uninhibited night many of them probably didn't get to enjoy very often. A couple of lessons had been learnt: firstly, to choose my attire much more carefully in future and secondly, to leave people who clearly didn't appreciate my presence well alone. But more than lessons learnt, it was depressing that the Polish boys had felt they needed to pretend to be English to better their chances of winning the affections of the girls. There would be many times in the next few years when, like now, this 'otherness' of western people, a perceived superiority, weighed heavily on me. There was a status and a novelty factor bestowed on us, an unfair and undeserved advantage over our fellow men, all brought about by an accident of birth that gave us the good fortune to end up on the right side of a political and ideological divide.

*

Maybe it was partly this novelty factor that attracted Doina and me to each other. By mid-August Alex and his tyrannical regime had gone, to the relief of everyone, although nobody seemed to know why. Barrie, Almut and a third cruise director, a genial Dutchman called Ernest, were joined by a female Romanian cruise director on *Carpati* and on *Oltenita*, and the atmosphere lightened on both. On *Carpati,* Alex's brashness and arrogance were replaced by Doina's humility and quiet reserve. Unobtrusive to the point of near invisibility, it was difficult to see why she had been entrusted with a position of authority, and one which carried with it such an insidious brand. That said, she had a child, a hostage against defection, and her bosses at the state tourism organisation (coincidentally also called 'Carpati') would surely have taken this into account when considering how to fill the void left by Alex. Whatever the explanation, one Wednesday morning I boarded the upstream cruise in Belgrade to meet my new group at breakfast, and there she was in the restaurant, shyly checking on the catering arrangements as I made my introductions around the tables.

Doina was slim and willowy. Her back was always perfectly arched and the joints in her elbows and wrists effortlessly supple, pointers to her earlier life as an accomplished gymnast some years before Nadia Comăneci struck gold at the Montreal and Moscow Olympics. The hue of her skin tended towards Middle Eastern rather than Dacian; she was convinced there was Turkish ancestry somewhere in her distant past. Deep, lonely brown eyes seemed to view the world almost unwillingly, trying hard to conceal themselves below a low fringe, her eye-matching hair an extended bob terminating at a prominent collarbone. Smallish in stature, she was exotically pretty, with no obvious artificial efforts made to graduate to beautiful.

Our early exchanges were formal and businesslike, as we followed the unwritten protocol that was supposed to govern dealings between Romanian cruise director and underling English rep, a protocol which made no allowances for interaction for any other purposes than to get our jobs done. Doina adhered to this to the letter, her demureness bordering on outright indifference at any straying on my part into light-hearted observations. My smiles were always answered with the same blank, dismissive expression, the kind a teacher might give a pupil who tests the established classroom order by daring to be ever-so-slightly flippant. The invisible fence surrounding her appeared to have no gate in it, and I resigned myself to a rapport in which there was no place for the sort of easy camaraderie which had come to mark out so many of my relationships on board the ships that summer and which, I had concluded, were the best sort of relationships to get things done.

I am not sure where the turning point was or exactly when the breakthrough came, and it's more likely there was a gradual thaw than one seminal moment. By August I'd expanded my entertainment programme to daytime and the airy space of the upper deck, and conducted regular exercise classes for my clients and anyone else who felt that a safely un-rigorous workout would provide a welcome alternative to cabin confinement. It's unlikely that the sight of me in my ridiculously brief, imitation silk red shorts and far-too-tight blue and white hooped T-shirt, persuading fifty or so mainly elderly passengers to bend tentatively forwards from the hips, stirred something in her. Or maybe Doina did indeed see that as a selfless and heroic act which allowed her to grab a welcome half an hour of respite from engaging with other human beings, and a chance to catch up on some reading in a quiet corner. She never said.

During the Cold War, it was perhaps unsurprising that a relationship between two people on different sides of the European divide often started out as a microcosm of this bloodless conflict. Nominally we were enemies, and as with any enemies a wall of separation had to be deconstructed so that trust and confidence could be won. These were not like relationships back home, and before the stage of mutual attraction there were pre-stages to work through and overcome, suspicion being uppermost of these. Not always a bilateral suspicion though, for the eastern party had more to lose from trust being abused and confidences betrayed, so was naturally more guarded and wary of getting too close and dangerously deep, with all the potential adverse consequences for career, for family and for quality of life. For his or her part, the western party was mindful of being an opportunity rather than a genuine object of affection, an opportunity for financial betterment or for escape to a better life.

Doina was a few years older than me, had a child, a flat with her estranged husband and this good job, some escape from a difficult domestic situation back home. The ice began to melt as we discovered a mutual fascination with each other's language, a relatively safe and uncontroversial canvas on which to weave the first threads of friendship. I recall introducing a few quirky English idioms into our rather mundane, matter-of-fact conversations, and her curiosity was aroused. What did these colourful phrases, so different from the bog-standard English she had been fed at school and college, mean? And how could we find equivalents in Romanian? Our daily meetings in the bar to go over timings, menus and excursions became lighter, cordial, and even fun, increasingly deviating away from the prosaic into territory beyond the dictates of our jobs. We came to extend each session to allow some time to teach each other new words and expressions; I would dare Doina to try out some of the more bizarre and useless ones on my customers, but her diffidence held her back. We told jokes and stories, ventured into revealing extracts from our lives before that summer, our paths to this point, dismantling the wall brick by brick, with caution and a frisson of excitement preceding each new revelation. It was like stepping apprehensively onto the edge of a frozen lake, wondering how far you can go before the glass below your feet gives way, listening intently for the groaning sound of the terminal crack that will put an end to your timid, yet bold, advance. But the crack never appeared.

Soon we were bold, and foolish, enough to take to sneaking

out onto deck in the early hours, after the last revellers had decided that bed was a preferable option to more music from the band. We put our trust in the cover of darkness, but this was folly on a ship where eyes and ears were ever alert for signs of non-conformity, and night offered no protection. Perhaps we knew this, and knew the risks we were taking, but the cool breeze coming off the river, gently ruffling our hair as we held hands and whispered and embraced, gave us a sensation of being immune to danger, of wrapping ourselves in something worth taking risks for. We were, literally and emotionally, on a journey together the likes of which neither of us had undertaken before, and as the preparation for the journey had been so complicated and challenging, we wanted to savour every forbidden moment, knowing all too well that these would be few, and would soon have an end.

On land we felt more free, free to hold hands for longer and, eventually, to dare to trade kisses. Being on neutral ground was the closest we could get to detachment from our real worlds, and the pavements of Vienna, Budapest and Belgrade turned from neutral into hallowed ground. On Saturday nights we'd meet in Vienna's City Park, where there was dancing on the terrace of the splendid, ornate café to Strauss and other classical masters. The dress was casual and incongruous with the sumptuous surroundings, and an easy vibe prevailed where no one cared if your rendition of the waltz was less than basic, as ours was. We would sit, chatting, laughing, sipping our beers, and I would do my best to persuade Doina to chance a few more steps on the dance floor after previous attempts at getting our footwork right and in sync had failed miserably. Then we'd amble along the Ringstrasse, dive off into the labyrinth of small streets in the city's inner core and seek out somewhere cosy for a final glass of white from the vineyards of Burgenland or Lower Austria.

Finally, a taxi would drop her off at the ship and deposit me at the Hotel Atlas, both returning to our caring duties, both harbouring a warm inner glow of elation, knowing we would be back together on board in a few hours.

When we were not on the same cruise we exchanged letters via one of Doina's cruise director colleagues, who she said was a trusted friend. Doina wrote passionately and expressively, with a confusion of love and longing, hopelessness at her situation and despair that I might not feel as strongly about her as she did about me. Her icy reserve in those first days had been replaced by an effusiveness that was raw, exciting and at the same time alarming, encompassing all the extremes of emotion that this unexpected, whirlwind romance had evoked in us both. I missed our stolen, clandestine moments on deck at night, as we drifted carefree past the silhouettes of tiny villages and stately buildings on shore, buildings which by day curious customers would quiz me on and about which I rarely knew anything. We reps had our default get-outs for when we were caught off guard. For example, we would say that the palatial edifice before us was a former monastery which had been requisitioned for use as barracks during some conflict or other, before becoming a boarding school for girls, but which since the advent of communism had been allowed by the state to fall into disrepair through lack of funds. All of this was highly plausible, if totally inaccurate, and enough to induce a grateful, enlightened nod from the enquirer.

Then one day, just after I boarded *Oltenita* in Belgrade, Doina's cruise director friend gave me a note, delivered with a blank but mildly threatening expression. Short, and clearly written in haste, the note was from Doina who said that she was in trouble and that we had to stop writing to each other. I had half expected, and hoped, to see her here on the upstream cruise, but my disappointment was nothing compared to the grinding anxiety and guilt that gnawed away at me over the days and weeks that followed. When I timidly asked the note's deliverer for information on what fate might have befallen her good friend Doina, there was a shrug of the shoulders and a look that telegraphed that she didn't want to be engaged on the subject.

Eventually, towards the end of September, I did come to learn what had happened to Doina. My letters had somehow found their way not only to her bosses at ONT Carpati but also to her estranged husband. I had a nagging suspicion that her supposed friend had something to do with this, but of course I couldn't prove it. I later learnt what happened in a heart-rending letter Doina sent to my home in Northumberland. Because no one else was available, they had assigned her to *Carpati* for the final fortnight of the season, and she was writing from Budapest. Her ex had been upset with her but seemed to have accepted the situation. She'd had problems in the office, but her transgressions were evidently not deemed sufficiently serious for her to be struck off the cruise director list. Or maybe necessity prevailed there. Her letter was full of passion, of pain at our being separated and of loathing for the 'spies' on the ship, and it made distressing reading.

Especially so as by then my summer on the river was over; I was back home and knew I would probably never see her again.

*

New recruits to the esteemed ranks of tour escorts, couriers, reps, tour guides, or whatever we end up being called by the group we are serving at the time, will often learn within hours of embarking upon their noble profession that the Boy Scouts' motto of 'Be Prepared' is its fundamental prerequisite.

At its most basic and obvious level, this means carrying

out a raft of checks which should always be made before your customers descend on you:

Has the hotel (or ship) restaurant taken note of any special dietary needs? Does the coach that is due to transfer the group from the airport to the hotel/ship have enough seats and luggage space? Has the hotel/ship reception allocated rooms/cabins correctly? And so on.

And then, as the tour (or cruise) progresses, it's about always staying one or two steps ahead by making sure everyone involved is fully apprised of any changes in schedule and participant numbers. Then there are the essential double-checks, for example that the folklore venue is actually open as planned, that the local guides know when and where to meet the group, and that they have a reasonable command of English. The mindset is to never switch off, to constantly be thinking ahead, so that when the unexpected does happen – as it inevitably will – at least the main cornerstones of the operation are in place. And once you have the experience of the first of a series of tours under your belt and have noted any potential pitfalls, such as the backlash from my SAGA charges after they first set foot in C deck cabins and, in some cases, refused to set any more feet in them again, your level of preparedness reaches new heights, and you are well on the way to honing this crucial skill.

In the Eastern Europe of the early eighties, 'being prepared' was never going to be enough. It wasn't just that individual service providers often lacked the motivation to perform, or even in some cases to turn up to deliver at all – although, in reality, there were plenty of excellent guides, drivers, waiters and waitresses and receptionists among the wholly inadequate or invisible. It was more the unique nature of some of the challenges that arose that left even the most able and best prepared of our number to go into a sudden, rapid nosedive from which salvation seemed unlikely. In such cases, the next grade up of 'being prepared for the unexpected' didn't provide sufficient insulation and, rather like Dante working his way down through the ledges of hell, you had to adopt a state of 'being prepared to be unprepared'.

One week I had embarked *Oltenita* in Belgrade to find something approaching mutiny among my new guests. They had all hated the food in Romania, were disappointed with the ship, and had been expecting to be able to spend on board the worthless Romanian lei they had ill-advisedly amassed, only to find that they couldn't. The mood was at best sombre, more accurately conspiratorial, as one clique endeavoured to outdo the other in contriving something new to find fault with.

Alex was the Romanian cruise director at the helm that week, and as we approached Budapest he summoned me for a meeting. I was expecting him to demand that I somehow quell the dissent and whiff of rebellion among my OAPs so as to stop the contagion of negativity spreading to the other passengers, and to come up with something to lighten the rather toxic atmosphere that had developed. Instead, he declared in a resigned and vaguely triumphant tone that the ship had run out of butter and so there would be no butter at breakfast the next morning. He had spoken to the captain, who had said he'd been unable to get permission from his superiors in Bucharest to purchase more butter supplies in Budapest, and nothing could be done about it. It was regrettable, but there it was.

The thought of my already simmering clients having to spread their jam straight onto naked, usually rather limp toast was chastening. This could be the spark which ignited a sizeable pile of smouldering kindling, and something had to be done. In desperation, I expounded in great detail to Alex the essential British cultural necessity of toast and jam being accompanied by an intermediate layer of butter, and that the absence of butter would only serve to increase the chances of an all-out riot taking place on board. His trademark sinister nonchalance seemed momentarily and partially ruptured by my appeal to national customs, and he grudgingly agreed to find some way of compensating my clients for the inconvenience of having their mornings utterly ruined.

After a sleepless night, I was in the restaurant earlier than usual for breakfast duty, half hoping – but not really expecting – that some overnight change in orders from Bucharest might have led to the magical sight of little ceramic receptacles of butter adorning the faded white tablecloths. Instead, I was greeted by the spectacle of two waitresses carefully placing four glasses of Pepsi-Cola on each table. Warm Pepsi-Cola, I discovered when I picked up one of the glasses. When I enquired why Pepsi-Cola was being introduced onto the breakfast menu, one of them meekly replied that Mr Alex had ordered it because there was no butter and to make the guests happy.

So this was Alex's idea of compensation, and predictably it was met with disbelief, then a blend of ridicule and anger, and the refusal of almost everyone to take so much as a sip of the flat, tepid liquid which was supposed to appease them. With the mid-morning air incendiary, a search party from among the crew was dispatched into the city with a brief to locate and procure butter as cheaply as possible. Their mission was successful, and breakfasts once again returned to being one of the less contentious and troublesome parts of the day. A raucous games session in the bar that evening and a punishing workout on deck the following day took the wind out of the sails of the insurrection's ringleaders, and the remainder of that cruise passed off without further incident.

*

The following week on the upstream cruise, a significant delay almost caused the homebound passengers to miss their flight in Vienna. The delay, however, was inconsequential compared to the tragedy that caused it. *Carpati* had pulled into the town of Komarno on the northern, Czechoslovakian bank of the Danube; it was the only occasion we would moor in that country during the whole summer. No announcement had been made as to why we had made this unscheduled stop, and as the hours rolled by a nervousness started to spread through the ship. Captain, Romanian cruise director and crew were tight-lipped, and even Almut didn't seem to know what was afoot. Everything became clear when I was called to sit next to the ship's entrance with one of the female crew members, a young girl who was clearly in considerable pain, her face a wan, greyish-yellow hue. The captain was in negotiation with the local authorities to have the girl taken to hospital, it transpired, but this was not a straightforward matter as there were permissions to be granted and a lot of forms to be filled in. I wondered where the ship's doctor was, why he was not attending to the stricken girl, and why I was there in his place, holding her hand and giving her what little comfort I could in my wholly inadequate Romanian.

Then the reason for the doctor's absence became clear. I learnt that the girl had fallen pregnant by one of the engine room boys, and had attempted a self-induced abortion using a wire coat hanger. It had gone disastrously wrong, and she had lost a lot of blood. As abortion was illegal in Romania, and she knew that a baby would mean an end to a life in which she could spend at least some time away from the drudgery of her homeland, she'd chosen the only course of action which, in her lonely desperation, had seemed open to her. And the doctor wouldn't have wished to be tainted by association, so had made himself scarce in her hour of greatest need.

After what must have been a terrifying eternity for the girl, three Czechoslovak border guards marched onto the ship and escorted her, bent double in agony, to a waiting ambulance. No sooner had the girl left than *Carpati* spluttered away from her mooring with even greater vigour and protest than usual, arriving in Vienna only slightly behind schedule.

I never found out what became of the young girl, nor whether she had survived her terrible ordeal, but at the very least her days on the Danube would have been numbered.

*

For all the unexpected events in the average week, there was one event which was guaranteed to happen, and happen in the early hours of Tuesday morning at a small port near the village of Bezdan on the Hungary-Yugoslav border. It was an event that anyone with the slightest vestige of authority on board came to dread.

At some time between midnight and four o'clock, depending on how many other ships they'd terrorised before they got to ours, we'd be invaded by a rowdy gang of Yugoslav border guards in the guise of performing a passport and customs check, a front for mild extortion on good nights and for something approaching wholesale pillage on less good nights.

As tension mounted during the evening before and we readied ourselves for what became our own weekly Battle of Mohacs, the Hungarian town just north of the border where the nation's army was routed by the Turks in 1526, we prepared our combat plan. This involved making sure the passengers were fully apprised of what might befall them in the small hours and how to mitigate the more serious misdemeanours of our assailants, based on past form. In contrast to the tame, page-stamping affair in Budapest, where parting with a lot of western tobacco ensured that no questions were ever asked, the robbers who masqueraded as Yugoslav officials had to be handled in an altogether different way, and would never leave empty-handed. Damage limitation was the name of the game, and the passengers had to play their part if they were not to become unwitting collateral. The guards, who would either be drunk or very drunk, subject to the tribute paid by the captains of ships ravaged in the hours leading up to the assault on our own, would routinely demand that the bar be opened up, music struck up and bottles of vodka offered up. That was on a good night. On a less good night they would scrutinise the passenger manifest and passports, noting down which of the female guests, on the strength of their passport photos, qualified for a personal cabin inspection. If the guards liked what they found in bed in the cabin, those same female guests could be invited to continue the inspection back at the bar. This would usually culminate in enforced drinking, singing and dancing, before the unfortunate passengers were allowed to salvage what remained of their dignity back in the now violated security of their cabins.

At other times they would simply charge through the ship, knock on cabin doors, wake everyone up and get back to enjoying the nightmarish party unfolding in the bar. Whatever form the nocturnal visitation took, the situation was bound to be exacerbated if the guards found that something was not in order, particularly if a passenger was found not to be in his or her allotted cabin. This was not a night to practise clandestine berth-hopping, a warning I drummed into my senior citizens at a meeting I always held with them the night before we arrived at the border. The veiled suggestion that one of our widows might have been contemplating spending the night in the discomfort of one of our widowers' cabins, and if so to resist the temptation at all costs, was always greeted with elated whoops and ribald laughter. While some saucy innuendo was no doubt good for group morale, it might inadvertently have tempered the gravity of the message, which was that things might get heavy that night and we stood a better chance of surviving intact if we all remained on our best behaviour.

On one memorable, near-disastrous occasion, one lady decided to put the system to the test and constructed an impressively lifelike effigy of herself out of pillows and clothes, placed it in a recumbent position in her bed, and moved into the cabin of a newly found friend. That night the guards decided to inspect every cabin and were incensed when they discovered the deception. Once the offending woman had been traced, which ended up being no easy task, she was summarily ordered to dress and report without delay to the bar, where her court martial awaited. A long and entirely unnecessary, monosyllabic interrogation then followed in shouted, broken English. The woman, in abject fear, was now sorely regretting her catastrophic error of judgement, while her inquisitors used the whole incident as a pretext to consume an uninterrupted flow of free alcohol, donated by the captain in penance and as compensation for the gross inconvenience caused to the guards by the woman's puerile prank.

What may have helped the lady escape a worse fate was my standing with the guards. Paul had warned me in Vienna that the Hungary-Yugoslav border could be hostile territory and, for the sake of my customers and myself too, to treat the guards with extreme caution. That first week, the palpable edginess on board *Carpati* as we neared the frontier signalled that the night ahead was likely to be challenging. I wondered how bad it could be. When the time came, at around 3 am, and five inebriated guards stomped noisily up the ramp, I'd dutifully taken up my position alongside the cruise directors and captain, next to tables piled high with passports and lists, a bottle of Finlandia and some glasses. To my amazement, one of the guards was carrying a football, and rather than heading straight for the tables and their liquid bounty, the five started to kick the football around the bar, showing off skills which would have made most Sunday morning pub teams look highly competent. When the ball ricocheted off the back of a chair and landed at my feet, I had a split second to decide whether to tap the ball back obediently or pursue the riskier option of joining in the game. Caught in two minds, I played for time by doing a few keep-ups which, despite my mediocre footballing talent, most recently displayed when turning out for Leeds University 4th team on the consistently muddy wastes at Boddington Hall, I'd pretty much perfected through years of stubborn patience and persistence.

'You good football!', bawled one of the guards, as the five stood around with hands on hips, contemplating the show of balance and dexterity before their eyes.

'Where you from?'

'England.'

'Ah England! What team you?' he enquired, aggressively.

'Newcastle United', I replied, praying that the guard didn't have a distant relative in Sunderland. There was a pause as the guard struggled to decide whether he'd heard of Newcastle United.

'You know Kevin Keegan?' I stammered, an attempt to move onto safer, more neutral ground, as the ball continued to bob up and down as if attached to my shoelaces. Doing this and holding a conversation at the same time was proving challenging, and adrenaline must have come to the rescue.

'Ah, you Kevin Keegan! Yes, yes, Kevin Keegan!' the guard came back at me, pointing in a gesture of recognition, face widening and excited.

'Erm...yes...yes...Kevin Keegan', I stuttered uncertainly, bringing the ball to rest under my right foot so as to pay full attention to the moment and mentally adjust to my new status as the England legend.

1982 was turning out to be quite a year for the real Kevin Keegan. That summer, he was considering a move from Southampton to my home team of Newcastle, having netted twenty-six goals for the Saints, been named PFA Player of Year and awarded an OBE for his services to English football, which included sixty-three appearances for his country. And by the standards of the times, he was no doubt being handsomely remunerated for his efforts. So quite why anyone would think Keegan would take a massive salary cut to spend his summer break looking after pensioners on a slightly shabby river cruise ship in the middle of Europe was difficult to fathom.

Wondering whether this was really happening, I contemplated my physical similarities to Keegan and concluded that except for shoulder-length, black wavy locks we had very little in common. At five feet nine I was a full two inches taller, so positively towered over him, and whereas he was stocky and powerfully built, I was skinny and visibly in need of proper nutrition. But I allowed the opportunity to confess to pass, and side-footed the ball back into the field of play with a swagger of authority, as if further participation was beneath me.

I never discovered, nor sought to discover, whether the guards genuinely believed I was Kevin Keegan, or just thought that I knew him or simply looked vaguely like him. Whatever the truth, whenever that band of guards boarded my ship I was jovially and boozily greeted as 'Mr Keegan', and something bordering on respect flowed. And I like to think that my fortunate SAGA clients benefitted from more lenient and less intrusive treatment as a result of what was probably all a colossal misunderstanding.

The end of an era in Yugoslavia

Two years earlier in May 1980, the man credited with holding six separate republics together in a single socialist federation for so long had died. Having successfully led partisan resistance to the Nazi occupation of his country in World War II, Josip Broz, nicknamed 'Tito', had ruled as President of Yugoslavia since 1953. After the war, Yugoslavia – born out of the collapse of the Austro-Hungarian empire in 1918, known first as the 'Kingdom of Serbs, Croats and Slovenes' and then, in 1929, the 'Kingdom of Yugoslavia' – comprised the six republics of Bosnia-Herzegovina, Croatia, Slovenia, Serbia, Montenegro and Macedonia. This coalition was called the Federal People's Republic of Yugoslavia and from 1963, the Socialist Federal Republic of Yugoslavia.

Such an amalgamation was no mean feat. There were stark differences in ethnicity and historical development between the individual republics, and it was a mark of Tito's strong leadership, and cult of personality, that he was able to sustain union and unity for so long. No doubt his policy of keeping the Soviets at arm's length, and what was seen as an enlightened approach to socialism in the economic sphere, greatly helped his cause. Workers were able to have a stake in the ownership and running of the businesses in which they were employed, and a certain amount of power and autonomy was devolved to the individual republics. Relative to other Eastern European countries, the economy performed well and Tito was lauded for rebuilding it in the years after the war. He shunned membership of Comecon, the bloc's economic pact, centred on Moscow and made up of socialist nations in the Soviet European sphere and further afield, and Stalin is reputed to have ordered no fewer than twenty-two assassination attempts on Tito to rid himself of this constant thorn in his side. Tito was undeniably a dictator, but he garnered popularity inside and outside the capital of Belgrade by allowing the leash to be strained.

Glueing together so many disparate ethnic groups for so long was a major achievement, and within months of Tito's death there were signs of the alliance unravelling, a foretaste of what was set to tear Yugoslavia apart so dramatically and bloodily some years later. There were early rumblings in the northern republic of Slovenia, where in June 1980 local politicians pushed for greater free speech and even the right to question government policies. In early 1981 riots broke out in Kosovo, then an autonomous province within Serbia, where Albanians, who formed almost eighty per cent of the population, attacked ethnic Serbs, killing nine and injuring over two hundred and fifty. And back in Slovenia, in the February of 1982, its capital Ljubljana was the venue for a pop concert held in support of the Solidarity movement in Poland.

The leash was showing early signs of the rupture to come.

The Tuesday evening folklore show, held in a restaurant in Belgrade's bohemian Skadarlija quarter, was an exhibition of ethnic equality at its colourful, high-octane best. There was a harmony of movement in the dancing – the performers, with smiles unflinching from start to finish, contorting their brightly costumed bodies with the strength and agility of gymnasts – and a harmony of representation, with each republic allotted slots of the same duration to show off its own vibrant culture. Towards the end of the night a mock wedding was staged where two hapless, usually unrelated onlookers were cajoled out of their front row seats and married off to one another. Throughout the sham ceremony they sat nervously before the giggling audience, wishing they were somewhere else, while the delighted dancers gyrated round them to bless their awkward union.

Folklore was politically safe and that's why, wherever western tourists were to be found, it was used to demonstrate the less dour aspects of life in Eastern Europe and to infuse some colour into cityscapes in dire need of some gloss. 'And we have popular culture, we have history shaped by our people and their sacrifices, we have traditions which we uphold even though our system may seem dreary and authoritarian. These provide the elixir for our people, there is no need for formal religion to nourish the soul here.' So read the subliminal message embodied in the light relief of the folklore show, which became a highlight of my week and one I always relished, even after watching the same show week after week.

After the show we returned to the river, I would bid my group farewell and wave them off from the quayside as the ship juddered grumpily into the River Sava, back to the Danube and on downstream towards Bulgaria and Romania. The upstream cruise would arrive at around five in the morning, and the powers at SAGA Holidays had decided that it would be perfectly acceptable for me to spend the six or so hours in between in the company of the Belgrade harbour police. So that first week, I reported, suitcase in tow, to a small, prefabricated hut on the quayside where I was to be billeted for the night.

It was immediately clear that the four policemen inside were not happy to be on night duty, and even less happy to have to share their cramped confinement with a fifth person, and a foreigner at that. Unfortunately for me, word hadn't reached them from the border that they were due to be joined that night by a famous international footballer, and with no footballs in sight I soon sensed that difficult hours lay ahead. That turned out to be a grave underprediction. Like their colleagues up the river, the policemen were embarked on the sort of booze-swilling, card-playing bender that would make any sort of meaningful work, let alone actually having to arrest anyone, practically impossible. Any attempt at greeting, handshaking and ingratiation on my part was curtly and rudely rebuffed and, after standing inside the doorway for some considerable time, I was directed to a stool in a corner where I sat down and stared at the floor, fervently wishing that I wasn't there.

After a while, and probably bored by the endless games of cards, one of the policemen produced a revolver and beckoned me over to join the group. It was time to spice up the fun and make it more explosive, at the expense of their new guest. I surveyed the scowling, sneering expressions around me and realised that my night was about to descend into new depths of misery, and there was no way to avoid it. In any typical group of drunk people there is normally at least one member whose mood has been lightened by the alcohol, sometimes the quiet one who casts off the everyday mantle of reticence and hesitation and is magically transformed into the life and soul of the party. Here, in contrast, the vast quantities being guzzled had led to a uniformly aggressive dynamic, and there was no way a beseeching glance would be met with anything other than scorn. The policeman thrust the revolver towards me and indicated by pointing thumb and forefinger at his temple then squeezing an imaginary trigger that I should follow suit with the actual gun. I let out a sort of stifled whinnying sound, raising both arms and shaking my head to indicate that I would prefer to be left out of this game. The gesture was met by howls of derision, and the revolver was passed to each man in turn, each pulling the trigger and simulating blowing off his head, making sure his accompanying facial distortion was more bizarre than the colleague's before. The last one launched himself sideways off his chair into a crumpled heap on the floor, and there were imaginary bits of brain everywhere. I was dismissed back to my stool in the corner amid guttural jeering, my humiliation complete, and, despite a lingering apprehension that there could be still worse in store, no one bothered me for the rest of the night.

Spotting *Oltenita*, instantly recognisable because it looked identical to *Carpati*, as it manoeuvred all too sluggishly onto its mooring, I grabbed my suitcase and exited the police hut as stealthily as possible, hoping that I wouldn't wake any of the policemen slumped like deadweights on the table covered in bottles, cards, shot glasses, cigarette stubs, ash and the revolver. It was five-thirty and the ship had been delayed, further prolonging my excruciatingly awful night. I groggily dragged my luggage up the ramp and onto my next assignment, hoping that an unoccupied cabin would be available so that I could catch up on some overdue sleep undisturbed, before meeting my new group at breakfast. There was nobody around, and I sat in the bar, dozing and waiting for someone to come on duty, which nobody did until after breakfast.

Even allowing for the fact that, as a keen new broom, I was prepared to go the extra mile to impress, the prospect of having to spend every Tuesday night that summer as an unwelcome and unwilling extra in games of mock Russian roulette was beyond alarming. My Letter of Engagement from SAGA had not made any mention of this, nor of having to absorb high levels of abuse in Serbo-Croatian. Something had to be done, so with the invaluable help of Wolfgang Lüftner, I petitioned SAGA to stump up for a hotel room, a hostel room, anything, never mind how basic, as long as it didn't involve spending the night with drunk policemen with guns. Surely a well-rested rep was going to be more effective, and able to provide a better service to their customers, than one who came fresh off the set of *Apocalypse Now*?

My pleas for clemency were heard and acted upon, and the following Tuesday, and every Tuesday thereafter, a taxi ferried me late in the evening to a modest guest house in the city centre where, quite apart from it not being the police hut, it was good to have a real bed for at least one night of the week, and some time away from the claustrophobic world of the ships. A huge disco always took place that night up at the Kalemegdan Fortress, a stunning setting for a spot of hedonism, and, residual stamina permitting, I would often nip up there for an hour or two before turning in for what remained of the night, before having to be back at the quayside for six-thirty.

Maybe, just maybe, those policemen did me a favour.

*

We reps had a 'C word' that summer, and the 'C' stood for 'Currency'. Currency was the bane of our lives, a necessary and nauseating evil of operating in different Eastern European countries, each with equally worthless currencies once you left the country and next to worthless within it too. In some countries, it was a requirement to change your UK sterling, US dollars, Deutschmarks or Austrian schillings into the local currency, but changing any remaining amounts back into our 'hard' currencies could be problematic, or restricted. Hungary, for example, only permitted half the amount of local forints purchased to be changed back. Exchange receipts had to be retained and submitted to one of a sparse collection of official exchange bureaus in order to get a portion of your money back, so if you were foolish enough to change large quantities of money on the black market, in the hope of going on a spree so productive as to solve all your Christmas shopping needs, you would be sorely disappointed on two fronts. Firstly, apart from some possibly novel stocking fillers, there was precious little in the shops to buy (and the best goods were often found in 'hard currency only' stores) so, secondly, you ran the very real risk of being left with a sizeable wad of unusable notes, which would probably end up stuffed and forgotten in the deepest recesses of a bedroom draw, never again to see the light of day, and certainly never to be used to buy anything.

And woe betide the eager tourist who joined the queue at an exchange bureau with his or her western banknotes in anything less than pristine condition. Depending on what kind of day the clerk on the other side of the glass screen was having, even a mint condition note could be declined if one of the corners was turned down. Anyone hoping to exchange notes that had been written on, or had the slightest of tears, or were in any way crumpled, was on a hiding to nothing and could expect morose and disdainful rejection.

Dabbling in a bit of black market action was often seen as being part and parcel of the Eastern Europe experience. This was not surprising, as the deal offered by the well-groomed, good-looking, confident young man who accosted you outside your hotel, offering four or five times the rate given at the official exchange bureaus, did indeed make your holiday pound go further. It was always highly advisable to inspect the roll of paper pressed urgently into your palm to make sure it really did consist of bank notes, and not partially of toilet paper, before completing the transaction. Many didn't, despite our warnings, and we frequently had to pick up the pieces and console our infuriated, defiled passengers that the loss of their tenner was down to pure bad luck. And to not heeding our warnings.

The upstream passengers I joined in Belgrade were often saddled with eye-watering amounts of Romanian lei, which they'd either been unable to change back into sterling in Romania or erroneously believed they could spend on board ship. Some also complained of dodgy tummies, something my penfriend Sharon in Sinaia attributed to the food served up a few nights earlier for the folklore evening at Bucharest's Parc Hotel. Both ships operated an identical system called 'Board Dollars', and this was the only currency that could be used to purchase drinks and snacks on board. It was a logical solution to the problem of having too many currencies in circulation, and of course circumvented any potential malpractice, misappropriation or temptation for self-enrichment on the part of the bar staff. We sold shore excursions in hard currencies only, which made life easier and meant local currency could be kept blissfully out of the mix, at least in that respect.

The Wednesday morning sightseeing tour of Belgrade posed a very specific currency problem. The tour was fairly arduous and involved a lot of time on foot, as our *Putnik* guide had been instructed to walk the group between some of the city's main sights so that her guests could breathe in the atmosphere of the city and fully appreciate its essential beauty close up. With temperatures regularly exceeding thirty-five degrees celsius, any atmosphere there was to breathe in was at best stifling and at worst life-threatening for the average SAGA holidaymaker. Moreover, the highlight of the tour, a visit to Tito's Mausoleum, a sombre affair in which visitors paraded slowly and with suitably gloomy expressions past the casketed body of the former president, flanked by rigid, stony-faced soldiers, could involve a lot of queuing up and standing around, especially if a few coachloads of admirers from the provinces were also in town to pay their respects to their recently departed leader.

When, to the visible and audible relief of all, the allotted forty-five minutes of free time was announced at the end of the tour, the tendency was to completely ignore the guide's exhortations to use the time to seek out more essential beauty and plead instead to be directed to the nearest café, and to desperately needed refreshment. But buying water, or coffee, or anything that might slake thirst, could only happen with some Yugoslav dinars, and that meant finding somewhere to change money first. This meant more walking, probably more queuing, and almost certainly no time left to collapse and recuperate in a café before heading back to the ship and waving goodbye to the city.

Only three hours on Yugoslavian soil, and of that only three-quarters of an hour in which local money, very small sums of local money, could be the difference between a successful conclusion to a moderately interesting tour and the onset of dehydration. I'd suggested to our guide that a word be had with head office to see if water could be provided on the coach, but that had fallen on deaf ears. The ship's bar was not open at breakfast time, so there was no opportunity for me to advise my customers to stock up with fluid for the trip either; and anyway having a bottle of water about your person was not as in vogue in those days as it is now, especially among the elderly.

After the first two Wednesday morning tours, and the experience of coaxing what was left of my gasping, panting band of senior citizens back onto the ship, I decided that I had to take matters into my own hands and find some sort of solution. The thought of a spell with one or more of them

117

having their heat exhaustion treated at a Belgrade medical facility, as the ship sailed away up the Danube, was a further, unappealing catalyst and cue to act. So I broke away from the sightseeing tour during the walking part and exchanged some sterling into sufficient dinars to allow for the equivalent of approximately one pound per person, easily enough to buy a couple of drinks. Our guide saw the sense in this but wouldn't let me change money on the coach, so she allowed me to announce at the end of the main tour that I would be available outside in the coach park to exchange minuscule amounts only – and at the official going rate.

This stroke of genius proved to be a lifeline, and over subsequent weeks my overheated tourists were able to avoid fainting, or worse, through my enlightened small-time banking operation. I was usually left with some spare dinars, and just held them over to the following week's float. Those who needed refreshment got refreshment, and it all went very smoothly.

Until, that is, one Tuesday afternoon in late August, by which time I'd extended my exchange activities to the downstream group too. I was standing at my usual place on the coach park, with ten or so of my flock gathered around me, and had commenced transactions, the bulge of banknotes in my left pocket gradually reducing and the contents of my right pocket swelling. None of us noticed the two casually dressed young men who'd attached themselves to the fringes of the group and, as the guide told me in her account afterwards, were taking more than a passing interest in what was going on. Once most of my thirsty customers had been supplied and departed for their liquid relief, the two men made their move.

'Your passport,' one uttered sternly.

I politely enquired who the man was and why he wanted

to see my passport, but the words were simply repeated by the other man, unsmiling, unmoving, brow furrowed, his tone even more menacing than his colleague's.

At that point the guide, who'd been observing the unfolding drama from a few yards away, sauntered nonchalantly over and greeted the two, beaming inquisitively, though she would already have guessed who the men were and to which organisation they belonged. As the two men took turns to talk at her, occasionally nodding in my direction and looking me up and down with blatant disdain, her expression settled into grim acquiescence, an acceptance that whatever she said to them in mitigation and my defence would only make matters worse, for herself too. She summarised the one-sided discussion that had just taken place:

'Mister Phil, these two gentlemen are from our secret police. They have watched you changing money with your customers and that is illegal in our country. They will visit you at your hotel tonight and check all your documents, exchange receipts and currencies. If they find something not in order, they will arrest you and expel you from Yugoslavia. Please, Mister Phil, what is your room number?'

Some weeks after the end of the season, a Mrs Esdon of Send, Surrey posted me a photograph of the unfortunate incident taking place, apologising for the poor quality of the picture due to her having had to snap the scene in secrecy and haste as she 'didn't hang around to check the camera settings'. She captured the coach park huddle of me, the guide and my two tormentors admirably well, however.

Any sort of resistance or disobedience at this point would have been futile and made me appear even more culpable of crimes against the state than I already was. So to counter any possible semblance of truculence or shiftiness, I offered up my hotel details and room number as if it were the most obvious thing in the world to divulge to complete strangers, with an alacrity which bordered on over-eagerness, practically welcoming the men to join me in my room at any hour of their choosing. In the second or so following the guide's proclamation, the full implications of what was happening had flashed before me. And they were troubling, to say the least. Being driven to the frontier and summarily banished from the country, with the order never to darken its borders again, would have damaging consequences. Why I'd been forced to abandon my group in such ignominious circumstances would take some explaining to the bosses in Folkestone and would almost certainly mean a rude and abrupt interruption not only to my summer, but to a career that had barely started and that I was quite enjoying. If the UK's tour operators ran a rep blacklist, I would probably be placed on it in pole position.

That night I carefully arranged all my various currencies in neat piles on the table in my room, even some board dollars I had, next to my main documents and anything which looked like it could be construed as a document of any sort. My current life story was there in its entirety, along with my very modest wealth and an array of exchange receipts. This time, there'd be no going up to the Kalemegdan disco for some moderate imbibing on a typically balmy Belgrade evening. Instead I waited, sleepless and anxious, for the sound of approaching, threatening footsteps on the corridor, and the ominous knock on the door that might seal my fate.

The knock never came, and the worst that happened was that I reported for duty on the upstream cruise at six o'clock devoid of any meaningful sleep, and had to tend to a succession of parched and heat-exhausted customers at the end of all the remaining Belgrade city tours.

*

That said, my next currency-related mishap may not have been entirely unconnected to the near-fatal incident in the coach park, and whether it was some sort of additional retribution, with my card having been well and truly marked, I never got to know.

Another Wednesday morning, this time a week later, I was ushering my group together on the quayside to board our coach for what would be another stifling three hours touring the city and paying our respects to President Tito. As we stood chatting and waiting for stragglers, and for the driver to open the doors, I suddenly sensed stirrings of disquiet among the four ladies I was talking to, who were casting alarmed glances towards something behind me. Before I had a chance to turn around to see what had aroused their consternation, a large hand appeared on and tightly clasped my right shoulder.

'Come with me,' rasped the booming voice, as the hand steered me forcefully away from the group and further down the quayside.

I looked up at my assailant, a monster of a man with cold eyes and unshaven jaw, whose dishevelled uniform struggled to contain his vast form. He pushed me further away from my group until we were well out of earshot, and I didn't dare to speak. What had I done this time? Surely I was not infringing any local laws by making polite conversation with a few elderly people outside a coach, with not so much as a single dinar changing hands? And I certainly couldn't be accused of illegal guiding. Such were the thoughts racing through my panicked mind as I was quite literally frogmarched off down the quayside.

We stopped and the man turned to me, getting straight to his point without any attempt at small talk or ceremony.

'I am Chief of Police for Belgrade. You are going to Vienna, yes?' he shouted.

'Yes, later.'

'Yes, I know. And you come back in one week, yes?'

'Erm, yes, next Tuesday,' I offered helpfully.

'So you must bring me one thousand Deutschmarks from Vienna next week. I will give you dinars. You understand me?' he frothed, as if this was already a fait accompli.

'But they don't have Deutschmarks in Austria,' I whimpered, 'they have Austrian schillings.'

'Austrian schillings, Deutschmarks, American dollars – I don't care. You bring me currency, a lot. Like one thousand Deutschmarks,' he said dismissively, as though my lesson on which countries had which currencies had been intensely irritating. And that Deutschmarks ruled anyway.

I summoned up some fruitless inner strength and argued feebly that importing large amounts of foreign currency into Yugoslavia was illegal, and I wouldn't be able to get my hands on that amount of money anyway. My meagre float from SAGA would certainly come nowhere near, I knew.

'You – bring – me – money,' he repeated, jabbing a bulbous forefinger into my breastbone. 'Next week. I meet you here.'

At that point, having absorbed quite enough intimidation for one day, I turned on my heels and made off towards my group, muttering back at the scowling giant that I would not be bringing him any money the following week. I was still shaking by the time I reached the coach, now with doors open and passengers in the process of boarding, which avoided my having to make a hastily contrived statement on why I had been led away in such an undignified fashion by a large policeman who clearly meant business.

Whether he actually was who he said he was was open to conjecture, and my first thought was that this was some sort of trap, a test to see if my encounter the previous week had been enough to bring about my rehabilitation from hardcore criminal to model visitor. And if it hadn't, then there were now irrefutable grounds for instant expulsion. So I'd played with a straight bat, and that had been extremely wise. If this had been the aim of the test then I had passed it, so I very much doubted I would see the man again, especially as I'd told him in no uncertain terms that I would definitely not be turning up in Belgrade next week replete with large amounts of western banknotes.

Six days later, I stood on deck and observed the scene. My clients were all at lunch, largely oblivious to the gurgling of *Carpati*'s bow thrusters doing their work to get us into landing position. I always enjoyed the spectacle of arrival, watching the captain leaning out of the window on the bridge, usually with a cigarette protruding motionless from the corner of his mouth, as he manoeuvred his vessel towards the quay wall. The sailors were perched below, crouching on the rim of the deck, ropes in hand, ready to lasso the capstans and hop nimbly onto the quayside to pull the ship the final few inches and secure her to her moorings.

Suddenly I was gripped by a sinking feeling, not because the captain had made some awful miscalculation, but by the sight of the towering figure down and to my right, standing hands on hips and legs akimbo, surveying the docking operation, a dour and uncompromising demeanour etched into his face. Our eyes met and his expression became triumphant, his head making a barely discernible nodding motion. As the ramp clattered onto the concrete I wondered whether he would board, and instantly decided that any confrontation was best played out off the ship, preferably without an audience. This meant breaking the bad news to the so-called Chief of Police sooner rather than later. I signalled that I would come down to see him, and set off along the deck and down the narrow, near vertical steps to B deck, and out onto the ramp to see what fate awaited me. The emotion that accompanied my walk was probably closely akin to the terror felt by a batsman on his England debut, making his way out into a packed Lord's or, even more intimidating, the enemy's Colosseum, the Melbourne Cricket Ground. Like that batsman, I was unsure of what the next few minutes would bring, but certain that a lot depended on them; my nerves were in total riot, but I also knew it was imperative not to betray any signs of fear to the opposition, nor to accentuate the smell of blood.

'You have my Deutschmarks?' he barked, circumventing any attempt at a greeting or enquiry about my journey or past week.

'No, I told you I could not do this, and why. Please understand,' I countered, pleadingly.

'Why you not have my Deutschmarks? I tell you to bring me Deutschmarks.'

'Look, it is illegal, and I cannot get such a large amount of currency anyway. I am just a tourist guide, I don't have much money,' I said, appealing forlornly to a better nature which surely didn't exist.

'Where is your cabin?' he retorted, almost certainly without the linguistic ability to have understood what I had just said, beyond realising that he was no closer to getting his bounty.

'On the ship, downstairs. Why?'

'We talk more in your cabin,' he ordered, pointing up the ramp. 'Come, we go.'

At least we'd be on friendly territory, I thought, as we marched purposefully onto *Carpati*, my tormentor squeezing himself ahead of me through the door, on down the steep steps to C deck and along the dim corridor to my cabin.

My suitcase was already packed and on my bunk, ready for my disembarkation later that evening. The Chief told me to open it and commenced a thorough search, casting clothes and papers into a disorganised heap on the floor, looking in the inner pockets and tapping against the sides and bottom of the casing with mounting desperation. He held up my ancient set of metal chest expanders and sneered. Why I had bothered to bring these with me anyway was a mystery. I should have known that trying to manipulate such equipment in the close confines of a cabin was always going to be a tall order and that they only succeeded in taking up valuable suitcase space. Severe underuse of the contraption meant my chest had not visibly expanded over the course of the last few weeks and I still looked like I needed a good meal, a point clearly not lost on the Chief.

All this was becoming extremely humiliating, but the worst was yet to come. Once he was satisfied that I wasn't concealing sizeable quantities of Deutschmarks, or any other desirable currency, he snappily told me to repack my case. As I stooped and knelt to gather up my offended collection of worldly goods from the cabin floor, and restore them to their original haven, I felt cautious relief that my ordeal might be nearing some sort of conclusion. He hadn't found anything in my belongings that might enrich him or incriminate me, and that should, I reckoned, be that. Unfortunately for me, the Chief had other plans and wasn't going to allow disobedience to go unpunished – especially when it meant that he was materially no better off now than when he'd gone on duty that morning.

He picked up the repacked suitcase and strode out of the cabin, with me following in a panic at this sudden, worrying turn of events. Where on earth was he taking my suitcase? Was he confiscating it to carry out a further, more forensic check on land, probably culminating in its effective destruction, along with all my garments and possessions?

That could mean plastic bags for the rest of the summer, not a happy situation for a representative who liked to look the part in appearance, dress and accessories in front of his customers.

I followed the Chief back up to B deck, but instead of heading out of the main door and down the ramp, he stormed along the corridor and into the restaurant, where lunch was still in full swing. He took up position in the middle of the restaurant and, to the astonishment of the assembled diners, opened my suitcase and with a flourish emptied the entire contents onto the floor. An appalled silence fell across the passengers who, moments earlier, had been gazing peacefully across the River Sava to the enticing cityscape, very much looking forward to acquainting themselves with the next gem of their holiday.

He was not yet done. Fishing out my chest expanders from the tangled mass of gaudily coloured shirts, unwashed underwear, crumpled receipts and expense claims, he held his trophy aloft and let out a thunderous, triumphant laugh. I stood there opposite him, feeling sick. To startled and aghast looks, the Chief proceeded to pull the expanders apart, further, further... until with a sudden, excruciating twang, they snapped.

He angrily flung down the remains of what I'd once hoped would be my body's salvation. *Nije dobro* ('Not good'), he ridiculed dismissively. He then stomped out of the restaurant, head raised defiantly, without giving me so much as a glance, the loaded cutlery of many of the stunned onlookers still suspended midway between plates and mouths.

My dignity, or what remained of it, lay haphazardly and cruelly dispersed on the restaurant floor, and not a soul spoke after the Chief had made his ostentatious exit. Then after a few seconds, during which people started to breathe again, a couple of my ladies began to gather up various items from amongst the carnage, a cue for other passengers to gingerly slide pieces of clothing with shoe tips or stilettos from beneath their tables towards the general direction of the loose mound of wounded life forming in the centre of the restaurant. This was humiliating enough, but well-meaning offers of help to repack my brutalised suitcase took abject degradation to a different level. Resistance was futile, however, and soon shock was replaced with sympathy: a feverish communal effort got underway to restore my belongings to their proper home, despite my protestations that I was quite happy to manage the task myself.

*

I never encountered the self-pronounced Chief of Police again, but came to dread my visits to Belgrade during what remained of that summer. Budapest and Vienna, both of which I fell increasingly in love with, were always welcome relief and sanctuary after the constant feeling of unease I had in Belgrade. There was always the sensation that something bad was about to happen, that I was a marked man and that my time there could be curtailed at any moment; something that would have an inevitable bearing on my career too. The threat of banishment if I put a foot wrong was ever-present, or so it seemed, and it always felt good when the upstream cruise pulled away, back into the Danube and up towards Hungary, with me on it, unscathed and going about the routine business of getting to know my new group.

What other highs and lows there were that summer were almost all to do with the vicissitudes of the river. A period of drought, or prolonged heat, often heralded low water, which meant we ran the distinct risk of not being able to moor the ship. That in turn meant we couldn't leave our current berth for fear of not being able to tie up at the next stop. On one such occasion, on the upstream cruise, we couldn't leave Budapest for that reason, and our group missed their flight home; replacement seats had to be booked on a later flight, which Wolfgang Lüftner duly did and paid for. And when the intensity of a days' long, suffocating Central European heatwave was finally and violently superseded by ear-shattering thunderclaps, jagged bolts of sky-splitting lightning and the ensuing torrents of lukewarm rain, we knew that high water was coming. At Novi Sad, now in modern day Serbia, passing under the then Marshall Tito bridge (destroyed in April 1999 by NATO bombs) was tight even when water levels were normal, so the bridge superstructure had to be collapsed; we would often get the passengers up on deck to see if they could touch the underside of the bridge as we glided beneath it. In high water it was unviable. As with low water, high water could also mean mooring was impossible, as landing berths were submerged.

This was very much the lot of the river cruise vessel, and of those in charge of it, and delays due to 'unforeseen circumstances' were sufficiently regular as to make the designation 'unforeseen' something of a misnomer. Far more unforeseen, even though the first buds of new growth were starting to appear, were the events that would unfold in Hungary, Yugoslavia and Romania within a matter of years, events which were still inconceivable as we navigated that grandest of rivers, and the idiosyncrasies of the countries through which it flowed, during that memorable summer.

Chapter Four

THE HILLS ARE ALIVE

High up in the mountains of Western Austria, at 1269 metres to be precise, lies a tiny settlement called Schröcken. Its heart comprises a church, a school-cum-tourist office, a small store selling souvenirs and its own baked produce, and two hotels, all wedged onto a narrow plateau. To one side the ground falls away precipitously into the ravine of the foaming Bregenzer Ache, while to the other perilously steep slopes of gentian, ranunculus, orchids and mountain rhododendron rise ever upwards, too often crossed rudely by stark, dark rows of steel avalanche barriers, vital protection against the threat of white oblivion during the long, harsh winters.

Just one road leads in and out of the hamlet. Westwards is the descent, following the course of the river down to more open, flat pastureland and on through the village of Au towards the provincial capital Bregenz and Lake Constance, where the Ache has its egress. To the east, the road zigzags and switches alarmingly back and forth up onto to the Hochtannberg Pass, before taking a more sedate route across high alpine meadows. Here, recovering from the terrifying ordeal of the

Hochtannberg, the fortunate driver might be rewarded with a glimpse of marmots or mufflons before arriving at the famed ski resorts of Lech and St. Anton-am-Arlberg.

This is the Vorarlberg province of Austria, and Schröcken lies at the most easterly point of what is known as the Bregenzerwald (or Bregenz Forest). Indeed, before colonisers arrived from the Wallis (or Valais, to use its French name) area of Western Switzerland in the fourteenth century, the valleys were thick forest. The dialect they brought with them is still spoken today by locals and is known as the 'Walser', linguistically poles apart from their overlords in Vienna. Politically too, there is a closer kinship with Bavaria to the north. Legend has it that one of those early visitors, a priest, took one look at what is now Schröcken and described the place as *schröcklich*, an old variant of the modern-day German word for 'dreadful', and the name stuck.

Anyone happening upon Schröcken today, if they don't miss it when passing through, would surely find kinder adjectives to describe the cluster of creosoted wooden edifices, their balconies bedecked with geraniums, flanking the gleaming whitewashed church with perfect sleek spire, perching happily on its grassy knoll. It was built and consecrated in 1639, burned down in 1863 and rebuilt by 1876. Across the ages, fire has frequently devastated Schröcken and other villages in the Bregenzerwald, and the visitor shouldn't be surprised to come across bands of fire brigade volunteers rehearsing their drills. This is a pure and healthy haven; in summer its peace is broken only by the reassuring, hollow clonking of copper cow bells from higher, flower-filled pastures and the intermittent, plaintive screech of an eagle, wheeling gracefully through a cloudless sky above the simple tranquillity.

The ancient Gasthof Tannberg is one of Schröcken's two hotels. The Tannberg, with its cosy, wood-panelled restaurant and intimate stüberl, the perfect evening retreat for a shot of peach schnapps or a home-brewed obstler,[21] is everything an Austrian alpine hotel should be. It's always prided itself on its extremely tasty, locally sourced food, and has been owned by the Moosman family since the late 1800s. In winter it welcomes skiers, up for the challenges afforded by the slopes of the Saloberkopf, and in summer its guests – hikers and flora lovers – wander through meadows and along the rough track to the Körbersee, a pristine lake nestling serenely in an amphitheatre formed by the dizzying peaks above. After wandering, hoping perhaps to spot rare orchids concealed amidst grasses gently buffeted by balmy mountain breezes, some hikers come to rest their weary legs at one of the rustic huts producing and serving up Schröckener Bergkäse, the local, delicious mountain cheese, an integral part of the area's dairy economy.

*

In the summer of 1983, the Gasthof Tannberg was the venue for the *TV Times* Austrian House Party, which ran weekly from the end of May to late September and was conceived and organised by Page and Moy Holidays of Leicester. Every Saturday afternoon a coach would arrive at the hotel containing around forty-five guests, mainly middle-aged and elderly couples interspersed with a few single and even fewer younger travellers. All would be fairly shattered after enduring the arduous overnight drive from home across much of Western Europe, and not yet quite ready for the week's schedule of more time spent on a coach and a veritable cornucopia of fun and games. The following Saturday a new group would arrive, their coach then returning immediately

---

21. *A traditional type of fruit schnapps.*

to the UK with the guests from the previous week on board. Saturday mornings were generally miserable for the homebound guests who, when they booked their holiday, clearly hadn't considered that it would involve two hideously long journeys. They were also usually exhausted from the programme of the past week: a continuum of full-day excursions to places such as Innsbruck, Mad King Ludwig's castle at Neuschwanstein, into Switzerland, to Appenzell and on the cable car up Mount Säntis, and to Vaduz in Liechtenstein. And in the evenings, the hilarity, frivolity and often physical demands of the party element of the House Party also took their toll.

Indeed, it was the evening entertainment on offer that made the whole thing different from the more traditional week's holiday in the Austrian Alps. It was its USP, along with an extremely attractive price achieved through the two torturous overnight coach journeys and by basing the eye-catching, lead-in offer on the hotel's most basic rooms, which had neither bathroom nor WC. There were rowdy, alcohol-fuelled games evenings, quizzes, a meat fondue dinner and a folklore show – with lots more local booze – up at the Diedamskopf alpine restaurant. There was also a farewell evening where most of the guests seemed intent on consuming enough beer and schnapps to ensure they'd be comatose during the bulk of their journey home, only regaining consciousness at Calais.

As the Page and Moy representative at the Gasthof Tannberg, I had the task of making all this happen. There were other house parties happening in two other hotels in Vorarlberg, in the villages of Damüls and Au, and with the season in Schröcken starting a week later than these (not least because the snow tended to hang around that bit longer than elsewhere in the Bregenz Forest, so the hotel spring closure lasted longer too), part of my induction week was to tag along on these and soak up those ingredients essential to making the house party tick.

When my turn came, however, the start was inauspicious. The coach was due to arrive at two in the afternoon, and since early morning my nerves had been in a state of heightened anticipation. By four there was no sign of the coach and I tentatively put a call through to head office, who had heard nothing. By six, Fritz Moosman, the Tannberg's owner, had talked me into accepting a shot of obstler every half hour the coach failed to turn up, ostensibly to reduce my tension levels to somewhere close to where they should be. We dined together at nine, two hours after the time scheduled for the group's dinner. Further calls to the office brought no fresh clues as to the possible whereabouts of the coach. By ten-thirty we had taken the decision to abort the planned hot dinner and send the chef home. Renata, Fritz's wife, suggested she rustle up some soup and salad if the group subsequently arrived.

Midnight passed and Fritz, I and a couple of the locals settled down at the bar to continue working our way through a vicious procession of schnapps made from apples, pears and various other types of fruit I'd never heard of, with the odd Jägermeister occasionally thrown in as a reminder that other, more mainstream drinks were also available at the Tannberg. We resigned ourselves to believing that a coach and its occupants would not now be troubling us that night, that some inexcusable administrative error had been made and someone had got their dates wrong, though even in the confused depths of our worsening inebriation we must have known that this was highly unlikely.

At just past one in the morning, two elderly ladies appeared at the bar. One of them said shakily: 'Hello, we're from the coach.'

'What coach?' I slurred, too drunk to take in the message properly.

'The coach. We're stuck up on the pass. The driver went over the edge.'

In a sickening flash, what remained of my ability to reason told me that these were people from my missing group, the group we'd given up on and which was now clearly in some sort of terrible predicament.

'Where are the rest of you?' I stammered.

'Some have got off the coach and are walking down, but there are a lot who are too frightened to move,' came the desperate reply. 'One of the drivers has had some sort of mental breakdown too.'

I staggered through the darkened, empty reception area, groggily heaved open the main door and emerged into the clear, pine-scented moonlit night, my two ladies at my heels. There, just about discernible, a phalanx of dark silhouettes was traipsing slowly and silently down the road from the pass towards us. Fritz and Renata were soon at my shoulder, and as the pairs and small groupings of shattered souls reached us, Renata ushered each inside and to a table in the restaurant. The hotel spluttered back into some sort of strange half-normality as the dismal nocturnal invasion of exhausted spirits gradually filled the room.

'You've saved our lives, this has saved our lives,' insisted one woman gratefully as she eagerly slurped down spoonful after spoonful of frittatensuppe,[22] hurriedly ladled into soup bowls from a large vat and placed on the red and white checkered tablecloths by Renata moments earlier. One of the drivers, the one who had allegedly cracked under the pressure of what happened on the Hochtannberg,

_____

22. *A clear soup made with pancake strips.*

had marched up to me and pleaded to be given a room immediately, muttering something about not having had any maps for the journey. The other was still in situ with the coach and some of the passengers up on the pass. Fritz called up a local coach company, Hagspiel Reisen, based in a village a few miles down the Forest, to alert them to the situation with the stricken coach. Within half an hour the owner's son, Wolfgang Hagspiel, had set about the not inconsiderable task of extricating the vehicle and the remaining passengers and driver from their cliffhanging plight.

The only good thing about the incident was that it occurred right at the start of the season, so there were no returning passengers. Otherwise, with the drivers evidently far from capable of embarking on the return journey, we would have had two groups in a hotel which only had capacity for one.

The next morning, the drivers, now able to express themselves coherently again, explained that their boss hadn't given them a map and consequently, and catastrophically, they'd taken a wrong turn when coming into Austria, a mistake which also added hours to their journey. Rather than heading straight up the Bregenz Forest road from the Swiss border, they'd headed south to Feldkirch, taken a left up the Ill Valley and tried to get over to Schröcken the 'back way' via Lech. By the time they started to snake down the Hochtannberg it was dark, they were shattered by the long drive, stress and hours of navigating mountain roads, and had miscalculated one of the Hochtannberg's notorious bends. The front of the coach had strayed off the bend and was left protruding over the edge of a precipice. And that, they had concluded, was quite enough driving for one day.

*

The day before this pre-satnav era debacle had come close to wiping out my first Austrian House Party group and with it, quite probably, continued publication of the *TV Times*, I'd received an important visitor. Paul Taylor was Assistant Operations Manager at Page and Moy Holidays, and he had a problem. Due to a sudden and unexpected resignation in his team, he was an executive down. And that executive had to be able to speak German, so he'd come to see whether I might be interested in the position. As we sipped our coffees at a corner table in the stüberl, Paul set out what the job of Operations Executive entailed. It was far-reaching and very appetising, almost mouth-watering in its scope: conceiving ideas for new holidays; putting together detailed tour itineraries; travelling throughout Germany, Austria, Switzerland and possibly beyond; finding the company new hotels and handling contract negotiations with existing ones; and doing the same with coach companies too, as these were needed to operate airport transfers and local excursions. Back at base, there were couriers and resort reps to be found, hired, briefed, kept in check, praised, reprimanded, even fired. Finally, there was the whole box of surprises that came with troubleshooting, including taking that call on emergency duty that might test your ability to solve, single-handedly, the thorniest of problems on the hoof.

It all sounded too good to be true, but was I ready for it? After all, I'd only been in Schröcken for a matter of days and hadn't taken delivery of my first group yet, let alone established whether I had what it took to keep a bunch of tourists royally entertained day and night in the middle of nowhere. Moreover I had sensed, even after just a few hectic days of getting to know the ropes, that that 'middle of nowhere' was a place I would be more than happy to spend the whole summer. Scenically, atmospherically, naturally and spiritually too, it seemed like paradise on earth, this almost forgotten corner of Austria where at the end of May the closest to a commotion was the sight and sound of herds of long-horned, lethargic cattle being coaxed by their drover minders up into the mountains, to their summer grazing grounds just below the snowline. Here, man and beast would inhabit the high pastures together until, months later, the weather would start to turn, and the time would come to begin their long descent back into the still-verdant valley below.

Every evening at the Tannberg, early at six o'clock, the same wizened old man took his customary place at a table near the bar, and tucked into whatever speciality of the day Renata laid in front of him. I had tried to engage him in conversation but he was a man of few words, and those I could understand were still fewer. Fritz told me his wife had died quite recently, and the old man couldn't cook. He was a roofer and had reroofed the Tannberg, and rather than pay him for his work in hard cash Fritz had agreed to feed the man nightly for a year. A perfect form of 'countertrading', where goods and services are exchanged without money ever being discussed, practised in these parts for centuries. I wondered what I could have offered, if I lived here, that would have been deemed valuable enough to trade, and drew a blank. But it was enough to witness the purity of a system where transactions were based on human need, and where for once money didn't make the world go round. It turned out that the bereaved roofer was also a man of wisdom, and as my efforts to build some sort of rapport with him in the early days began to bear fruit, he would often take his leave stating:

'And remember: there are only two things in life we truly know. We'll never be able to change the weather; and whether rich or poor, you'll still die'.

This sobering, rather gloomy message did nothing to dampen my rapidly growing attachment to my new surroundings. One evening that first week, I'd sat in on the house party up at Damüls and, amid the general mayhem, hit it off with a pretty waitress called Barbara, who was studying in Graz and had made the long trip across Austria for a summer supplementing her meagre grant. A highly competent English speaker, in the weeks to follow she would unwittingly be exposed to the full panoply of British dialects, delivered in differing degrees of drunkenness and with a variety of antics to match. After the frenzy had more or less abated, we shared the dance floor with a couple of remaining diehards and chatted over wine after wine. We agreed to meet up again the following week if I could somehow extricate myself from my duties in Schröcken for a few short hours.

So when Paul Taylor made his proposal to swap the healthy mountain air of the Vorarlberg for immersion into city and civilian life in Leicester, there was much to mull over; and as alluring and enticing as the job sounded, there were some increasingly heavy counterweights.

*

Nine months earlier, I'd returned home from the Danube and headed straight to my bedroom, instructing my mother not to wake me up under any circumstances. Two days later I crawled out of bed and started to contemplate my next mission, due to start in a matter of days: a two-week Nile cruise that Paul Bowden had warned me would be tough for a relative newbie. Still, he appeared to have every confidence that I would be up to the task. Feedback from those passengers who had been kind enough to submit their post-cruise questionnaires, or even kinder, to write a letter, had been positive, and it was felt that a spell on the Nile would provide a suitable next step on my learning curve. I would later learn that being assigned the Nile cruise was considered a thoroughly bad thing by the vast majority of seasoned reps, something to be feared rather than welcomed and definitely not a reward for good behaviour. I suspect I was probably chosen because no one else had raised their hand when approached to take on the job, or had had a plausible excuse for not accepting the offer. But by then it was too late, and I spent a largely hellish fortnight dragging collapsed pensioners out of tombs and onto non-airconditioned coaches, and trying to procure black market supplies of a drug called Lomotil, the only known antidote to extraordinarily violent bouts of vomiting and diarrhoea, when stocks ran out after the first few days. These bouts afflicted most of my sixty customers, and had an annoying tendency to strike suddenly and without warning when we were deep underground in some archaeological wonder.

The next escorting role was an altogether tamer affair: a Christmas cruise on Fred Olsen's Black Prince around the Canaries which, after a rough passage through the Bay of Biscay that saw all but four of my sixteen passengers declare themselves too ill to attend the Captain's welcome dinner, turned out to be far less demanding than both Nile and Danube. And for that reason perhaps also a little dull, though a warm Christmas reclining with the crew on a beach in Gran Canaria was a welcome and novel festive highlight; I was more accustomed to celebrating the big day shivering at my grandmother's farm in the Lake District, due to her insistence on trying to heat her entire, sizeable house with an ancient kitchen Rayburn.

After a winter spent largely in my bedroom, translating a very technical and mind-numbingly boring book on ships' propulsion systems from German to English, I was relieved to be back on the rivers of Europe in April. This time I was doing stints for SAGA on the Rhine and then the Dutch waterways, the 'Bulbfields' cruise, so-called because the focal point was a visit to the mesmeric Keukenhof Gardens, resplendent with tulips of every conceivable colour. The weather on the Rhine was atrocious, and at Königswinter the water level rose so much that our jetty was submerged. The crew and I, along with any bystander unfortunate enough to look sufficiently fit to be of service and who was therefore press-ganged into the team effort, managed to construct a rickety pontoon bridge from the upper deck of the ship into someone's back garden, allowing us all to disembark for shore excursions. Disembarkation was a long and nailbiting process, as one by one we coerced and manhandled each terrified elderly passenger along a wobbling, swaying structure only two plank widths wide, while just feet below the river frothed and thundered its way inexorably to the North Sea. After three days stranded on our mooring, that particular cruise was brought to a premature end and – to a mixture of dismay and relief – everyone was coached back to England.

There was high drama on the Bulbfields Cruise too, although this time the outcome was tragic. I may have also been partly responsible for the tragedy. My efforts the previous summer to raise passenger fitness levels through mass participation workouts on deck had gone to my head, and I'd got into the routine of putting my guests through their paces every morning, more or less come rain or shine and whichever stretch of water I was working on. It was proving to be a great bonding exercise and morale booster, and a useful way of filling some of the morning downtime. And nothing bad had ever happened. Until now.

After the first couple of morning sessions, as we worked our way up towards the Zuider Zee, it was as if the whole ship was becoming consumed by a singular desire to get very fit. People who for years hadn't engaged in anything more strenuous than a gentle walk to the shops were suddenly hell-bent on attaining levels of cardiovascular perfection last enjoyed in their school days. Midway through a session, and as numerous arms were valiantly trying to emulate the windmills close by on shore, my assistant rushed up to me in a state of panic. There had been an incident in the table-tennis area, and one of the male guests had collapsed.

I hurried over and arrived to the incongruous sight of an upended table-tennis table and one of the handful of American passengers on board lying in a gasping heap where the table met the deck, his frantic wife standing over him.

His last words were: 'I think I overdid it', and despite the best efforts of a retired doctor in our group, he passed away minutes later. He had been grossly overweight, and according to his wife had never played table-tennis or done any other kind of sport in his life, so was probably a heart attack waiting to happen. It was an awful, shocking moment for everyone; the communal mood became sombre and pensive, and for the rest of the day the whole ship retreated into a shell of silence and introspection, with barely a word audible at dinner that night.

Then something extraordinary happened. Early the following morning, I went up on deck to find that queues had formed at the table-tennis tables. Everyone seemed to want a go, and I had to impose maximum limits of ten minutes to meet the demand. By evening, the atmosphere of bonhomie and good cheer had fully returned, possibly even more vibrant than before, and it was as if the death on board had become a distant memory. As one of the ladies commented sagely to me: 'there is a certain competitiveness that comes with advancing years.'

Meanwhile, the other Paul in my life, Paul Bowden, my route into SAGA, who had kept faith with me despite some indifferent reports from some of the Nile passengers, had metaphorically jumped ship and headed up the M1 to Leicester to join Page and Moy Holidays as Operations Executive for Germany, Austria and Switzerland. Once he'd found his feet in the role, he duly signed me up to run the Austrian House Party in Schröcken – before, only weeks later, resigning to join Miki Holidays in London, just days before the season was due to begin.

So there was a sudden and unexpected vacancy due to Paul's untimely departure. Paul Taylor needed to plug the gap quickly, and his search had led him to our alpine meeting. And, for me, to a life-changing moment.

*

I walked apprehensively into and on up the long, narrow Operations Room, running the gauntlet of enquiring eyes sizing up the new broom, nodding with a forced smile to right and to left as I made my way to my desk in the far corner.

First, a world away from where we'd last met, a reunion with Paul Taylor, who seemed greatly relieved that someone was there to fill the void. Then onto introductions to my new colleagues, culminating in an audience in his glass box with the manager himself, the very genial and laid-back Brian, who offered me an outstretched hand from a recumbent, almost horizontal position which he maintained throughout our discussion. At one point, one of the directors' secretaries walked in to give him some papers and have a quick chat about something. After she'd gone, Brian whispered to me that she had 'the best tits in the company'. Later, as I stood up to leave his office, Brian said: 'Phil, here's a piece of advice. If it's gonna happen – it's gonna happen. No point worrying about it, mate.'

Brian was the antithesis of what I had imagined someone bearing such responsibility to be like, and was also genuinely warm and caring. His parting words of wisdom that day, delivered with no more gravitas than someone conjecturing that we might be on for some rain soon, but not to worry, we had umbrellas, turned out to be some of the most valuable I would ever hear.

The decision had not been an easy one, but I reckoned that a bad move could always be rectified, and a swift return made to head-counting, microphones and missing suitcases if things failed to work out. On the back-of-envelope list of the pros and cons of upping sticks prematurely and heading home, the pros outweighed the cons, though there were some sizeable cons, including leaving behind the newly discovered wonder and beauty – in physical as well as human form – of the Bregenzerwald, and the sense that I was leaving this insecure, peripatetic, usually stressful but never dull or predictable life too soon. I'd come to revel in the satisfaction of knowing I was helping, in a small way, to make dreams come true in those few cherished days that so many had saved up for, waited long months for, lived for. Dreams were not always realised, of course, as there were still disasters and expectations not met; so the pros column included being able, I hoped, to make sure that holidays were impeccably planned and executed from the start.

My confidence and self-belief had reached scarcely anticipated highs during the past months, and I loved to entertain and reveal new places, new games, even new ways to exercise to the constantly changing myriad of faces. And this was about to begin again in one of the most stunning locations in Europe.

And yet: here was an opportunity to keep the German going, to keep the travelling going and, just maybe, a chance to get back to Eastern Europe. Paul Taylor had been open to the idea of ploughing new furrows, of introducing some fresh ideas into the portfolio. After all, Page and Moy did much of its selling through magazines, the IPC empire, encompassing big household names like *Woman's Own, Woman's Weekly* and *Woman's Realm*, and the editors of these who had final say over what was featured were always on the hunt for innovation, prestige, anything to keep their readers happy and loyal, and for good commission earnings. I felt a latent appeal in this need for inventiveness and creativity, and there was surely a strong chance that my knowledge of those parts of Europe that were relatively unknown – and full of eastern promise – might be put to productive use.

So Paul Taylor and I struck a deal. I would spend a month in Schröcken, a high-altitude swansong to my brief but happy immersion in the world of the rep, before switching from the grassroots to the inner sanctum, the nerve centre, the place where the dreams were made. In that month, four groups came and went, each partying as hard as the last, each dreading the homeward trek when the time came, exchanging envious, drained glances with the new arrivals and raising expectations with laudatory comments as their paths crossed. Barbara and I met up whenever we managed to synchronise the rare gaps in our duties, and were boyfriend and girlfriend for the next three years.

Within days of taking my place in the Operations department, I was dispatched to Geneva and given one week to set up a 'Lakes and Mountains' programme, featuring Swiss and Austrian resorts, for the following year. One of the directors felt that the time was right to sell our expertise through retail agents, and not solely rely on the IPC account, but in the annual contracting merry-go-round we were already late to the party, and much of the best hotel capacity would probably have already been snapped up by our competitors and other foreign tour operators. With pricing and print deadlines to consider, and to ensure we were on the travel agents' shelves in time for the autumn booking season, there was no time to lose; and it was decided that this would be an appropriate baptism by fire, and test of my mettle.

A whole raft of new hotels had to be found, prices negotiated, contracts signed, along an arc from Lake Geneva, through the Bernese Oberland, and eastwards to the Tyrol and Salzburgerland. My first find was the palatial Hotel Eden Palace au Lac in chic Montreux where, after striking a decent and confidence-inspiring deal with the very dapper Director of Sales, I encountered problems with my hired Opel Kadett; I struggled getting it into reverse, and ended up creating a large hole in one of the hotel's perfectly manicured hedges, much to the horror of my host and new business partner.

Despite this early and rather embarrassing setback, the week was a success and the mission accomplished. I even managed to squeeze in a detour to Schröcken (and, of course, to Damüls), where I found myself sitting opposite Fritz in earnest debate over next year's prices, in the same restaurant where a few weeks earlier I had been holding beer-drinking races, arranging games involving blindfolds, and tying people together at their wrists.

By November of that year, 1983, I was back in Budapest, much sooner than I had dared hope. The notion of combining the grandeur of the three imperial capitals of Prague, Vienna and Budapest into one irresistible week-long winter tour, and infusing it with a cookery course for the lady readers along with wine tasting for their menfolk, had been instantly and enthusiastically embraced by the travel editor of *Woman and Home*. And quite against the predictions of the head of the Hungarian Tourist Board in London, who couldn't fathom why anyone would want to visit his country in the depths of the Central European winter, sales were going through the roof. We had struck a rich seam.

Buoyed by this victory, I wondered – was there scope to push still further east? If there was appetite for venturing into the relative unknown at a fairly awful time of year, could there be a 'curiosity factor' for places even further afield, places far deeper behind the Curtain than Hungary, places seen as more communist, more closed, and far more repressive?

Chapter Five

INTO THE CRADLE

The rise and rise of Mikhail Gorbachev

On December 15th, 1984, Mikhail Gorbachev, accompanied by his fashion-conscious wife Raisa, arrived in London to meet Britain's Prime Minister Margaret Thatcher. If a pretext was needed to invite a senior Russian official to the United Kingdom, Gorbachev's appointment in April of that year as Chairman of the Foreign Affairs Committee of the Soviet Legislature provided it. Margaret Thatcher had formed a close bond with US President Ronald Reagan, and all three saw a visit from Gorbachev, who Thatcher had heard was approachable and open-minded, as a chance to initiate a thaw in relations between the US and USSR.

For those of us looking for any ray of hope that relations between East and West might improve, that memorable visit stands out as one of the most transformative moments in the course of the Cold War, and in the lives of millions of people. Thatcher and Gorbachev clashed over basic human freedoms and rights as well as over the key economic differences between socialism and capitalism, but – crucially – got on well with each other and established an early, mutual respect. Thatcher found Gorbachev confident and easy to debate with, and not wedded to the usual convention of Soviet leaders and politicians of sticking to bland, cautious dogma interspersed with unconvincing aspirations for better relations. Her summary of their time together was captured in her famous words in Downing Street: 'I like Mr Gorbachev, we can do business together.' And for many of us watching the news on December 17th, those words were the first glimmers of a new dawn.

Mikhail Gorbachev was born in 1931 in the North Caucasus region of the Soviet Union into an impoverished family of peasant farmers. The first fifteen years of his life were extremely harsh: millions in the countryside had died in the Great Famine of 1932 to 1933, and the Stalinist purges of the thirties had visited his family when his grandfather was arrested, beaten and tortured in 1937. His village was devastated by the invading Nazi forces and, with his father fighting at the front, young Mikhail stepped up and took on his work on their *kolkhoz*, or collective farm. The end of the war saw more famine, more starvation, and more purges. Meanwhile at school, Gorbachev marked himself out as a good actor and organiser, who relished playing any roles which had an element of leadership. Out in the fields he learnt how to drive and repair a combine harvester. At the age of seventeen he was awarded the Order of the Red Banner of Labour for his efforts in gathering in the local grain harvest (his father receiving the Order of Lenin), and this in turn led to his being accepted to study law at Moscow State University without needing to pass the entrance exam.

By this time, Gorbachev had developed an ambivalence towards the system in which he'd been raised, and many of the philosophies, and indeed tensions, which formed the basis for his future actions began to take shape. Despite Stalin's bloody iron grip on the nation and the resultant loss of innocent life on a terrifying scale, there was nationwide pride in both the wartime achievement, in snatching victory from the jaws of defeat through a heroic communal effort, and in the leader's drive for massive industrialisation, which was seen as setting the Soviet Union on course to become an economic world power. So, surely socialism as an effective system was vindicated? While sharing this essential belief in socialism, Gorbachev had also concluded that the way the state exploited the peasantry was wrong, both morally and economically, and that the peasants themselves derived few – if any – benefits from the imposition of rigid, top-down policies. He'd also witnessed violence in his own community during the purges and the Nazi occupation, and it is quite likely that his reluctance in later years to resort to using state force as a valid means to an end was a product of his first-hand experiences in early life.

By 1953 Stalin was dead, and so was the policy of terror. At university, Gorbachev had befriended a young, liberal-thinking Czech called Zdeněk Mlynář, who went on to become one of the main proponents of the 1968 Prague Spring uprising in Czechoslovakia against Soviet rule. There too he met his wife-to-be, Raisa, the two marrying in September 1953; in him she apparently saw strength but also kindness, with a respect for the dignity and rights of others.

As Gorbachev climbed the party ladder in the years ahead, Raisa would be his closest ally and confidante in a world where loyalty and trust were in woefully short supply. In 1956, the year of the Hungarian Revolution, Nikita Khrushchev delivered his landmark speech to the

Twentieth Party Congress, denouncing Stalin, his brutality and cult of personality but stopping short of criticising the system outright. Nonetheless the speech triggered a process, effectively the first embryonic stirrings of reformist thoughts. The core principles of Marxist–Leninism were starting to be questioned, and even in Moscow the Budapest protesters were not without their sympathisers. Twelve years later, the Prague Spring, and Alexander Dubček's failed attempt to give communism a 'human face', gave fresh voice to a growing, pent-up desire for basic freedoms: freedom of speech, freedom of the written word and of movement; and for economic decentralisation.

In return for educating you, the state decided where you went and what you did, and Gorbachev was sent back close to home, to the largely agricultural Stavropol region. Over the ensuing years, he made his way up the local party hierarchy, doing what he could to improve the lot of his people, a people he saw as trapped in hopelessness, poverty and subsistence living, and making sure he managed to stay on the right side of officials who might potentially jeopardise his progress. It was a balancing act which required all his powers of persuasion, charm and oration, a feat made somewhat easier by his insights into and grasp of how the rural economy of the region worked – or didn't. He went on to run the local branch of 'Komsomol', the body tasked with mobilising and exhorting the youth of the region to fulfill the objectives set by the party, and by 1968 was deputy party chief of the Stavropol area. By 1970 he was its First Secretary, all-powerful in his domain and answering directly to the Central Committee in Moscow.

Gorbachev's experiences in the Stavropol period helped him formulate his philosophies on the economic ills of the system. He saw an economy built on corruption, in which the laudable ideal of people caring for both the collective and themselves was wrecked by those in positions of responsibility caring for neither. As officials blatantly prioritised their own advancement to the exclusion of practically any meaningful action of benefit to their communities, those communities could not be expected to produce what was asked of them; there was a complete absence of moral example and guidance and, after Stalin, no longer a way to coerce through terror. Targets set were often unrealistic; the system of rewards was illogical and only further stoked already corrupt practices; machinery was outdated and there was no scope or allowance made for initiatives promoting innovation and renewal. Every last detail of people's lives was subject to control from on high. Gorbachev could clearly see the consequences of and privations caused by the communist party's monopoly of political and economic power. But to survive he had to conform and play officials off against each other. While he walked the tightrope, he still managed to help his drought-stricken region with some notable achievements in irrigation, with the Great Stavropol Canal at the forefront of these.

Fortunately for Gorbachev, Brezhnev, who succeeded Khrushchev in 1964, held him in high regard and liked his youth, energy and obedience. The Brezhnev era marked a return to conservatism following the false dawn under Khrushchev. The early sixties had witnessed advances in science and technology, and the launch of Sputnik, all heralded as triumphs of communism and pointers to a rosier future, but ideologically the brakes had been applied and any reformist zeal throttled. Outwardly Gorbachev supported Brezhnev but he also forged important ties elsewhere, including with Yuri Andropov, head of the KGB and another son of Stavropol, who would go on to succeed Brezhnev. Like Gorbachev, Andropov toed the party line without being blind to its glaringly obvious failings, but believed that a total overhaul would be going too far. As ambassador to Hungary during the 1956 uprising, he considered that too much freedom came at an unacceptably high price. And like Gorbachev too, he saw there was scope for much-needed reform; there were limits to this, however, and ultimately any reform could and should only take place in a socialist context.

A visit to Czechoslovakia in 1969, a year after the crushing of the Prague Spring, was almost certainly decisive in cementing in Gorbachev's mind the idea that nothing good came of intervening in another country's affairs using force. He left Czechoslovakia in no doubt of the vehement and deepening anti-Russian sentiment that the invasion had caused. And what the reformers there were proposing – greater democratisation within the party and more freedom outside it – did not seem unreasonable.

Between 1970 and 1977 he undertook five visits to Western Europe, a concession which underlined how highly his talents were regarded, as only officials likely to cut an impressive figure were permitted to venture west. Gorbachev felt comfortable in the West, became attuned to the atmosphere of unrestricted speech and debate, and saw that despite some of the self-evident downsides to democratic society – unemployment, unoccupied houses and apartments, poverty – overall, people lived better than in his own country.

Admission to the uppermost echelons of the party came in September 1978 when Gorbachev was elected to take on the agriculture portfolio in the Central Committee, a promotion which took him back to Moscow. The late seventies was a period of stagnation on all fronts: food shortages and price rises were rife, and despite twenty per cent of the population working on the land, decent quality fruit and vegetables were hard to come by. Much of the nation's farming equipment dated from the war years, and even though there were combine harvesters aplenty, grain still had to be imported. There was a lack of capacity and facilities for storing and transporting what the frequently poor harvests produced. Industrial output was woefully low: the USSR only produced twice as much steel as the USA while boasting eighty times more iron ore. At the helm, an increasingly old, physically infirm leadership indulged in bouts of self-congratulation and occupied an opulent realm, divorced from the masses and sheltered from the true, stark reality of the nation's equally infirm condition.

The earlier spirit of détente between Brezhnev and American presidents Nixon and Ford, when arms control agreements had been hammered out, had dwindled and been replaced by renewed brinkmanship, fresh tensions which ushered in the latest escalation in the Cold War, leaving the Politburo more fearful of a US attack than ever. The USSR built up its stockpiles of SS-20 nuclear rockets; the Americans answered in kind by deciding to base Pershing II missiles in Western Europe; there were flashpoints in Africa and Central America; Russia moved its troops into Afghanistan; the US responded with sanctions; intervention in Poland was threatened, but then watered down to the imposition of martial law; on September 1st 1983 Korean Airlines flight 007 strayed into Soviet air space and was mistaken for a US spy plane, and shot down with the loss of all 269 passengers and crew on board.

Gorbachev watched and waited as the situation, and inertia, worsened, and three General Secretaries – Brezhnev,

Andropov and Chernenko – died in quick succession. His innermost circle agreed that the system was rotten and that basic principles like rewarding good work with good pay were being stymied by rigid economic centralisation, but no heads raised themselves above the Kremlin's parapets. On a visit to Canada to investigate how agriculture functioned there, Gorbachev confided in the Russian ambassador that workers back home were alienated from both the means of production and the results of their labours, so had no motivation to work efficiently nor, therefore, knew how to work efficiently. With the passing of Chernenko in March 1985 and his unopposed election, first by the Politburo then by the party's Central Committee, to the top job of General Secretary, Gorbachev's moment had come. But with hardliners in the Politburo intent on guarding their own power and fearing their positions would be undermined by too rapid change, the way to reform was unlikely to be straightforward or smooth, and a gradual approach to reform would have to be adopted.

How one man would go about trying to transform his country's economy, political system, society and role in the world was set to become one of the twentieth century's greatest dramas, a sequence of events which would touch the lives of countless millions of his own people and have even deeper ramifications for the citizens of those satellite nations living under the Russian yolk.

Back in the eighties, anyone standing in Red Square and marvelling at the remarkable, gaudy assemblage of domes crowning St Basil's Cathedral, surely Moscow's most iconic sight, could not have failed to notice the architectural monstrosity a few degrees to its left and wondered how even a regime not known for taking aesthetic considerations into account in its city planning could have allowed its erection so close to this hallowed place. For this was the Hotel Rossiya, at that time arguably the world's best and worst located hotel. It was also, at that time, the world's largest hotel, with its almost 3,200 rooms, the majority no larger than eleven square metres in size, able to accommodate just short of 6,000 guests. These guests included, up to its overdue demise in 2006, George Bush senior, Mike Tyson, Gorbachev himself and armies of MPs and officials from far-flung corners of the empire, billeted there while doing their stint of duty at head office across Red Square. And millions of foreign tourists.

The gargantuan twelve-storey glass and metal box that was the Rossiya – rising up to twenty-one stories in a tower which erupted from the north building – had been completed in the late sixties on the site of the former residential area of Zaryadye. The area had been completely obliterated, save for haunting traces of its former glory in the shape of a few elegant churches and historic buildings along Varkava Street, which were now usurped by their hideous new neighbour. Varkava Street was the ancient route into Red Square, and the seventeenth century Church of St George, impressively tall by any normal standards but utterly dwarfed and unable to make its presence felt in the looming shadow of the Rossiya, was its most notable survivor. Indeed, these few remaining gems, concealed almost to oblivion by the hotel's offensive bulk, were competing against a vast edifice consisting of four component parts (north, south, east and west blocks), covering the area of twenty football pitches. Inside there were restaurants, a health club, nightclub, post office, a theatre-cum-cinema, the 2,500-seat State Central Concert Hall and a barber's shop. The barber's shop is worthy of mention because of some very ordinary-looking black doors located close to it. These were the unbroadcast entrances to a police station which contained a number of cells, presumably to temporarily house any visiting officials who may have fallen out of favour, or other hotel guests whose behaviour may have aroused suspicion.

The Rossiya's notoriety came to include death-trap status when on February 25th, 1977, forty-two guests died and fifty were injured in a fire on the upper floors of the north block. The duty manager responsible for that part of the hotel committed suicide two days later. A performance taking place in the theatre at the time was extended so that departing audience members wouldn't get in the way of guests fleeing the fire. The disaster was largely hushed up by the authorities, as far as a fire of that magnitude could be. As time went on the hotel's grim reputation came to be more about its uninvited guests, the rats and cockroaches. But it wasn't all bad. Dominating the bank of that section of the Moskva River, and so close to Red Square, the Kremlin and St Basil's, the views could be sensational, depending on which part or side of the box your room was located in. The stark, bleakly lit interior was on occasions used as a film set. But neither the filmmakers nor many other visitors would have known about the series of secret underground halls and tunnels supposedly uncovered during the hotel's later demolition, and running as far as the Kremlin.

*

As our coach drew up alongside the entrance to Rossiya's south block, our Intourist guide handed me a voucher and instructed me to proceed with the group to the reception area for check-in. She would meet us here at nine o'clock the next morning for the city sightseeing tour, she confirmed, in the sort of tone which implied there could be grave penalties for any late arrivals.

Some hours earlier, our British Airways flight had touched down at Sheremetyovo airport. After a protracted wait to get through passport and visa control, we'd collected our luggage and stood, with enforced and wise patience, in a queue which led up to rows of tables where our suitcases might or might not be inspected by one of the expressionless customs officers. As we edged closer, our collective anxiety and anguish increased at the sight of four Hasidic Jewish gentlemen being ordered to empty the entire contents of their luggage onto the tables in full view of the long line of onlookers, all fearing a similarly humiliating fate. Clothes were rifled through, books were pored over by furrowed, deeply quizzical brows, and bulging toiletry bags were left flaccid as their guts were rudely disgorged onto the cold steel surface. What had started as carefully, neatly assembled piles of belongings were finally reduced to something resembling a church hall jumble sale at three o'clock on a Saturday afternoon. The final ignominy was the toothpaste. Each gentleman watched aghast, as did we, as tube after tube was squeezed empty onto a piece of paper by pumping, clenched fists, giant worm casts of Colgate and Aquafresh, white streaked with red and turquoise, each one as harmless, non-subversive and innocent as the next. The officers then gesticulated to the men to repack their cases, toothpaste included, and move on.

I presented the hotel voucher to one of the glum-looking ladies at the reception desk. She disappeared into a back office for what seemed like an eternity, my group silently surveying their stark new surroundings as I waited to arrange their lodgings. For a few hours I was back in my old role as a rep, though I was formally there to see how our Russia programme was running and hold meetings with Intourist, the monolithic state travel organisation controlling all foreign tourism into the Soviet Union. Our usual rep was over in the outskirts settling another group into the Hotel

Cosmos, and it felt good to be back at the helm. Until the receptionist reappeared.

'No, you are wrong here. You must go back outside. You must go to west building. Your group will sleep there. But you must eat here,' she stated emphatically, before handing the voucher back and readying herself unenthusiastically for her next task.

I repeated her words back to her, to be sure I had fully comprehended the unwelcome news, whereupon she lifted her head to deliver a curt and perfunctory nod, indicating that no further intrusion on her time should have taken place as the matter was already settled. I gathered my group together and informed them that we were going to be sleeping in a different part of the hotel, and that getting there would involve them carrying their suitcases a not inconsiderable distance. And given it was – not untypically for a December evening – minus fifteen degrees outside, they should wrap up warmly. I then added that, by the way, our restaurant for dinner later on was back here in the south block, and that it was just over there, across the lobby.

The hotel was stiflingly hot, and there would be a lot of wrapping up and unwrapping that evening and over the course of the next four days. We entered the west building, our shivering bodies met by a thick wall of heat, only for the debacle in the south block to be played out all over again. We were in the wrong place, came the verdict after the voucher was compared to a manual ledger; we were to sleep in the north building and must go outside and report to the reception there, in the north building.

The receptionist in the west building turned out to be true to her word and, hovering precariously between hypothermia and asphyxiation, we finally stood huddled before our Key Lady on one of the upper, north block floors, relieved to have got a significant step closer to some sort of sanctuary.

As is so often the case when there is the barrier of officialdom to overcome before achieving the end goal, a straightforward request ('here are our papers, can we have our keys, please?') was peppered with smiles, jolly greetings and enquiries into how the Key Lady's day was going so far – none of which impressed her one iota. In a deliberate breach of strict grammatical correctness, I capitalise **Key Lady** for a good reason, namely, to emphasise the elevated position these ladies – who sat at simple wooden tables next to the lifts – held in the hierarchy of this and many other Russian hotels. As well as dispensers of keys they were sentries, much like the Swiss Guards at the Vatican or the Queen's Guards at Buckingham Palace, who are similarly afforded the honour of capital letters. They were also known as 'Floor Ladies' and nothing that went on along their long patch of grimy, very weathered carpet escaped their notice, so it was wise to at least try to enjoy good relations with them. If a towel or bar of soap happened not to be in your room on your arrival, which was entirely possible, your Key Lady was your salvation. If you wanted to make an overseas phone call, it could only happen via the Key Lady. Your *dezhurnaya*, to give her her Russian name, could be the difference between a trouble-free and a troubled stay, and you chose not to pay her due deference at your peril.

*

I'd arranged to meet two of my reps at the National Hotel for a late drink that evening, so after marching my guests back to the south block, where our earlier check-in ordeal had started, and taking a passable dinner of borscht,[23]

---

23. *The famous 'borscht' is made from beef, beetroot, cabbage and other vegetables.*

pork chops and ice cream with them in its restaurant, I headed out across a freezing, almost deserted Red Square to the rendezvous. There was no wind, yet the bright red Soviet flag with its hammer and sickle insignia fluttered energetically above the Kremlin's towers and crenellations, a constant stream of air being forced upwards through its sleek pole. The star perched atop the Saviour Tower was closer to a wine red, and looked cosmetic and awkward, like a plastic toy left thoughtlessly on a priceless, elegant piece of period furniture: an unsightly blemish, an affront to this otherwise magnificent place, this stunning and unique centre of culture, and of power. In one direction, there lay the crazy conglomeration of multicoloured domes that make up St Basil's Cathedral, in another the massive fortress walls of the Kremlin, dwarfing Lenin's Mausoleum beneath them, and to the third side the GUM department store, a building so grand that Raisa Gorbachev wanted it turned into an art museum. Only ahead, as I made my way across the square, lay the spoiler to this awe-inspiring aspect: the faceless, twenty-storey banality of the Intourist Hotel, a foretaste of the miles of high-rise concrete wasteland which made up much of the Moscow beyond it, and which stretched deep into the suburbs.

I never tired of standing in Red Square, grateful that it hadn't gone the same way as the large patch of land the Rossiya occupied close by. It was a lone, defiant jewel preserved from a glistening age of architecture, music and writing, surrounded by something worse than mediocrity. The contrast could not have been starker, but it had endured the upheavals that followed the Bolshevik revolution of 1917, that violent break with Russia's past, and now stood at the heart of a totalitarian state, albeit one in the process of major transformation, and all the dreary bleakness that went with it. Might it, one day, witness continuity with the past resumed? Maybe they were just wishful imaginings, but whenever I stood in this beautiful place, this symbol of not only a nation's power but of its survival too, I had a strange sense of better times to come – not just for the people of Russia but also for the citizens of its satellite states, desperate for their master's grip to be loosened, who now had an emerging ally inside the Kremlin's walls.

After weeks of fairly bland and predictable fare at the Hotel Cosmos and the Intourist, my reps were keen to be treated to the altogether more appealing offerings of the kitchen at the National, so we made our way upstairs to its ornate restaurant. I asked the man at the door for a table for three, but the response came that the restaurant was full. There were no free tables that evening. This was surprising as the restaurant appeared to be completely empty. I explained that there were only three of us, and might a small table be found for us in some remote corner of the room? No, came the uncompromising reply, they were full. No table tonight.

At this point one of the reps stepped forward and, without any pretence of secrecy, thrust a one-dollar bill towards the man, who immediately turned on his heel, waved us into the restaurant and led us to a large table in the middle of the room. Next, a platoon of smartly dressed waiters materialised from nowhere, made a beeline for our table and then busily began to straighten up knives, forks and spoons, which already seemed perfectly straight. With great ceremony, napkins were placed on laps and our chairs pushed firmly closer to the table. Glasses were inspected, and in some cases replaced. My request to see the menu was silently ignored, and within minutes silver platters loaded with smoked salmon, caviar, butter and a variety of bread rolls and slices were being ferried from the kitchen, along with jugs of water, bottles of beer and an even larger bottle of vodka. That was just the prelude to a sumptuous

dinner of beef stroganoff, dumplings, blini, okroshka[24] soup
and my evening's second helping of borscht. As more and
more dishes were produced, in what was fast becoming a
minor banquet, my fear over the likely size of the bill grew
exponentially, but I comforted myself with the thought that
here was a good opportunity to reward hard work, even if it
meant a shattered expense budget.

After a couple of hours of overindulgence and royal
treatment, Soviet-style, we ground to a boozy and satisfied
halt, and I braced myself to ask for the bill. At this point, one
of the reps, the same one who'd bought our way into the
restaurant earlier, stood up, walked across to the head waiter
and counted out ten more one-dollar bills. There was a hint of
a nod from the head waiter as the notes disappeared into his
jacket pocket, and we exited. On the way out, the rep asked
me whether it would be okay to put the meal on expenses,
and I replied that it would be absolutely fine. He went on
to tell me how a few weeks earlier he'd been in charge of a
group of twenty-five businessmen on a four-day 'incentive'
to Moscow, all owners of car dealerships being rewarded
by the manufacturer for a year of highly impressive results.
On the first evening the lead client, the sales director at the
manufacturer, had approached him and said:

'Here's three thousand pounds. I want these guys to be
given anything they want. Anything. The best food, the
best vodka and champagne, great nightlife. And I mean,
ANYTHING, if you get what I mean. Make sure they are
happy. And if there is anything left at the end, keep it as a
tip. If they're happy, you'll have earned it.'

By the end of the four days, and despite his best efforts, the
rep had spent just under six hundred pounds, and assured me

24. 'Blini' are a type of pancake; 'okroshka' is a type of vegetable soup
containing the green seed pods of the okra plant.

that he'd pulled out all the stops to provide the group with the best Moscow had to offer, in every sense. This chimed with a letter I'd received from the group leader shortly before my trip, eulogising about how successful the incentive had been, what an ideal place Moscow was for entertaining a bunch of salesmen hell-bent on having a good time, and how he intended to repeat the exercise the following year. And what a tremendous job our rep had done, on such a tight budget too, in ensuring the group's complete satisfaction.

*

At just past nine o'clock the following morning, I waved my group off as the coach pulled away from the Rossiya to start the city sightseeing tour. Over the next two days, the tightly controlled programme would not afford much time for spending money on what little there was to spend money on. A visit to one of the 'hard currency only' *berioska* stores was, however, as compulsory as queuing to pay respects at Lenin's Mausoleum, where the USSR's founding father had lain in state since 1930, with a break in Siberia during the War, and was looking distinctly pallid. His embalmed corpse was regularly removed for essential maintenance, a delicate process which had succeeded in preserving his unmistakable facial features. The day's tour, much of which played out inside the Kremlin's walls and included time in the magnificent Armoury and Grand Palace, featured a guided stroll along Arbat Street, the only other shopping opportunity, lined with stalls selling replica religious icons and, for any tourist, the must-have wooden Russian dolls, each containing several more wooden dolls, ever smaller in size as each casing was removed. Every now and then, a long static line of people would appear though the freezing mist, silent, heavily coated and booted souls, each waiting patiently for a portion of morozhenoye, the ice cream prized and eagerly devoured even on the harshest of winter days.

While my group immersed themselves in the dazzling array of relics and palatial piles inside the Kremlin fortress, I had a meeting at Intourist (literally 'Foreign Tourist') at their head office, just a few paces from the National Hotel where I had dined so gloriously the night before. Intourist was the sole state agency responsible for regulating and arranging tourism into the USSR, and what little travel there was out of it. In each socialist country tourism was run along the same lines, with one body in overall control of the human flow in and out, and as a buyer, as I was, it left little room for manoeuvre and an almost total lack of negotiating power. The programmes tourist groups had to follow were pre-ordained, as were the prices paid by the tour operators for those programmes, and a set, very limited number of hotels were allocated to accommodate foreigners; the main ones in Moscow at that time were the Rossiya, Intourist, Cosmos and the Stalinist skyscraper that was the Ukraina. There was no choice of menu, nor of which coach company ran the airport transfers and excursions; all vehicles were state-owned. Concerns over quality could be raised, and were listened to, and occasionally superficial improvements were made, but beyond small concessions it was a case of having to accept what was offered, as there were no alternatives.

To a consumer society used to the concept of the client generally being regarded as king, and where there is always another eager and willing supplier to switch to if standards fall short, all this seems intensely frustrating. And to a point, it was. Getting some form of tacit agreement, though far short of a binding one, that our guests would be accommodated whenever possible in the Rossiya or Intourist, hotels preferred by dint of their superior location so close to the heart of the city and to Red Square, was about as close to a breakthrough concession as we could expect to get, and was proof of a job well done and a strong relationship which Intourist, in their own way, were showing they valued. That often involved getting certain types of merchandise to the right people in the hierarchy. Once client numbers increased, I like to think that our impressive sales figures were to some degree reflected in relatively low year-on-year price increases, but we came to accept very early on that the (to us) normal, capitalist version of the buyer–supplier relationship held absolutely no sway whatsoever, as indeed was the case in every aspect of economic life throughout the entire country and the wider socialist bloc.

And for the man on the street, the quality and choice of goods were practically irrelevant. What mattered was what basic goods were available to buy in the first place.

Thanks to an emerging brand of customer behaviour, the frustration over lack of control and choice only went so deep. One Friday evening at around six, I was in the Operations department, tying up a few loose ends before heading over the road to join my colleagues at The Marquis of Wellington for the customary and unconstrained end-of-week binge, when a concerned-looking duty manager scurried into the office waving a telex.

'Phil, I think we might have a problem with the Moscow group flying out tomorrow morning. Seems like they won't have a hotel.'

The telex was from Intourist, and was short and to the point:

Dear Page and Moy,

This is to inform you that your clients arriving tomorrow will be accommodated on boats.

Sincerely,

U Bagrov

We had never come across a 'U Bagrov' amongst our many contacts at Intourist, and wondered whether this was some sort of sick wind-up. The name, when said slowly and with a cockney accent, sounded like a coarse insult. We tried to call Intourist, but to no avail, leaving us no choice but to spend the rest of the evening phoning all the lead names on the passenger list, some seventy calls in all, to pass on the bad tidings that, regrettably: they and their travel companions would be sleeping in berths, not beds, for the next three nights; we had no idea of the whereabouts of these boats, on which body of water they were located or what sort of boats they were; and finally, we didn't know whether they would be fed on these boats, or elsewhere.

Despite the scant information and the fundamental material change from what the brochure had promised, there was a general, occasionally resigned acceptance but no cancellations. This was no doubt in large part because suitcases would already have been packed and check-in for the flight was due to open at seven-thirty the next morning.

But there was more to it than this. A trip to the Soviet Union was not undertaken with any illusions of enjoying a luxury break, of staying in flashy, modern hotels or sampling top-notch cuisine. There were certainly places and sights of justifiable world renown, as well as the mouthwatering prospect of evenings at the Bolshoi and Moscow State Circus. But more than anything, people were paying for the chance to be inside the inner sanctum of our Cold War adversary, in the cradle of communism, to dare to discover what in 1983 Ronald Reagan had referred to as the 'evil empire' was actually like now that it was becoming more accessible. Not only that, but there was a strong sense of witnessing, being a small part of, a developing political event which could have far-reaching ramifications not just for the Soviet Union, but the entire world. In this respect alone, the growing volume of visitors during this period from non-socialist countries to Moscow, and to other parts of the USSR, represented a completely unique trend in tourism, a phenomenon that hasn't been repeated anywhere in the world since: the urge for large numbers of people to venture into what was considered by many as 'enemy territory' to experience first-hand what was happening there.

So as things turned out, Mr Bagrov's (I later found out that 'U Bagrov' did exist, was male and high-ranking, and I went on to meet him in person) shock last-minute announcement didn't make too many waves, nor cause a tidal surge of complaints, even though the boats were no better than glorified barges and were moored some way out of the city centre on the further reaches of the Moskva River. Indeed, we rarely received complaints about anything that inadvertently went wrong on our Russia programmes or that was well below the standards and norms taken for granted on other holidays. People had no expectations. It was enough just to be there.

Gorbymania?

Be there to see what exactly? By the end of 1987, as I was going through the tribulations of checking my group into the Rossiya (where the man himself had often taken a room on the tenth floor after his return to Moscow in 1978), Gorbachev had been in power for more than two and a half years. His initial steps had been faltering: a drive for stronger law and order, for stricter discipline, backed up by a crusade against alcohol, were effectively a continuation of Andropov's policies and deeply unpopular. Alcohol was ruining the economy, but getting it off the shop shelves and failing to replace it with a wider range of quality consumer goods left little else for a population deprived of its daily dose of vodka to spend its money on. And as long as there was an absence of consumer goods people would continue to stash what money they had in safe corners of their bedrooms instead of putting it back into circulation. This, in turn, made economic restructuring problematic. Gorbachev wanted to accelerate the economy, and proclaimed that Soviet output would overtake that of the US by the year 2000, but was unsure how to do it. He longed to kick-start a scientific and technological revolution, but the structures needed to make that happen were not yet in place, as central planning made no allowance for innovation.

The old, well-worn mantras about socialism being the way forward had cropped up in his maiden speech after becoming General Secretary, but there were references to democratisation too, along with the concept of 'Glasnost', something he'd first referred to in a speech at an ideological conference in 1984. 'Glasnost', broadly meaning 'openness', bordered on an acceptance of free speech, and was an exhortation for greater transparency in the way the state operated. And this signalled a sea change in the way information was handled and disseminated. Officials at every level had always been accustomed to telling their superiors what they thought they wanted to hear; Gorbachev personified his concept of Glasnost by openly mixing with the people, letting them question him, listening to their views and making sure they felt it was their right to know the facts. He went on walkabouts, he spoke off the cuff, not from a prepared text ridden with platitudes and dogma, and hoped that if people knew the truth about the ills of the economy they would feel empowered to help bring about positive change. Magazines and journals saw new, progressive editors appointed, over one hundred banned films were rehabilitated, and novels laying bare the evils of totalitarianism were allowed to circulate. Late in 1986, Gorbachev ordered the dissident Andrei Sakharov to be released from exile in Gorky, boosting his own popularity but alarming some of his more cautious colleagues.

Gorbachev's problem was that all this Glasnost presented a platform to those who wanted to highlight his failings, including opponents who felt he was moving too fast, or not fast enough. Nevertheless, the nuclear explosion at Chernobyl on April 26th, 1984, and the aftermath of cover-ups in what had been one of the few truly respected Soviet industries, further persuaded him that the entire system was riddled with incompetence, self-serving and falsification. He launched into diatribes on everything from the lack of vegetables in Moscow to government ministers well past their sell-by date, and from the embedded, sinister practice of denunciation to the lack of democracy in all areas of society. Gorbachev was on the warpath against the system he had grown up in and inherited, and word was reaching the West.

And it wasn't just about one word – Glasnost – but about 'Perestroika' too. In 'Perestroika' Gorbachev was alluding to the urgent need for a restructuring, not of the entire communist party system, but in the way the economy was managed and government and social policy were run. The new openness in debating should extend, he believed, into political and governmental realms and be reflected in the way the institutions of both society and state were structured.

In Britain, a nation often accused of languishing in the linguistic lower leagues, the two words – Glasnost and Perestroika – rapidly became assimilated into the conversation of the day, proving that our ability to import useful foreign language went beyond Angst, Schadenfreude and ménage à trois.

The fact that word was reaching the West was not purely down to Gorbachev's reputation at home, but because he was demonstrating the same traits, the same desire for a change to the status quo, in his approach to the Cold War too. With the exception of Khrushchev's promotion of peaceful coexistence, relations with the capitalist world had always been antagonistic. Soviet leaders saw capitalist and imperialist powers as their sworn enemies, and Stalin maintained that peace with the West was impossible. Encouraging the working classes, and the more left-wing political parties they may have subscribed to, to detach themselves from their overlords ideologically or, if possible, in more fundamental ways, formed an ever-present thread throughout decades of Soviet foreign policy towards the West. Gorbachev was not going to abandon national security interests or the interests of the global socialist movement at a stroke, but he recognised that most of the countries considered to be the USSR's adversaries were in better shape economically and technologically than his own. He surmised too that the western powers weren't about to attack the Soviet Union, but knew that trying to outpace Reagan's plans for a strategic defence system in space to thwart a nuclear attack – the so-called Star Wars programme – was a battle the USSR couldn't win, and trying to would almost certainly bring about economic catastrophe. Moreover, Gorbachev held a deep-seated abhorrence of nuclear weapons, not just for the destruction they would cause to humanity, but to the natural environment too. And if only he could halt the arms race it would leave him more money for domestic regeneration, so an anti-isolationist, pro-engagement strategy made more sense on all fronts.

The war in Afghanistan had been dragging on since 1980, and was deeply unpopular at home. Thousands of Russian soldiers were dead, but a speedy withdrawal would send a message that the massive loss of life had been in vain, and unjustified, and Gorbachev had to be careful not to be seen abandoning territory only for it to be swallowed up by imperialist, or other unfriendly forces. Nevertheless, in 1986 (although it was 1989 before the last Soviet troops finally pulled out) he told Afghan president Babrak Karmal that any future intervention would be limited to military equipment rather than men, and that a peaceful solution should be sought in the ongoing, bloody conflict with the Mujahideen.

This in itself was a notable – and, to the onlooking world, a welcome – switch in direction, but it was undoubtedly Gorbachev's (and Ronald Reagan's) efforts to end the Cold War, and with it the arms race, which propelled him into the international limelight in the mid-eighties. The impact of Gorbachev's fresh, charming, thoughtful and more natural style – so radically different from what had come out of the Kremlin before – on the American leadership and his wider western audience cannot be overstated. A series of summits, starting with their meeting in Geneva in November 1985, saw the chemistry between Reagan and Gorbachev grow, and with it came agreements and a de-escalation in tensions. Before travelling to Geneva, Gorbachev had visited President Mitterrand in Paris and been given a warm welcome by the French public, and his popularity kept on rising wherever he went.

The talks in Geneva were characterised by an atmosphere of informality, and achieved a mutual understanding that a nuclear war must never be fought and could never be won. A year later, in the autumn of 1986, a hastily arranged summit at the Hofdi House in Reykjavik saw the two leaders come close to agreeing to scrap nuclear weapons within the next ten years, but Reagan refused to rein back on the Star Wars programme. Although this would remain a deal-breaker, a rapport of trust had been established and the threat which had hung over Europe, and beyond, for so long was vastly diminished. By the end of 1987 the two superpowers had signed the Intermediate-Range Nuclear Forces Treaty in Washington, eliminating each country's short and medium-range nuclear weapons.

Back home, 1987 – the seventieth anniversary of the Russian Revolution – was turning out to be a year of mixed fortunes for Gorbachev. Economic performance was worse than the previous year, and there was ongoing disagreement over what type of reforms were needed. The old problems of low-quality manufacturing and a lack of a viable market for goods persisted; there was no real competition in the economy. Gorbachev continued to signal his intent by exploring ways of making the electoral system more democratic, and of allowing enterprises to set their own targets rather than have them dictated from above. But often, this simply resulted in more expensive products generating bigger profits for the bosses of those enterprises, leaving all but the wealthiest consumers with the same dearth of choice. And giving workers more say was all well and good, but the voices raised would frequently appeal for higher wages rather than for the greater democratisation that Gorbachev cherished. At least in the provinces, Glasnost was spreading, and journalists and writers there felt increasingly unbridled to say what they wanted. At the heart of the matter was a cultural reality: having been ruled autocratically for centuries, Russians were not accustomed to engaging in open debate and discussion to resolve an issue or decide a course of action, so trying to bring about change via consensus was an alien concept. In contrast, Gorbachev's book 'Perestroika: New Thinking for Our Country and the World' sold millions in the West.

A further bold step, and break from the past, was Gorbachev's open condemnation of Stalin's crimes and assertion that the former leader had known full well what was being perpetrated under his rule. It was bold because so many had died heroically defending Stalin's Soviet Union against Nazi occupation during World War II, so Gorbachev had to be careful not to offend patriotic citizens, alive and dead. As with the majority of his pronouncements and policies, there were those around him who felt he went too far and those who criticised him for not going further faster. In the latter group, Boris Yeltsin, head of the Moscow City Party, had emerged by late 1987 as one of the chief protagonists and a vocal opponent of Gorbachev. Yeltsin, who had sacked practically everyone in his team when he assumed the role in 1985, cut a larger-than-life, brash, authoritarian figure, no doubt more in keeping with what Muscovites were used to, and courted popularity by travelling around the city on public transport and getting amongst the locals. He made no secret of his frustration at the slow progress of transformation and portrayed himself as an alternative people's champion, much to Gorbachev's annoyance and displeasure.

It was a toxic relationship which would ultimately come to define Gorbachev's later years in power, and the outcome of his drive for reform. For now, though, he was attaining superstar status on the world stage, and we in the West were getting very excited about what he was doing.

The train hauled itself reluctantly out of Moscow's Jaroslavl station and trundled through the desolate, colourless blocks of the city's suburbs, a dreary and monochromatic start to what the Page and Moy brochure described as 'the world's greatest train journey'. It was March, raw, and the short walk from coach to platform had been enough to unleash an outbreak of collective relief when, after heaving their suitcases up vertical metal steps, my small band of passengers entered the warm, sticky air of the train's corridor and started to search for their compartments. Compartments were second-class and four-berth, though most had paid the £140 supplement to keep the number of occupants down to two, creating some essential extra luggage and breathing space. The accommodation was spartan, and the brochurespeak had hinted as much: 'On the Trans-Siberian Express you will travel in comfortable 4-berth compartments during your journey, and you'll find the corridors wider than on most European trains.'

The fact that the relative width of the corridors was apparently the train's only selling point worth highlighting, spoke volumes. As an example of how to be creative and find something to accentuate that appeared to confer advantage and benefit when there was really nothing of the sort, it took me back to Germany's Mosel Valley two years earlier. Ever in search of cheap winter holiday ideas to boost our lean low-season cash flow, I'd set up a series of four-day coach tours to a hotel in a relatively unknown village in the area. The hotel was normally closed in winter, and its owner had agreed to a stunningly low price of just five Deutschmarks per person per night (then equivalent to around two pounds). This was for bed and continental breakfast, on the condition that dinners and a wine-tasting evening would be arranged in-house and charged out to the guests – as were all the excursions, to places such as Bernkastel, Cochem,

Koblenz and the Rhine Valley, so that we too could actually turn in some sort of profit on a lead-in price of £39. Apart from the coach transfers and ferry crossing from the UK to the Mosel and back, the bed and the breakfast, nothing else was included in the price of the holiday. This prompted our marketing people to go big on the breakfast, which they described as consisting of 'bread rolls, butter, jam, ham and cheese – and a choice of either tea or coffee!' I'd been horrified at the inclusion of the exclamation mark after 'coffee' and felt that 'choice of tea or coffee' went quite far enough, without the added insult of the exclamation mark. But I'd lost the day and, whether it was due to that choice of tea or coffee or, more likely, the irresistible price of the holiday, the whole programme sold like hot cakes and was repeated for winters to come.

If the brochure couldn't find many virtues in the train to extol, it was far less challenging to whip up enthusiasm for the journey itself, an odyssey of 'almost five thousand miles, passing through seven time zones and across Siberia, the "sleeping land", over four million square miles of mainly forests, rivers and lakes.' The name Siberia itself conjured up terrifying images of a vast, closed wilderness, where the state's undesirables, dissidents and sundry unwanted denizens toiled in appalling conditions in labour camps, the *gulags*, from where escape into the endless miles of frozen tundra was futile and meant certain death. Yet, this closed wilderness was now open enough for us to venture into, though still very much within strict limits.

It soon became apparent how strict those limits were. Like the hotels, the train was stiflingly hot. The early euphoria we felt when boarding the train at leaving the piercing bitterness of the Moscow winter soon gave way to grumbles about the withering heat of the compartments. The corridor was little

175

better. An upper, narrow window in the compartment could be hinged partially open, and there was a row of these on the corridor too, but each time we opened any of them the visibly peeved guard would make a show of snapping them shut again. A sort of stand-off developed in which we'd see how long we could manage to keep the windows open before the guard responded. I asked our Intourist guide, a friendly, helpful lady who accompanied us on the journey, why it had to be this way:

'He says it is because the air outside is too cold, and you will get sick. But really it is to stop you getting out of the train, or people from outside getting on.'

This defied logic. For anyone, even the leanest, to have squeezed through the aperture that called itself a window would have required an inconceivable level of physical dexterity, a lot of inhaling and probably the removal of some limbs. Even when the train's speed reduced to a leisurely trundle, landing on the frost-bitten earth below would have been at best highly destructive and at worst fatal. And which 'people from outside' would want to travel even deeper into Siberia, even if they had been able to scale a moving train and force themselves through a slot high up on its side?

We rolled on through the uniformly flat landscape, grove after grove of silver birch trees punctuated now and then by the dark, wooden houses of another drab, unpretentious small community, where rough streets were unmetalled and unedged, a throwback to an almost early industrial, Dickensian age, with figures trudging who knows where, each so completely and anonymously wrapped up against the cold as to rob them of any individuality. It was peaceful, strangely serene, often sleep-inducing, observing this other, this harsh, world from our own privileged isolation, always to the barely discernible, rhythmic swaying of the train. It was mesmerising too, the effect of passing nothing that took the breath away but being hooked spellbound to a very long, very rare film. There was a ripple of excitement as we gathered in the corridor, between Perm and Yekaterinenburg, to witness the mighty Urals. But the Urals, at least here where they form the Central Urals, were far from mighty, and before long we were once again moving drowsily onwards through the plate-flat sylvan wastes.

A few of the eighteen members of my group needed some sporadic animation to break up their days spent gazing out of the window, dopily transfixed by the images floating before them or nodding off in the oppressive heat of their compartments. To the rescue came a couple of packs of cards and my set of 'Pass the Pigs', always certain to engender both hilarity and fierce competition, which involved tossing two small plastic pigs into the air and scoring points depending on the positions they land in ('making bacon', a rare achievement where one pig lands on the back of the other, scoring particularly highly). I tried to absorb some basic Russian from our obliging Intourist lady, who would test my growing knowledge of the Cyrillic alphabet by getting me to decipher the names of stations we passed through. After a couple of days of intensive tuition, my conversational Russian was starting to shape up well, thanks in no small part to our guide's unswerving patience.

This patience turned out to be quite a godsend. There was an elderly lady in the group, well into her eighties, whose energy and zest for life, new discoveries and adventure, was truly uplifting. She apparently had some health issues, so travelled with a younger female companion, in her forties, her friend and helper in case anything went wrong on tour. And something did go wrong, but not to the elderly lady.

On the third night on board, shortly before reaching the

city of Krasnoyarsk, the elderly lady's younger companion had a suspected minor heart attack. The guide and train staff decided that she needed to be taken to hospital in Krasnoyarsk and, understandably, the elderly lady insisted on accompanying her. And the guide had to go too, so as to interpret at the hospital and ensure her two western charges were not left to their own devices in what was at that time a 'closed' city. It was agreed that I would continue with the group to Irkutsk, where we were due to disembark later that day and spend two nights at a hotel, and all being well the guide and two ladies would rendezvous with us there.

So I found myself catapulted unexpectedly into the role of 'Russian-speaking' tour escort, meaning that exchanges of fire with the peevish guard, ordering everyone tea from the rather gloomy woman who operated the giant ceramic *samovar* at the end of the corridor, and liaising with the waiters in the restaurant car were now all down to me, and my worryingly basic knowledge of Russian. To add to my titles, I had overheard one of our louder group members refer to me a couple of times as 'the travel man' ('the travel man said breakfast starts at 8 am'; 'the travel man said we arrive at the next station in one hour', etc). I decided to take this as conferring a certain status on me, although I did wonder whether it was because I'd failed to announce myself properly at the start of the journey, and my former tour guide skills had slipped.

And by this time, a situation had developed in the restaurant car too. Each day we trekked three times – for breakfast, lunch and dinner – through several carriages to get to the restaurant car at the opposite end of the train, always arousing curious looks from our fellow passengers. To many of those, maybe all, this would have been their first time at close quarters with anyone from beyond their own borders, so any curiosity was unsurprising. With the faces we came to recognise, the same people always standing in the corridor rather than sitting closeted in their compartments, nods and even a word of greeting came to be exchanged: a fleeting, refreshing bridging of the wider chasm that separated us. Once we reached the restaurant car, the waiters silently ushered us to our allotted seats and brought out our allotted food, portions not generous but covering the essentials, fairly balanced and relatively tasty and certainly nothing to arouse dissent in a group which had demonstrated a positive, 'ready for anything' mentality all trip. This was fortunate, because by the end of the second day it was evident that the menu had become decidedly less varied and a lot more repetitive. Vegetables had disappeared from the daily fare, and breakfast consisted of bread, butter and a plain omelette. By the final morning before reaching Irkutsk, the only food left on board seemed to be bread and tinned pineapple, served that day for both breakfast and lunch.

Had we, and our co-travellers, really eaten so much that we were down to starvation rations? Apart from stopping at the main cities – Perm, Sverdlovsk, Novosibirsk, Krasnoyarsk – the train, especially during the night hours, would make shorter, unscheduled stops at smaller cities and towns. The guide had successfully negotiated us short bursts of temporary release from confinement, and the guard had agreed to allow us to disembark for a couple of minutes to stretch our legs whenever the train pulled up. We were to stand by our carriage where we could be observed. What we observed, however, at almost every stop, was a tightly packed huddle of freezing humanity further down the platform outside the restaurant car, where some sort of semi-clandestine activity seemed to be taking place. Items and objects were hurriedly passed down by one of the waiters, standing in the doorway, into outstretched arms darting upwards from within the crowd. A figure, then another, would peel away from the crowd, a bag swaying from a clenched hand, and scurry off the end of the platform and disappear into the penetrating cold of the night. We realised that the Trans-Siberian served not only its paying guests but also communities along its route which were prepared to part with money for some of the onboard experience, for the food they had no hope of procuring any other way. Even out here, the black market was alive and well.

We arrived in Irkutsk on the fourth day, our bellies having had their fill of bread and tinned pineapple and all of us craving a hot shower. The washing facilities on board had been rudimentary, and necessity had proved to be the mother of invention: there was a small cabin with a toilet and washbasin (cold water only) at the end of the carriage, and one of our group managed to find a length of rubber hose, heaven knows from where, which we attached to the tap and then tossed up and over a metal bar near the ceiling, letting it dangle down to make an improvised shower. It flooded the cabin every time it was used, but for the hardier, brave enough to endure the shock, it provided a short, sharp, thorough wash, and a welcome boost to the circulation after the distinct lack of physical movement. On the final evening of our two in Irkutsk, the guide and two ladies caught up with us, but by then had missed the highlight of our time there, the trip to an ice-locked Lake Baikal, the deepest freshwater lake in the world and almost four hundred miles long. To get from A to B, and to avoid taking a long and arduous circumnavigation of the lake, convoys of lorries would drive across the ice, and we stood on the shore watching in stunned amazement as one such column, far in the distance, crept slowly and tentatively across its frozen vastness. The ice close to our feet strained and groaned, and we wondered how many drivers each year made a tragic miscalculation, with the risk proving fatal.

As the group prepared to head back to the station and continue the journey east to Khabarovsk in the far east of Russia without me, I was taxied to the airport for my flight back to Moscow. At Omsk I had to change planes, and as I entered the airport building I was segregated from the other arriving passengers and directed to an empty lounge to await the departure of my connecting flight. There was a two-hour wait, and as departure time approached I was still, to my surprise, alone in the lounge. This was shaping up well, I thought, as I contemplated having the entire plane to myself, some compensation for the austere experience of spending several hours on a clapped-out Aeroflot Tupolev with no food and, at best, a plastic cup half-filled with warm water, warm Cola or warm lemonade. As the flight from Irkutsk had shown, conditions on these turboprop internal flights were cramped, smoky and bumpy, so at least having some extra space would make things more bearable.

Finally I was summoned to board, and a smartly dressed lady official cautioned me to put hat, scarf, coat and gloves on for the walk to the plane, as the outside temperature had dropped to minus eighteen. She led me out, and as she marched me across the snow-covered tarmac towards the waiting plane I thought I could make out what looked like a mass of people gathered around the foot of the mobile stairs, a soldier standing two steps up barring their entry to the aircraft. As I got closer, it was clear that despite thick coats and headwear they were shivering, bitterly cold, and must have been waiting there for some time. The lady barked out an order as we approached the edge of the crowd, the soldier gesticulated in a sort of breaststroke motion, and a channel opened up before us, like Moses parting the Red Sea. Purple faces, taut with cold, turned towards us as we made our way through the group to the bottom of the stairs, and there were mutters, even muffled shouts of disapproval and useless defiance as we passed. Then a thick, gloved hand plonked heavily down on my shoulder and jerked me backwards; the soldier jumped off the steps into the crowd and pushed my assailant aside, issuing a sharp rebuke for what had been no more than a token show of anger. The revolt quelled, the soldier then turned to push me briskly up the stairs towards the plane door, where the lady official was already waiting, ready to lead me down the aisle to my seat in the front row.

The next four hours were amongst the most uncomfortable I have ever spent on a flight, as I felt the full weight of freezing opprobrium bearing down on me from behind, and from next to me. My singling out for preferential treatment hadn't been a blessing but a curse, and one which could only serve to further widen the east-west divide in the hearts of my fellow fliers.

*

Next day, back in Moscow, I had a lunch appointment at the National Hotel with Tanya Panova, my main contact in the British department at Intourist. Tanya was softly-spoken, blond with classic Slavic features, and it was understandable that our MD – and prime mover behind the Soviet Union programme – seemed to have a crush on her. At this time, in March 1988, Page and Moy were approaching their zenith, the peak of their success, in the Soviet Union, and Tanya clearly took pride in our achievement and her integral part in helping make it happen. With our debut just two years earlier, our customers now numbered several thousand each year, and apart from the mainstays – the Moscow City Breaks and the eight-day Moscow/Leningrad (now St. Petersburg) programme (three nights in each city and an overnight train ride in between) – our offerings featured the Baltic States,

Kiev, the Silk Road, the Black Sea resort of Dagomys and, of course, the Trans-Siberian Express.

When British Airways were no longer able to meet our demand, we upped capacity by chartering weekly flights with Britannia Airways into both Moscow and Leningrad. Such was the interest and curiosity, we even launched day trips to Moscow: a crack-of-dawn departure from Gatwick, three-and-a-half-hour flight, lunchtime arrival (with the three-hour time difference) in Moscow, a city sightseeing tour, sometimes partially at dusk or in darkness, all culminating, naturally, with a visit to a *berioska* shop to load up with wooden dolls and other local handicrafts. Then it was back to the airport for the homeward flight. When your neighbour asked 'What have you been up to recently?', being able to reply ' Oh, not much, just went across to the Soviet Union for the day yesterday' carried some serious kudos with it, and certainly some one-upmanship over the Joneses.

Tanya was eager to know how our maiden voyage east had gone.

'Well, Mister Phil, how was your trip to Siberia? Were your customers happy with their experience?'

I replied that despite the absence of a staple diet, hot water or any ventilation, we had all had a great time, and that the trip was memorable in every respect. As, indeed, it had been. And a medical emergency in a closed city, which fortunately had a good outcome, had added some spice to it. Tanya dutifully noted down the shortcomings, but we both knew that that was an exercise in futility. And in the final analysis, none of them really mattered anyway. They were all just part of the experience.

After lunch we went to the Hotel Cosmos to attend a travel exhibition, a fledgling concept in the USSR and a sign that the tourism authorities were starting to take promotion of their huge empire's regions and cities to the outside world more seriously. I'd arranged to meet two gentlemen from North Korea there; Tanya and I had previously spent some time brainstorming over the Trans-Siberian timetable, and she'd raised the mouth-watering prospect of taking the train as far as Irkutsk, then heading south into Mongolia and across to Pyongyang. This would involve cooperating with the North Koreans, so I'd made contact with the national tourist board and arranged to meet their representatives at the event in Moscow. The two men, sporting identical suits and hairstyles and polished Kim Il Sung lapel badges, spent half an hour with us, showing us a range of accommodation and programme options, and we agreed that they would send us proposals by telex in the following weeks. That, however, was the last we heard from them and, despite further overtures from our side, the idea never progressed beyond the drawing board.

That was a matter of great regret, for to have blazed that trail, and arranged tours to North Korea in the late eighties (and indeed, now), might have been a sign that parts of the world, destinations even more impenetrable than Russia had seemed some years earlier, were opening their doors, and that a new union between separated peoples, a union so important as a small step towards wider harmony in the world, was at last becoming a real possibility.

Chapter Six

'THERE ARE NO PROBLEMS. ONLY DIFFICULTIES'

Curiosity alone cannot be expected to attract large numbers of people to a new, unknown destination, even one cloaked in the alluring mantle of secrecy and intrigue. But if the ingredient of affordability is added to the salesman's recipe, the dish instantly becomes more enticing. Any tour operator worth its salt will be on constant lookout for extremely attractive deals, especially cheap offers from airlines looking to kickstart a new route or boost takings on an existing one. Indeed, many new holiday ideas are built on the back of an airline rep wandering into a tour operator's head office and proceeding to make the operator's day by announcing a sensational offer, well below normal market rates. Frenzied excitement follows as the planners get their heads together to look at what sort of itineraries might be constructed around the airfare, the points of entry and departure, and the flight schedule. The sales team is then brought in to assess whether any of the brainchildren have legs, and viability within existing sales outlets. Numbers are crunched and re-crunched to see whether something ending in a '99' is achievable.

And so it was with Moscow, with Japan Airlines (JAL) the provider of some very unexpected manna from heaven. JAL had recently launched new routes to Tokyo via Rome and Moscow respectively, with permission for the routes granted on the basis that at least one hundred seats had to be available to sell on the London–Rome–London and London–Moscow–London sectors. The London–Rome airfare of £60 return might not sound like anything special in our present world of low-cost fares, but back in the eighties there was no Ryanair and no EasyJet, and today's intra-European network, linking capital cities with often unknown semi-rural towns, was a baby that hadn't yet been conceived. In 1984, Richard Branson's Virgin Atlantic started operations and was giving BA and the established US airlines a run for their money on transatlantic routes, but Europe was dominated by national flag carriers charging prices that by modern standards seem viciously high.

The JAL Moscow fare came in at £85 return, more than £100 below British Airways, and allowed us to sell four-day breaks in the Russian capital at a lead-in price of £199. Curiosity plus affordability equalled a winning new product, and the scene was set for Page and Moy to become a major force, possibly *the* major force in group travel in the developing USSR market.

It was a golden time of opportunity and innovation, and a surplus of aircraft available for charter, which got the creative juices flowing even faster. In late 1986 we chartered the legendary Concorde daily over a couple of weeks before Christmas, each day laying on one supersonic and two subsonic flights between cities around the UK, the ultimate, dream, experiential Christmas present. It turned into something of a family affair when my 84-year-old grandfather took his first ever flight, and I managed to arrange for my brother Mike, who was embarking on a career in photography, to have a pitch at the bottom of the aircraft steps, where he took a snap of each excited passenger before they boarded, selling to each the resulting cardboard-framed souvenir photo for a tenner a piece. My role was to arrange coaches to get our one hundred customers from their destination back to their departure airport for each of the thirty-six flights we organised.

The following spring we re-hashed an old idea from the thirties: the 'Air Cruise', a luxury escape to four top cities in nine days, with the captain and crew of our chartered plane staying with the passengers throughout and joining them at meals and on excursions. The 'cruise' featured two nights in each of the four cities, Vienna, Athens, Rome and Paris, five-star accommodation, opera and theatre visits and sumptuous fare throughout. We'd placed an ad in the *Sunday Times*, as conspicuously as budgets allowed, and hoped it might catch the attention of at least a few readers as they pored over the paper's pages during a leisurely breakfast. Expectations amongst the sales team were fairly muted, so only one 'Reservations Girl' had been persuaded to give up her Sunday morning to cover the office phones, after a suggestion that we might get the odd enquiry. After half an hour, with phones ringing off the hook, the poor girl was calling for urgent backup. And after three hours, all one hundred and thirty seats had been sold.

And then there was Romania: the Black Sea coast, the lure of sand and sea, with sunshine virtually guaranteed, and ludicrously low prices. The Scandinavians, and even a couple of niche British companies, were already tapping into the all-too-tempting mix of perfect bucket and spade conditions at an absolute bargain in the (to western holidaymakers) unknown beach resort of Mamaia. Occupying a long, thin strip of land and sand between the sea and a large inland lake, Mamaia consisted of a string of mainly three and four-star hotels, a small number of shops and restaurants, a few discos, and not a lot else. The resort catered for the local market and holidaymakers from other socialist countries, and ONT Carpati (in effect the National Tourist Office, those old friends from the Danube days) felt that standards there had now reached sufficiently high levels for it to be acceptable to westerners too, westerners who would, of course, provide much-needed hard currency for President Ceauşescu's depleted coffers.

No sane tour operator could ignore the hotel – and other – prices on offer from ONT for the summer of 1985. It was proposed that our guests should be allocated rooms in the three-star Hotel Junona, with daily prices starting at £1.10, all meals included and, for the more discerning, the Hotel Dorna at a rate of £1.40 per day, again with all meals thrown in. On top of that came a return airport transfer from and back to nearby Constanţa airport at a quid per person. The national airline, TAROM, contributed to the feast with a return airfare from Gatwick at £50 and from Manchester at £60. With all the prices in and some fairly simple maths conducted, the prospect of selling a beach holiday in a brand new destination for just £169 all-in proved too much to resist. *TV Times* bit our hands off and pushed for exclusivity, which was denied as we realised that the IPC magazines were also keen to climb on the bandwagon. Unbelievably, there were decent profits to be made too, even on such a ridiculously low price, further boosted by some of the excursions laid on from the resort. Relatively close at hand lay the ornithologist's paradise of the Danube Delta, and every week tourist flights took off on day trips to Cairo and Istanbul, a real eye-catcher on the brochure page and a source of some serious commission revenue. Indeed, it's hard to think of any other beach resort in the world which provides access to such an extraordinary range and variety of possibilities to explore further afield as Mamaia did back in the eighties.

And that, as it turned out, was a very fortunate thing.

*

'Mister Caldwell, welcome to Romania.'

I looked down to see a small, neatly dressed woman eyeing me shyly, slightly suspiciously, but confidently. I wondered how she'd managed to squeeze herself through the tightly packed crowd of overheating passengers who were desperately waiting for the doors to open so they could finally leave the sweltering prison of the shuttle bus and have an end to their suffering. The bus had stood defiant for a good fifteen minutes, imposing enforced incarceration on its occupants, all drenched in sweat and in critical need of air, even warm air. I also wondered how this woman knew who I was. Dressed in shorts and T-shirt, to blend in with the clients of the operator whose charter flight to Constanţa I'd hitched a ride on, there was nothing to betray my businessman status; and my casual attire made the ordeal on the shuttle bus a little bit more bearable. I'd never met the lady before, and this was my first visit to Romania. It was August 1984, and I was doing a recce.

Suddenly the doors jerked open, the throng disgorged itself in a frantic surge of shoulders, elbows, gaudy bags and the odd traumatised child, and my diminutive new companion and I allowed ourselves to be carried from the coach on the human tide. Silently but resolutely, she led me to the front of the long queue forming at passport control, where we were waved through after blissfully short formalities. In the car on the way to Mamaia I tried to make conversation, but to no avail. I enthusiastically recounted how much I'd enjoyed working with her compatriots two years earlier on the Danube, but there was no interest, not even a flicker, no desire to engage. As we pulled away from the airport, she announced that we were going to Mamaia, but that was it. Even my very British efforts to pass comment on the weather, and elicit predictions on the forecast for the days ahead, were met with stony silence.

Despite that frosty first encounter, over the course of the next couple of days the red carpet was rolled out as I was escorted from hotel to hotel to inspect Junona, Dorna and a number of other candidates for our programme. Each one was much like and as utilitarian as the last, though Dorna did do just enough to warrant its four stars. I managed to accost some British and German customers during late evenings at the Dorna's bar and, aside from some comments about bland food, their stays generally passed muster. The weather was fabulous, they'd paid next to nothing for the experience and continued to pay next to nothing for anything they might happen to find to purchase in the resort. The excursions were arduous, involving phenomenally early starts, but the opportunity to fly to Egypt to see the pyramids for under £100 was too good to pass up and well worth the discomfort.

I was driven down the coast to Neptune, wholly different from Mamaia and centered on its futuristic Hotel Amfiteatru, then to Saturn and Eforie Nord, still off the radar of all but the most intrepid, niche operators, and certainly offering no obvious advantages over Mamaia. And further south still, we passed to within touching distance of Bulgaria, whose better-developed resorts such as Golden Sands were already attracting a steady flow of sunseekers from the West and being enviously eyed by the Romanians, keen to emulate their success and grab a slice of such lucrative action.

By Christmas our allocations at Dorna and Junona had almost sold out so, early in January 1985, our MD John Elsom, realising from the volume of booking forms pouring in daily that we were onto something very big, insisted he go to look at taking on more capacity, with Paul Taylor and me in tow. The three of us flew out to Bucharest, and to the bleak and desolate reality of a nation in the cruel grip of crippling, lethal austerity.

Whenever I came to the capital I was always put up at the Hotel Bucharest, always in room 101; years later I would learn that my phone calls were always monitored. At a brutally early five-thirty, John, Paul and I emerged into the freezing mist from the relative comfort and warmth of the Bucharest and wedged ourselves into the back seat of a waiting car. John was a big man and took up most of that back seat, with the front passenger seat occupied by our ONT escort. We set off, and before long it became sickeningly clear how desperate the existence of the city's inhabitants had become. Almost all the streetlights were extinguished, and as our car gingerly made its way through the eerily empty, black-icy streets of the inner suburbs, the only signs of life were gangs of elderly women wearily hacking away at the hillocks of packed snow, piled grey along every pavement and roadside. Shoveling it onto yet more hillocks, the women's only solace was that the rigour of their exertions might give their bodies some defence against the biting cold.

Not a light shone from any of the apartment blocks lining our route, not even in their hallways. This extreme, grinding austerity, like nothing I have ever encountered anywhere before or since, extended to a mandatory ban on heating dwellings of any kind for more than a couple of hours a day, purportedly causing many to die from hyperthermia.

As a bruised dawn broke, we left the city and continued along an almost deserted highway, six hours to the coast through dreary whiteness occasionally broken up by a dark, cheerless town. Settlements appeared empty, devoid of humanity, except a few brave souls tramping and slipping, heads bowed, through the chill wasteland to an unknown destination; acts of courage, or necessity, or foolhardiness. Dismal factories, shabby blocks of flats with no light nor sign of life: this was another world, a sombre and miserable one, which put the minor discomforts on our seemingly endless journey into stark perspective.

We reached Mamaia, no less frozen than the hinterland, with ice fringing its vacant, forlorn beaches, a place which seemed to beseech us to go away, to wait until late spring when it would emerge from months of abandonment and show its real colours. All the hotels were closed, but their managers had been enlisted to put on some show of welcome, to try to project what summer season normality looked like, which of course was impossible. Thankfully for us, a tray with glasses full of a schnapps-like liquid greeted us at each hotel, more than anything to ward off the gnawing cold, as we proceeded to traipse around unheated hotel rooms and silent, gloomy restaurants, wondering why we had made the effort and what benefit we hoped to derive from viewing a resort in such deep, unshakeable slumber.

After two hours of drudgery we set off back to Bucharest, returning to the same unsettling and depressing scenes we had left fourteen hours earlier as the city prepared itself for another night of anguish, and almost certainly of death.

*

Just after I arrived at the Hotel Dorna it started to rain. It rained incessantly for the next two days. This was troubling, as our first guests were due on the third day and having to acclimatise to their new surroundings in a monsoon would surely dampen spirits. On my first evening, the local tourist office organised a welcome dinner for me and my team of reps at the Hotel International, the jewel in Mamaia's crown and the one officially five-star property in the resort. Misjudging the distance from the Dorna, I sloshed along cratered roads, sometimes ankle-deep in water as I failed to negotiate a succession of deep puddles, arriving to the formal event soaked to the skin and ill-prepared to make a speech to my hosts and team.

I'd started to assemble the resort team in the weeks following that depressing January mission, and after a protracted interview process had settled on a blend of youthful inexperience and local nous. The local nous was provided by a Romanian national, Sorin, and his English, Romanian-speaking wife Susan, who lived together in London. Sorin would head up the team, and a few days earlier he and Susan had made the arduous drive across Europe to take up their positions in Mamaia, along with their new baby Emily, whom the couple hadn't mentioned at the interview. The fact that Sorin had a car, and a foreign one at that, meant that he could keep an eye on what was going on down the coast in Neptune relatively easily, as foreign cars were able to go straight to the front of the horrendously long queues ever-present at the few petrol stations there were in the area.

The junior team members in Mamaia were Maxine, Clare and Jenni. The former two had no previous repping experience but personality, enthusiasm and promise in spadeloads. Jenni, who'd worked on a *kibbutz* in Israel and more recently on a campsite in the south of France, had all of the above plus those bits of experience too. She was also fun-loving and mischievous (she adopted a stray cat, which spent the next five months concealed in her hotel room) and turned out to be the life and soul of the party.

We had a much smaller programme in Neptune run by a girl called Lynne, while Sally looked after those in search of breathtaking scenery and evidence of Count Dracula up in the mountains in Sinaia.

None had any conception of what awaited them, as they prepared to welcome the first of what would be thousands of guests that summer.

So great was the demand for Black Sea sun that we'd been forced to take on more space in some of the hotels I'd seen the previous summer and on our winter mission, most notably the Siret and the Pelican. The latter would greet its guests, and anyone else who might wander into its lobby, with a large stuffed pelican. Whether through particularly shoddy taxidermy or having been on show for far too long, or both, the poor creature was practically falling apart and seemed to be held together by a few remaining feathers and some exposed, discoloured bones.

At the Siret the lunch menu offered a choice of (typos included):

Pork meat with cabage
Potatoes with meat fried in grease then stwend
Beefsteak douguetiier
Omelette with chips
DESERT, BREAD, MINERALWATER

Dinner consisted of a choice of tomato or vegetable soup for starters and beefsteak with eggs or pork chop with chips as the main course.

And herein lay one of the main sources of complaint that summer. The food was, for the most part, shocking. Reports from the reps of significant numbers of clients being laid low with a variety of gastric illnesses grew, as did the mailbag in the Customer Service department. A picture of carnage started to emerge, with local doctors frequently summoned to hotels to dispense what succour they could, and the beleaguered reps coming under a barrage of fire from poorly customers and their relatives. We urged the local tourism authorities and our partners at ONT to intervene and do something to ameliorate the problem, and prayed that salmonella wasn't endemic in the kitchens. Up in Sinaia, at the Hotel Caraiman, a palatial, nineteenth century pile which hearkened back to a time when its well-heeled guests arrived on the Orient Express, standards were noticeably higher, and gripes far fewer. But on the coast things were decidedly grim, and it was the reps who bore the brunt of the flak.

*

A few weeks into that first season, after an indifferent start to our debut in Romania, the austerity measures President Ceauşescu was imposing on his stricken citizens almost derailed the entire programme. Overnight, a governmental decree was issued forbidding any electricity consumption in homes, hotels and resorts after ten o'clock in the evening, meaning that all restaurants, bars and entertainment venues were forced to close by that time. All lights had to be switched off. Any thoughts of enjoying a late-night glass of Murfatlar[25] in a bar along the beachfront before proceeding to one of the (albeit relatively few) discos for some serious partying were, at a dictatorial stroke, scuppered for the foreseeable future and with immediate effect. The collective protests and high-level representations of travel companies across Europe fell on deaf, powerless ears. The President had spoken, and no amount of lobbying would, or could, change the situation.

Letters went out to customers, with the option to cancel with a full refund, but surprisingly few cancelled. This might

---

25. *One of Romania's best-known wines.*

have had something to do with the age profile of the typical Page and Moy client, making it unlikely that the urge to party in a beachfront disco was a decisive factor in the choice of destination; or maybe an early bedtime was a price worth paying for the bargain of a lifetime. Or perhaps it was a bit of both. And like staying on the Moskva River on a boat, it may also have been tacit acceptance that this was a very different world, one in which the abnormal was normal.

A couple of weeks after the 'curfew' had been declared I flew out to Mamaia to get a feel for how disruptive it was proving to be, and to see if there had been any improvement in the quality of meals: we had stressed and re-stressed to the authorities that if the complaints kept on coming, we would have to consider pulling out. To my amazement and relief, after-hours life was alive and reasonably well, not in bars and clubs, nor in darkened hotel lobbies, but in hotel rooms. Small throngs of people would squeeze themselves into someone's room, and an impromptu party by candle or torchlight would break out, with boisterous card games and raucous singing, all accompanied by bottles of whatever spirit the revellers had managed to procure during the day. There was a camaraderie over and beyond any normally experienced on holiday, a determination to make the best of this strange experience, communal defiance of a regime which was heaping agony upon depredation on its country, and a common and heartfelt desire to show solidarity with its people. Our reps and some of the local guides would join in, jokes would be told, in Romanian and English, each one greeted with howls of laughter irrespective of whether or not it was remotely funny, or even understood.

Jenni had been sent the page of a daily tabloid from home, and at one of these soirées read out an article on the sort of political humour covertly doing the rounds in Romania.

Headlined 'Zic, Zic, Zic ('I say, I say, I say')...this is no joke', the article went as follows:

Heard the one about the dictator who was so afraid of criticism he called in the secret police to stop people telling jokes about him?

In Romania it's no laughing matter.

The country's dreaded Securitate has set up a special Section for Subversive Jokes and Rumours to stem the flood of taunts about President Ceauşescu, who this year celebrates 20 years as head of what is probably the most oppressive regime in Eastern Europe.

Under Ceauşescu, agriculture and industry have almost collapsed and the nation has been hit by major shortages. The Romanian people try to make light of their misery by making jokes about the way the country is run, but they now risk being sent to prison. One current favourite, based on the claim that few understand Ceauşescu's policies, has him riding in a chauffeur-driven car with Mrs Thatcher and President Mitterrand of France.

She tells the driver: 'Signal right and turn right.' Mitterrand says: 'Signal left and turn left.' But when it's his time to give directions, the dictator says: 'Signal left and right then drive straight ahead.'

During that same visit, I arranged to meet Mr A, the head of the Black Sea Tourist Board, at his office. As the most senior tourism official in the area, and with direct responsibility for running everything that went on in the resorts, I hoped that an appeal to him might at least have some chance of bringing about improvements in food and concessions on activities after ten o'clock, even keeping the hotel bars open for an extra hour or so. I was ushered into his office and directed to sit down on the other side of a large desk at which Mr A was sitting. A radio was broadcasting a speech, and the secretary whispered to me that it was Mr A who was the speaker. The speech went on for fifteen minutes, during which time he sat staring over my head, never once acknowledging my presence nor uttering a word to me. I could just about understand a few sentences, about how tourism and socialism went hand in hand, how a socialist economy was the only way forward, and how many, many tourists from western countries were now flocking to the beaches of the Black Sea coast and its modern hotels.

After the speech finished, he proceeded to summarise its main points to me in English. After ten minutes of this, and just as he seemed to be winding down and I was readying myself to finally make my long-awaited pitch, the secretary scurried back into the office, gabbled something to him, and hurriedly turned the radio back on. Mr A raised his arm, indicating that he needed to listen. Incredibly, his speech was being re-broadcast, only minutes after its initial broadcast, and he wanted to revel one more time in his commanding pronouncements, his wisdom from on high. So I continued to sit, passively, seeing whether I could decipher any more of his nuggets, wondering whether the opportunity to debate whether chicken might be added to the menu, and whether the chefs could find something other than grease to fry it in, would ever come.

When it did come, the opportunity was brief. Mr A had a pressing engagement, due to start very soon. But I should understand that tourists, when asked, had declared themselves quite happy to retire to bed at ten o'clock as there were so many daytime activities available in the resort, and by evening they were tired out, but happy. And as for the food, a lot of work had been done to ensure that menus conformed to the tastes of western tourists, and everyone was happy with what was on offer. As I started to make my way out of his office after a curt handshake, he stopped me and said:

'Ah, Mister Caldwell, one more thing. When you come back, please bring with you the new Argos catalogue. My wife loves to read the Argos catalogue. She likes to look at all the goods in it. Please don't forget this, or maybe you can send it to me when you get back home?'

*

Jenni seemed to be bearing the brunt of the onslaught and was struggling. Her natural exuberance was being slowly throttled out of her by an endless tirade of moans from afflicted clients, and she had written to me. In mid-July I wrote back to her to try to boost her spirits, and stop her from jumping on the next flight home:

Dear Jenni,

Thanks for the letter regarding complaints about you. I thought I would jot down on paper to you a few of my thoughts on the situation to try to give you some form of reassurance.

First of all, you must not take all this so hard, although I can understand why you are doing so. Personally, I fully appreciate the position and the complete difference in set-up between Sinaia and the Siret, and there is no way you could hope to emulate that set-up in the Siret. The very fact that a) you have got more pax,[26] b) the different facilities at the hotel, and c) perhaps more importantly, the nature of a beach holiday means that you will never be able to get people together as Sally has the opportunity to do.

---

26. *Tour operator lingo for 'passengers'.*

So for heaven's sake don't worry! I hope you will understand things at this end as well, and I realise that when we receive complaints about a courier[27] then it is necessary to follow this through in case that particular courier is having problems. I think it is fair to say that we only start worrying once we get a deluge of protests.

However, every courier receives complaints at some time or another. These have to be seen in perspective and in relation to the number of good comments which are received. I hope you will see from some of the letters and questionnaires that have been sent out that there are those who are responding most favourably to your services!

Furthermore, I ought to add that I realise that you are all working under difficult conditions and I am sure you will all be glad when the summer is over. With 250 pax per week arriving, and many of those being bitterly disappointed through no fault of anybody's, I am afraid that you are always going to get a fair bit of flak. But I think you will find that (and this is certainly coming through in a lot of letters) the majority of the people realise that you are up against it, again through no fault of your own, and they are amazed that you manage to keep smiling.

Anyway, I hope to see you soon and, of course, will be only too pleased to discuss any of this with you should you so wish.

Yours,

Phil.

As the summer wore on, small groups of recently returned customers would insist on coming to our office in Leicester to have their grievances heard. We held audience up in the Operations department, and let people vent their spleen. We asked ourselves whether it was all worth it: the travel editors at

---

27. *The word 'courier' was generally more in vogue in those days than 'rep'.*

TV Times and *Woman's Realm* were also coming under attack from disgruntled readers, so the pressure was mounting. In the more serious cases compensation was paid, though on a holiday so cheap this was never going to be a fortune. The fact that some of the programme – the mountains component – was proving more popular gave us some heart, and our friends at ONT managed to engineer some improvement in the food situation on the coast, so we stuck with it. Volume did seem to be talking: the tourism authorities in Bucharest appeared to be genuinely impressed by how we had conjured up thousands of tourists in our initial year of operation, and could therefore justify their appeals for a raising of the bar to their political masters, who in turn were seeing the sterling currency account filling up nicely.

But any enhancements came too late to prevent the ultimate bottom smack, a visit from Trading Standards. To an operator like Page and Moy with a solid and proud reputation, this was the summer's nadir. The cumulative anger being generated by scores of disillusioned travellers, many claiming they had been poisoned, had become too great to ignore, and an official investigation was launched into what was going on on the Black Sea coast. This was whole new territory, and as Harry Whitehead, the local trading standards officer, opened his notebook and stated that the information I was about to give him could be used in any proceedings taken against the company, I wondered how we could ever get through this unscathed.

It was a gruelling hour, which seemed a lot longer than an hour, and it was a relief when the roll call of accusations finally came to an end. I'd insisted we were doing everything we could to resolve the food issues, that we'd repeatedly inspected hotel kitchens and called in local health agencies to see whether there was any obvious reason for the gastric problems so frequently being reported. There was not a lot else we could add in our defence, but what helped, and gained some traction, was that we were operating for the first time in an environment where there were barriers and limitations to what we could realistically achieve. The fact that we had taken steps to be completely transparent about the impact Ceaușescu's austerity measures would have on people's holidays earned us brownie points, and some sympathy. In the event, we got off pretty lightly, and no serious action was taken beyond a warning. And for our part, we promised to do everything in our power, constrained though that was, to ensure that stomach and other upsets became a thing of the past.

*

As Jenni's fragile state of mind showed, getting the reps through the season without partial or wholesale defections was going to be a battle, and without Sorin's fatherly presence (alongside his fatherly duties with the concealed baby), his language, local knowledge and understanding of the system, it could have been a battle quite easily lost. The pressure was unremitting, and with nowhere open to escape to after dinner to let off steam the reps understandably felt trapped. Every Saturday we would send out documents and supplies via our company mail on the TAROM charter, and always threw in a few 'luxury' items to make the reps' lives more bearable, including: tomato ketchup; boxes of Mars and Marathon (to make a change from the German Merci and Toffifee bars sometimes available in the resort); Walkers cheese and onion crisps; plus shampoo and several pots of hair mousse, a necessity for the well-groomed rep back in the eighties.

Sinaia, where Sally was working, seemed like an oasis compared to Mamaia, a small slice of paradise where things functioned well and the food was relatively decent. It was true, the tourism people up there appeared to take a degree of pride in the impression the area made on visitors, and operated in a sort of microcosm, floating above the morass of dismal mediocrity that pervaded the rest of the country; but even here there were shortages, and the unobtainable. In one of her weekly reports to me, Sally apologetically added a PS: could I please arrange for a consignment of condoms to be sent to her with the next company mail? She had fallen head over heels in love with one of the guys at the tourist office, but the nationwide lack of any means of birth control meant that their relationship couldn't safely take its natural course. We duly obliged, hoping that customs officials at Constanţa airport wouldn't intercept our contraband shipment, which fortunately they didn't. Sally was extremely grateful, and more than a little embarrassed, when I next visited her, and I was happy that we'd been able to provide some meaningful comfort to at least one of the reps.

*

The reps themselves did their bit to provide some meaningful comfort too, but to the locals. As, unwittingly, did the tourists.

Each day the chambermaids would arrive to begin their shift at whichever Mamaia hotel they had been ordered to service. Whether they then proceeded to do any work was a different matter. Either way, they would still receive their wage from the state. The reps soon came to realise that the presence of the chambermaids in the hotels didn't necessarily mean that their rooms, let alone those of their guests, would actually get cleaned.

Many years later, Jenni revealed how this obstacle had been overcome. The reps agreed among themselves to add a pound to the price at which they were supposed to sell the excursions to their customers. The fund created was used to persuade the chambermaids to do what they were being paid by the state to do in the first place, i.e. clean hotel rooms. In a roundabout way, and without knowing it, the tourists were paying for the privilege of occupying rooms which, at the very least, would be filled with the acrid smell of Romanian detergent.

As well as taking care of the cat, Jenni also took care of her chambermaid. When her son needed to have an operation, and his mother needed to grease palms at the local hospital to make sure the operation happened, it was Jenni who provided the essential grease.

*

September came, the season tapered down and the last charter flights touched down at Gatwick and Manchester. In the office, we breathed a collective sigh of relief. We felt battered, exhausted, yet there was a palpable sense of elation, of achievement, that we'd managed to avoid cutting short the summer in spite of everything that had been thrown at us. Our mettle had been severely tested, and we'd probably done as well as we could have realistically expected. Operating under such restrictive conditions had presented us with challenges that were entirely new to us, in a time when many of our holidays almost ran themselves, unhindered by anything too far from the norm. Now we'd been well and truly wrenched out of our comfort zone and, though it had been painful and frustrating at times, we'd learnt to work within a very different system, with little leverage at our disposal, and had just about pulled it off.

The question then was: did we care to repeat the experience? Mike Voicu, our main contact at the Romanian National Tourist Office in London, was already brandishing next summer's contracts and, chuffed that all his efforts to woo us had resulted in over five thousand tourists in our first year and a mass of advertising in mainstream mags, was keen that we should not only repeat it, but expand. He was also keen to add the paltry sum of ten pence to the hotel rates, but was persuaded that a price hike of such magnitude would negatively impact sales, and quickly beat a retreat. Buoyed by this victory, and a large dose of misplaced optimism that our new position as a major provider of tourism to the Black Sea could bring about significant improvements, we resolved to persist with Romania. And persist we did, into the nineties, albeit with reduced client numbers. Price had talked; we learnt to manage expectations and the complaints abated – though they would never disappear entirely.

In the end we had adapted, and had bought in to Mike's mantra, always aired with laconic irony, that 'there are no problems. Only difficulties'. Working with the system, not against it, was the key.

*

The highlight of the company's social calendar was the annual Christmas party, when the year's reservoir of pent-up emotions was well and truly emptied as we all assembled in festive mood in the function room on the first floor of the former Grand Hotel on Leicester's Granby Street. For the Reservations Girls, it was a well-deserved reward for months of pacifying awkward customers and sticking pins in wall charts to record bookings and coach occupancies. That year there was a group of them, infiltrated by a couple of the sales team, who donned bikinis, sunglasses and sun hats and walked, cocktails in hands and with a slightly nervous swagger, up onto the stage in front of the massed ranks of their colleagues, who wondered what on earth they were about to witness.

Five chairs had been set out in front of the stage, and the five directors were guided to sit on them so that they could enjoy the show with unimpeded views. Somewhat gingerly, they obliged. Then one of the performers announced that this year, the theme of the show would be HOLIDAYS, before the scantily clad troupe duly launched into a rendition of Cliff Richard's *'We're All Going On A Summer Holiday'*, the first couple of verses of which went like this:

We're all goin' on a summer holiday
No more eating for a week or two
Not much laughter on our summer holiday
And lots of worries for me and you
For a week or two

We're goin' where the lights shine dimly
We're goin' where there's a curfew
We're goin' to Romania
And when we get back we'll sue – YOU!

And on 'YOU' the singers pointed accusing forefingers in unison at the row of suited, visibly uncomfortable men before them, who did their utmost to feign amusement; but failed to convince.

The rest of the room erupted into whoops of laughter and applause, and the party was underway for another year.

*

When reactor Number 4 at the Chernobyl Nuclear Power Plant exploded on April 26th, 1986, sending radiation and shock westwards into Europe, the ensuing silence from the Soviet Union was deafening. In contrast, within hours of the accident, the tourism authorities in Romania were hard at work firing off telex after telex to tour operators in the West, assurances that Romania was unaffected and safe followed by tables of statistics claiming to show minimal levels of radiation in the nation's atmosphere.

With a dearth of nuclear scientists at Page and Moy, and certainly no one who possessed an intimate knowledge of microsieverts, microroentgens or even microrems, these figures were a bit of a mystery to us; as the relentless flow of missives out of Bucharest persisted into May and June, we came to accept that they must signify consistently low radiation levels, if indeed the radiation levels were low in the first place.

The Romanian authorities were clearly terrified by the potential of the incident to completely derail their summer season, so went into overdrive to reassure us all that the country was open for business as usual. But there was a less than subtle, more than subliminal message in the rolls of telex paper being expended, a blatant piece of anti-Soviet propaganda: 'It was the Russians that caused this, not us, yet we must bear the fallout. The Russians say nothing, but we are transparent; we want to keep the world informed, even though it was not us who caused this problem. It was them.'

*

Russia-bashing was a national sport, and one not limited to the machinations of government departments.

In the relative cool of the Mamaia early morning, I took a pre-breakfast stroll along the beach, bare feet making shallow indentations where water had recently retreated from virgin sand. I caught sight of one of the local guides assigned to our groups as he sauntered lazily along further up the beach, no doubt, like me, soaking up the peace of the place in preparation for the day's travails. I waved, he altered course and headed towards me. We fell into conversation.

He told me how much he enjoyed looking after our tourists, how appreciative they were, how interested in everything he told them; how generous too.

'Not like the Russian tourists. They are terrible. They think they own us and our country. They never smile. They are always complaining about something. So we guides have a trick we play on them when we take them to a restaurant for lunch.'

He went on to explain that some time ago the guides had noticed that many of their Russian guests had clearly never seen a teabag in their lives, so when tea was served at the end of the meal some instruction was required.

'We tell the Russian tourists to place the teabags in their mouths, then fill their mouths with the hot water from the cup, keep the hot water in the mouth for a few seconds, then swallow. Then repeat, several times, until the cup is empty. Then remove the teabag from the mouth.'

He described how the sight of forty or so miserable-looking Russians, sitting at their tables with bloated faces and thin white threads dangling down over their chins from pursed lips, made the guides' work that bit more bearable, and how more than once he had very nearly collapsed in convulsions of laughter.

*

The flat tedium of the Romanian Plain gave way to the first gentle gradients of the Carpathian foothills as the road north penetrated the Prahova Valley. Entering the valley always brought a sense of relief, of better things to come, of being blissfully far away from the searing, repressive heat of Bucharest and, instead, in the fresh fragrance of the mountains.

Ninety minutes earlier we'd taken the accustomed route out of the capital: setting out along Calea Victoriei, past the Grand Arcul de Triumf, erected to celebrate Romanian victory in World War I and from which, in part, Bucharest gained its label of 'Little Paris of the Balkans' in a previous more carefree and opulent life; continuing past the domestic airport at Băneasa and its larger international brother further down the highway at Otopeni, offering passage to a different world to those fortunate or privileged enough; then travelling out onto the plain, spirit-level flat and colourless, with a famished cow here, sometimes two, a half-finished concrete structure there, detached from any visible urbanisation – maybe the first blocks of one of Ceaușescu's notorious 'agro-industrial complexes' into which whole villages were due to be forcibly relocated; and driving on past Ploiești, its dismal sprawl of ghastly black refineries belching uncountable parallel plumes of leaden smoke inexorably skyward.

A cement factory provided an inglorious entrance to Sinaia's past glories and the town's array of brown-timbered, whitewashed buildings of which the Hotel Caraiman – stately home to guests of Page and Moy and, long before, the Orient Express – was one. Turreted and red-tiled, the Caraiman refused to bow to the ugly, brutal modernisation elsewhere in the country, clinging defiantly to its illustrious history. Further on lay the resorts of Bușteni and Predeal, popular with locals in summer and winter but considered too basic to tempt western visitors, so the car never stopped in either.

Then we drove onward into Transylvania and to Brașov, a gem of a city, isolated and insular in so many ways. Its cobbled alleyways and squares, its churches and towers, its profusion of splendid gothic and baroque edifices were all perfectly preserved as though in a time warp, its ethnic Hungarian and Saxon peoples now holding out amid growing repression from the regime. It was an enclave nestling, almost seeming to want to hide, in a bowl of antiquity beneath its Tâmpa Mountain. In 1987 workers here went on strike, but the strike was crushed, and many workers were imprisoned.

We continued a few more miles up to a plateau, on which lay the jewel of Romania's upland resorts, Poiana Brașov.

*

This time, the three-hour journey from Bucharest had been unusual in one very striking way. Physically, our positions inside the car were the same as always: I occupied the back seat, my escort – normally an official guide, or more often a fairly senior member of the ONT Carpati staff – sat in the front passenger seat, with the driver (rarely the same one twice) at the controls. I always felt sorry for the driver: there was rarely any attempt at conversation from the occupant of the passenger seat. At meals the driver never sat at our table, being consigned instead to an inconspicuous part of the restaurant where he ate what he was given. His attire was always simple and functional.

But this trip was different. The driver appeared affluent: he wore a pristine white suit and black shirt, and a lot of effort had clearly gone into polishing his shoes and the gold buckles adorning them. His hair, black medium-length with signs of balding on the temples, was gelled into an immutable sheen that even the most violent wind would have been unlikely to impact. He was tanned, his eyes piercing and bright, and a chunky silver chain bridged the gap at the top of his shirt, unbuttoned to expose a clean-shaven chest. His broad belt shone, and might feasibly have been real leather. And the conversation between him and his front seat neighbour was almost incessant, with the driver always taking the lead.

That evening I was a few minutes late for dinner, and arrived at the Hotel Ciucaş restaurant to find the driver and my ONT escort sitting at the same table and chatting, starters already served. I took my seat and tried to join the conversation, but the driver didn't seem to want to talk to me and my ONT escort appeared more interested in talking to the driver. It remained that way for most of the meal until the ONT man announced, as we finished our desserts, that the next activity was a walk down to the Hotel Alpin to watch a folklore show. So off we went. And the driver came too.

Taking in a folklore show had become par for the course, and a regular feature of the orchestrated hospitality laid on for me during a typical business trip to Romania. On summer visits, participating in an open-air barbecue in a forest clearing became almost mandatory, and I was usually and somewhat unwillingly cajoled into joining in the fun, feasting and frivolity of a group of western tourists who curiously always happened to be wherever I was being escorted to that day. I came to relish the colour, music and vibrancy of a Romanian folklore show, though one was very much like another and generally followed an established format. The costumes too tended to be standard issue, and blurry images of jolly peasants dancing together happily after a productive day's toil in the fields filled the pages of what few promotional publications existed.

But what was on offer for our delectation at the Alpin that evening was something quite different, something which went a considerable way towards breaking the traditional mould. The dances were still essentially folkloric, but the music had been jazzed up and the six female dancers, the 'ballerinas', as my escort called them, were decked out in scanty, revealing, vermillion dresses more akin to cabaret garb. The usual sideways shuffling was punctuated by a lot of high kicking and near gymnastic convulsions. The girls were all equally athletic, and had their hair tied up in identical buns. It was George Zamfirescu mixed with Moulin Rouge, Poiana with Pigalle, panpipes with pulse. It was exciting, even intoxicating, and delightfully unexpected. These were not the type of ballerinas who perform Swan Lake or the Nutcracker. The audience was engaged, enlivened, far beyond some infrequent, forced or passive clapping that happened at the normal folklore shows. The atmosphere in the hall was genuinely electric, with approval at the spectacle blending with unspoken surprise that this was possible in a country so woefully downtrodden.

As we walked the short distance back to the Ciucaş after the show, my ONT colleague announced that some of the ballerinas would be joining us later in the restaurant. And so they did. Half an hour later, three of them, now dressed in tracksuits but with hair still in the trademark identical buns, hovered uncertainly at our table before being instructed to sit down by the driver, who poured each a large glass of red wine. As the girls started to look more relaxed, I struck up conversation with the one to my left, Antonia, who turned out to speak very good English and was highly intelligent; with almost-blond hair and clear, silver-blue eyes, she was evidently descended from Germanic or Hungarian forefathers who had made home in the forests of Transylvania centuries before. From time to time Antonia's eyes would flash nervously in the direction of the driver and my escort, her speech faltering or delivered in hushed tones, or she would direct her talking to a position behind my left ear, her head tilted away from the table. There was measure and a formality to her speech and what she said; her smiles were infrequent, polite and never broke into a true, natural beam. Yet she was enchanting, a lovely, unaffected girl, and it was a pleasure to be making her acquaintance.

As the restaurant became a disco, a DJ having taken up residence in a corner of the room, people began to dance and the atmosphere around our table lightened. The red wine had been supplemented with stronger potions and the driver was starting to raise his voice, hold court and look increasingly in command of those around him. I asked Antonia if she wanted to dance, not knowing if that might break some protocol which the ballerinas were bound to in our presence, and she shyly accepted. I led her to a space as far away as possible from our table, wondering how I could possibly match up to anywhere near the skills she had demonstrated a couple of hours earlier at the Alpin. But we talked more than we danced, swaying unadventurously and vaguely in sync while we exchanged experiences, questions and simple jokes, with Antonia becoming more open and animated, more casual and less constrained as we ventured into the early phases of getting to know each other, away from prying eyes and inquisitive ears. Her smiles became broader, more genuine and radiant, and more frequent. She laughed, and we laughed together, and there was a sort of liberation in her laughter, in both our laughter.

She told me that she came from Oradea, in the northwest of the country, had wanted to study but had been told to work in Poiana after her talent as a dancer had been spotted in her home city. But that was OK for now, she said; she loved mountains and loved walking in the mountains. She just missed her family and hoped that next year she could start her studies.

After twenty minutes or so we returned to the table. Before Antonia could sit down, the driver took her by the arm and led her back to the dance floor in a manner which seemed to leave her no choice but to accept. They took up position in the middle of the floor, the white suit centre stage, mouth pressed ever closer to the side of Antonia's face. He gyrated around her, arms in a semi-flail, talking constantly into her ear with his head rocking from side to side, his face a constant sneer as he looked to be chiding her about something. And Antonia was clearly uncomfortable. She tried to keep a distance, as far as was diplomatically possible, between her head and his encroaching mouth, occasionally nodding and issuing a smile which was more grimace than smile.

And then they were gone. I had turned back to the table to drink some water and devote myself to whatever discussion was going on between my escort and the two remaining ballerinas, but also wanted to keep an eye on what was unravelling on the dance floor; I was concerned that our protracted session might have put Antonia in a difficult position. Had we overstepped the allotted time for a local to be in the company of a westerner? Had we talked too much? Moments later I glanced back, but they were nowhere to be seen. There was still a void where the white suit had been, as though the other dancers dared not stray into a zone which might shortly be reoccupied. I looked back at my escort, anxiously, quizzically, but the response was a blank, unblinking stare, not a suggestion but an order to let things take their unnatural course.

An hour later, and feeling somewhat light-headed, I made my way back to my room. It was approaching one in the morning and I had a meeting with some local tourism officials at nine. I fell asleep quickly but was soon awoken by a knocking sound at my door, quiet but persistent, insistent, almost frantic in its rhythm and duration. I opened to see Antonia standing there, hair down and straggly, matted in places to her cheeks and forehead, traces of mascara forming coal-dark, irregular patches beneath her eyes and on her reddened cheeks. She was sobbing and looked utterly distraught.

'Please, please – can I come in? There is a bear, I cannot get home. I am scared.'

This rang true. I'd often seen the relatively small brown bears in the resort after dark, scavenging in waste bins outside hotel kitchens after venturing out of their forest habitats to look for rich pickings. But they were generally shy, and attacks were rare. The larger ones were caged and on show as an attraction; the poor creatures were often emaciated, much the worse for wear and visibly distressed.

'Of course, come in,' I beckoned, casting a wary glance up and down the corridor before closing the door as silently as possible behind us.

'How did you know my room number?' I asked, a banal question given the state Antonia was in, but my curiosity got the better of me.

'I asked for the Englishman at reception and they said you are the only Englishman here,' she replied. 'I had to give the lady some lei then she gave me your room number.'

I sat Antonia on the bed and poured her a glass of the rather bitter mineral water provided in the room, then rummaged around for some reimbursement for her bribe.

'Ok, let's wait a while,' I suggested. 'Maybe the bear will go away, and I will walk you back home. But why are you so upset, why have you been crying?'

'He raped me,' she stammered, bursting into a torrent of tears punctuated by deep, gulping intakes of breath. 'He raped me,' she repeated, clenching the bed sheets and sobbing louder as she seemed to relive the terrible memory.

'He did WHAT!?' I exploded, unable to quite take in the magnitude of the three short words she had uttered. 'You mean the driver?' I blurted, knowing full well who she meant, but for some reason needing to have verbal confirmation of who had visited this dreadful injustice on such a sweet, young angel.

'Yes, him. I hate him. But you know what Securitate is? I had to let him, otherwise they will never let me study, and make me stay here and dance,' she protested, almost pathetically, before dissolving into fresh floods of tears.

It all made sense. His behaviour from the start, his clothes, the deference towards him by my ONT escort, his constant controlling of the conversation; all of this gave more than a hint that he was more than a humble driver. That one of the feared, dreaded Securitate had been assigned to keep an eye on me was, however, beyond belief. Precisely what did the state expect to gain by tracking the movements of an equally humble contractor as he went about his business inspecting hotels and researching new excursions for tourists up in the Carpathian Mountains?

'He was very angry that we talked so much.' Antonia had calmed down, and wanted to rationalise what had happened, as far as that could ever be possible. This only succeeded in elevating my growing feelings of guilt even further, and I internally kicked myself for not having sized up the situation before it went too far. And I felt nothing but a deep loathing for the driver, who had so brazenly and brutally taken advantage of a beautiful girl who had wanted nothing more than to have some small modicum of enjoyment, a fleeting break from her normal existence.

'I'm so sorry,' I said. 'This wouldn't have happened if I hadn't asked you to dance. This is my fault.'

'No,' she insisted. 'He would have taken me somehow. I saw him already at the show, staring at me. When they told us to come to the hotel I knew it was because he wanted me. If Securitate want something, they take it. You cannot fight it. When he danced with me he told me I had talked too much with you. He wanted to know what we discussed. He told me I was bad to talk to you like this, and I must go with him if I did not want problems.'

We talked some more, and then I walked her home. She was sharing a room with some of the other ballerinas below one of the big hotels on the other side of the resort. We walked down a deserted lane through the cool, pine-scented night, then took a short cut she knew across a meadow, further away from any bears that might still be nosing through the discarded dinners of hotel guests long asleep. In fifteen minutes we were at her digs. We gave each other a tight, prolonged hug, some closure to a night of both happiness and horror, an embrace filled with deep sympathy and understanding: hers to thank me for listening and to try to dispel my feelings of guilt, mine to acknowledge her pain and suffering and to convey closeness after her horrific ordeal. We resolved to try to meet sometime during the following afternoon.

Despite a lack of sleep I went to breakfast early, praying that the driver wouldn't have the same idea. I'd decided that if he did, I wouldn't sit with him, even though that table was allotted to us for all meals: it would be my own silent protest, the furthest that I could probably safely go towards expressing disgust at what he had perpetrated the night before. He didn't show, and I hurried to finish my breakfast as quickly as possible.

The morning dragged by, and thankfully was conducted on foot. There were hotel viewings, discussions with and feedback to the local tourism guys, lunch with some of them, and by two o'clock I had returned to the hotel with my ONT companion. I was tired after the celebrations of the previous evening, I told him, and would just work in my room that afternoon. We agreed a time for dinner and parted. I waited ten minutes before setting off in the direction of the Sport Hotel, below which Antonia and her friends were billeted.

It was a glorious midsummer day, extremely warm but with enough breeze to make a vigorous walk up a mountain a very appealing prospect. Some much-needed exercise, and a way to clear a troubled head. It would be a bonus if Antonia were free, and I wanted to see how she was, but otherwise I would still head up Postavarul, Poiana's local peak, a summit I'd often contemplated conquering if time allowed. My childhood in Northumberland, holidays at my grandmother's in the Lakes, and parents who loved the outdoors and gave me and my brother every chance to love them too, had all ensured that I'd learnt to cherish the sensation of standing on a mountain top, drinking in far-reaching panoramas and savouring the buzz of achievement. And this would be my first proper Romanian mountain.

I passed her window, which she'd pointed out the night before, and could see down into the basement room where Antonia was feverishly scrubbing her dance clothes. A soggy grey tracksuit hanging in the window partially obscured the view. I knocked on the pane and she spun around, fear giving way to a look of reprieve.

'Do you want to climb a mountain?' I asked her.

'Of course! Five minutes. Walk up the path into the trees and I will meet you there.'

I did as instructed, concealing myself off the track behind a tree, and Antonia appeared moments later, jogging towards me in a white T-shirt and light blue shorts. After a quick embrace, we were off up the path, up through dense, then less dense, pine woods, out into the searing heat of the open, parched hillside, then once more back in the fragrant, temperate shade, relief from the onslaught of the July sun. At first she was pensive, reserved, possibly through knowing that she shouldn't be doing this, or from a psychological hangover from the events of the night before. But as we ascended away from Poiana, leaving the resort far below us, her mood lightened, her stride lengthened, and if my comparatively slow pace hadn't held her back she would doubtless have bounded straight up the mountain, a free spirit, gratefully unshackled.

We found a grassy spot just below the summit and sat in the warm, southerly breeze, quiet contemplation interrupted by snippets of talk about nothing of great depth or importance, at least at first. For me, to hike up a mountain is to escape the burdens of everyday life, albeit fleetingly, and the sense of liberation is intensely nourishing. We find peace in our natural world, and perspective: the mind is given a good clean, a proper airing, and returns refreshed to the challenges it was struggling to confront. But here in the East it was different. The land below was a prison, both physically and mentally; it was a land empty of choice and opportunity and the mountain and its breeze offered neither escape nor sanctuary, just a short period of parole with an inevitable end, the descent back into the abyss of repression. It was impossible to feel free, more so because the girl next to me was living proof of what went on back in that prison. At the risk of destroying her short respite from reality, I shared these thoughts with her; I wanted her to know that I was on her side despite being from another, more fortunate world. We held hands and wished that one day the prison gates would be flung open, and the mountain air would be truly free too.

An hour later we shared a final, secluded embrace, this time longer, more a clasp than an embrace. I pressed my cheek against Antonia's, soaked up some of the tears there in solidarity, kissed it, then after a simple, almost formal goodbye, she was gone.

I was dreading dinner that evening. I resolved not to attempt any conversation with the driver, nor to acknowledge him at all, but to stick to safe, business-related exchanges with my escort. For the first time in my travels in Romania, I wished that the driver could be banished to anonymity on a faraway table, in time-honoured fashion.

This evening his shirt had changed from black to brown, but the suit, shoes and belt were the same as before. And something else had changed. He sat there, taciturn and exhausted, a shadow of his former self. He looked totally drained, broken, made no effort at conversing with his compatriot and picked wearily at his food with a reluctant fork, as though the effort could bring about total bodily collapse at any moment. His face was bright red, his eyes empty. Dessert was waved away. He rose, slugged back a mouthful of water and feebly wished us *Noapte bună* ('Good night'), before tottering away in the direction of the restaurant entrance.

'What was wrong with *him?*' I asked my ONT friend.

'Let me ask you something, Mister Phil. What did you do this afternoon?' he responded, sounding ever so slightly menacing.

A couple of options, including the sore temptation to tell a blatant lie, flashed through my mind before I rationalised that taking the afternoon off to explore Poiana's natural surroundings could only be seen as a positive thing. It was conducive to my gaining an even deeper appreciation of the manifold wonders of the area, which in turn would of course result in even more lyrical, enticing brochure descriptions, and surely not, I reasoned, something that could be punishable in any way.

'Well, I decided to take advantage of the amazing weather and climb Postavarul. It seemed such a waste of a perfect afternoon to sit in my room when I could be getting to know such a famous natural attraction,' I put forward, hoping it might lead to a less sinister tone from my inquisitor.

'I know you did,' he proclaimed, almost triumphantly. 'And I think you were not alone?'

The conversation was taking a turn for the worse. It was one thing to slip out alone unescorted after claiming I'd be spending the afternoon in my room: a clear breach of trust. But doing so in the company of my dance partner from the previous evening implied more than a little forward planning and connivance and, for all I knew, might already have caused some very unwelcome collateral damage. I wondered how I could most cleanly extricate myself – and Antonia – from what was edging towards becoming a full-blown diplomatic incident.

'You know how I know this, Mister Phil? The driver – he followed you,' he continued, the victory and humiliation almost complete. 'He saw everything.'

'What, you mean he followed me up the mountain?!' I exclaimed, affecting just enough outrage to be credible, reckoning that attack was probably now the only means of defence. 'But *why*?!'

'Mister Phil, do you know who this man is? He is a Securitate officer. His job is to watch you. And to watch me. This is our life in Romania.'

With this almost resigned confession the conversation opened up. I told him that I'd worked out he was Securitate, first from his abnormal behaviour and then from the events of the evening before. I asked him if Antonia would be OK and he assured me she would, and wasn't in any danger: he had had his way with her, so she was of no further interest to him.

'So this is why he was so quiet tonight. You both walked too quickly for him, and he didn't believe you would go to the top. You finished him!'

We both laughed, clinked glasses, and I knew we were on the same team after all. An unintended act of resistance had gone some very small way towards awarding Antonia a modicum of retribution for the atrocity she'd suffered at the hotel the night before; but I knew that even if I had been able to tell her the story, it would probably only have frightened her and made her fearful of some sort of reprisal.

The three of us, the driver, my ONT friend and I, left Poiana early the next morning. Unwillingly but necessarily together, acting out a futile three-hour façade in the close confines of the car, cocooned in a tense and suffocating silence that concealed emotions of anger, hatred, fear, deception and betrayal; stinging emotions which were beyond raw and threatened to seep out into open confrontation. There was no sign of guilt or repentance, but surely, and hopefully, at least some embarrassment.

It was impossible that any words could be exchanged, even the most banal, as our black Dacia wound its way back down the lush Prahova Valley, out onto the endless plain with its distant chimneys, then back into the subdued bustle of the metropolis.

The Winds of Change

The day of that awkward journey was July 12th, 1989; I often wonder whether the driver had had a premonition of what was to come, and had taken what he could while he still could, and from a girl probably of an ethnic group, the Hungarians, whose national leader (across Romania's northwestern border) had incensed his own leader only days earlier. Maybe it was more than a premonition, and word of what had transpired five days ago at a meeting in Bucharest, where the great, the good and the not so good of the Warsaw Pact had gathered, had gone out to Ceaușescu's network of adjutants. The word was that all was not well, that the leader's rant against Miklos Nemeth's reforms in Hungary, though supported by Honecker and Bulgaria's Zhivkov, had not moved the man whose mindset mattered most at the meeting, Gorbachev himself. Had the driver's actions been some sort of vengeful swansong, a warped reaction to what he'd heard emanating from that assembly?

Nemeth had only been in power since November of the previous year, but possibly as further affirmation of what

Hungary had so often exhibited in the preceding decades, that desire to keep ahead of the pack, to plough its own furrow and be less unfree than the pack, he was forging ahead with what looked more like a comprehensive dismantling of the socialist system than mere tinkering around the edges. There was the promise of free elections, which included new political parties, free speech and untainted human rights, and – most significantly for the trapped peoples of Eastern Europe – a promise to remove the physical border with Austria. Gorbachev is said to have given Nemeth a sort of knowing wink at the meeting, tacit acknowledgement that there would be no Soviet intervention if that was what he decided to do. Immediately after, Nemeth went home and set about fulfilling those promises he had not already set in train.

A month earlier, in June, the Solidarity party had recorded resounding victories in the Polish elections, and by August a non-communist leader was in power. The bond between General Jaruzelski and Gorbachev had deepened, and by now the Poles were confident there would be no Russian attempts to stand in the way of their country's startling progress towards self-determination. Gorbachev was clear that socialism needed to be more democratic for it to be truly fit for purpose and that, provided that the nations of Eastern Europe remained part of the Warsaw Pact and Comecon, the two spheres could coexist in a common, peaceful European home, whatever political views their leaders espoused. Indeed, he considered what was happening in Hungary and Poland as a potential model for his own country, where it was proving much harder to push reforms through.

What appealed to people throughout the world about Gorbachev was his abhorrence of violence, and how this ran counter to the traditional perception, so often borne out by bloody action, of the totalitarian communist state. The massacre of peaceful protesters in Tiananmen Square in Beijing on June 3rd and 4th by a ruling party that had introduced economic reforms but was not prepared to court even the slightest degree of criticism, the faintest assault on its hegemony, had come in the wake of a visit by Gorbachev to the Chinese capital, where he had been given a rapturous welcome by its citizens. The repressive, brutal and uncompromising old juxtaposed with this new and almost adventurous phenomenon heralded hope for a brighter future, not just for Europe, but for the world at large. In Western Europe too, Gorbachev's star was at its zenith. In April, he had made a speech at London's Guildhall and dined with the Queen and Prince Charles at Windsor Castle, inviting the former to Moscow. Meanwhile his relationship with the West German leader Helmut Kohl was proving to be his most fruitful with any of the Western European leaders. Gorbachev suggested to Kohl that the number of short-range nuclear missiles be reduced, a further unmistakable sign that he wished to eradicate the possibility of a conflagration in Europe. His message to the GDR's Honecker, in contrast, was that no military assistance would be forthcoming, were Honecker to request such support to quell any revolt from within his increasingly restless population.

And that restless population was on the move: south to Hungary, to the shores of Lake Balaton, tantalisingly – and deliberately – close to the border with Austria, a border already made porous in recent months by the Hungarian authorities under the pretext of removing and repairing sections of decrepit fencing. On August 19th the inevitable happened: a 'pan-European' picnic had been organised next to the frontier (precisely who was the moving force behind the picnic is still the subject of speculation, but it seems highly likely that it was a Hungarian–West German joint venture, and had Austria's blessing), an exhibition of the harmony that could and should exist on both sides of the divide. The weather was inclement and not conducive to picnicking, but that didn't prevent the mass gathering from taking place, nor the tide of human aspiration – including around seven hundred East Germans – bearing down on a flimsy border gate and simply walking through it to Austria. The Hungarian border guards turned a blind eye, preferring to examine the credentials of any Austrians returning to their homeland than trying to resist the joyful exodus.

It was an historic exodus, possibly the most significant political event in Europe since the end of World War II, and one that signalled the beginning of the end of the communist order in Eastern Europe.

Spying on Russian military
manoeuvres, Rerik, GDR, August 1976

Hotel Warnow, Rostock, GDR,
August 1976. The location for my first
night behind the Iron Curtain

A warm welcome at the Wilhelmstal
Pioneer Camp, near Erfurt, GDR,
July 1981

A work of art, and cherished possession, from the
Wilhelmstal Pioneer Camp, July 1981

Postcard purchased in East Berlin,
August 1981

'Get those knees up!' Putting my SAGA people – and a few
extras – through their paces, River Danube, summer 1982

MV Carpati moored in Budapest,
summer 1982

Caught red-handed: Yugoslav secret police (the two gentlemen facing the camera) quiz me (far right) as our guide (to
my left) interprets, while two of my SAGA ladies and our
driver look on. Belgrade, Yugoslavia, August 1982

Taking time out below Schröcken,
Western Austria, May 1983

The beach at Mamaia, Romanian
Black Sea coast, summer 1985

IT IS FORBIDDEN
TO ENTER IN THE
RESTAURANT IN BATSUIT

EST INTERDIT
D'ENTRER DANS LE RESTAURANT
EN MAILLOT DE BAIN

ES IST VERBOTEN

A misunderstanding at the
Hotel Siret, Mamaia, Summer 1985

Page and Moy reps in Mamaia,
Summer 1985.
Left to right: Clare, Sue, Jenni, Maxine

It's all about promotion: Romanian and British efforts
to entice tourists to the Romanian seaside in 1985

With Moya in Red Square, with the Hotel Rossiya looming
large to the left of St Basil's Cathedral, Moscow, March 1988

Rudimentary Viennese street art?
Or homage to a liberator...
Vienna, November 2021

Chapter Seven

CZECHING OUT

Our relationship with the Czechoslovak Tourist Board, known as ČEDOK, had had an inauspicious start. Towards the end of 1983, with the first few months at Page and Moy under my belt and my zeal for launching holidays in Eastern Europe gaining pace, I arranged for a lady and gentleman from their London office to visit us in Leicester. Prague, combined with Vienna and Budapest, seemed like a good idea, and might appeal to those women's magazine travel editors upon whose whims our fate rested. It would need to be something new, but not too off-the-wall or adventurous, as this would be breaking untested ground. Something including references to 'imperial cities' or the Habsburgs would probably go down well, and have a chance of passing first base.

As they took their seats opposite me, Mr Dvořák and his colleague Mrs Kramperova looked a little uneasy. Both were new to the role; it was their first sales trip outside London, their first time promoting their country in the provinces, and they had no idea how they would be received. Czechoslovakia was not high up on the shopping list of most mainstream tour operators, and they had clearly been briefed to focus on the niche, probably as a way of standing out from their other Eastern European competitors. They handed me a dossier of ideas which they were sure, they said, I would like.

The first page featured a series of courses on beekeeping. Overleaf was a tour of Czechoslovakia's most famous caves. This was followed by a programme of visits to Jewish heritage sites, then one centring on places specialising in the production of lead crystal. With the exception of the beekeeping extravaganza, all were undoubtedly worthy of inclusion on a broader-based tour, but as first-timers we were looking for something a bit more … conventional. I wondered how I could let my enthusiastic guests down gently, after all the preparation they'd evidently done for the meeting.

'Well, thank you very much indeed, those certainly look very appealing. But do you have anything with sightseeing and stays in Prague?'

'Prague? But why? Everyone knows Prague, and we have such wonderful countryside in Czechoslovakia.' Mr Dvořák looked discombobulated. Clearly the gentle deflation hadn't been performed with a sufficient measure of diplomacy.

'Yes, I'm sure, and no doubt in due course we can work up to such incredible experiences, but for now, to start moving forward, we just need two or three nights in Prague to see the most historic and famous sights there, and something traditional in terms of food and drink, if possible, please. And we'd like to start in January.'

And that is how that part, the Prague part, of our highly successful Prague–Budapest–Vienna winter tour came to pass. It remained prominent in several of our client magazines for many years to come, so prominent that we eventually had to operate charter flights into Salzburg and Linz to meet the growing demand. We got our two, then three nights in the capital as we soon came to realise that there was so much to see in and around this relatively small, compact city. Much of its splendour was best appreciated on foot: the ascent up Nerudova Street to the skyline-dominating Castle and St Vitus' Cathedral, then down along Golden Lane where the artisans sold their crafts; poking around the narrow, cobbled alleyways which abound in the Castle district; popping into a shop to buy, yes, some lead crystal; gazing patiently up at the astrological clock in the Old Town Square, willing its hands to strike the hour and its diminutive figures to appear. To the west, we ventured to the spas of Mariánské Lazně and Karlovy Vary, returning via the tragic village of Lidice, dwelling of the ghosts of innocents slaughtered by the Nazis in retribution for the assassination of Heydrich by the Resistance. And we went on to uncover much more of this enchanting land as we transited to and from Austria: the hills, forests, vineyards and villages of Moravia and Bohemia, quaint provincial towns with incongruously large squares flanked by baroque and renaissance perfection in shades of every colour. Our ČEDOK friends in London were pacified, even though scaling down into the caves of the Moravian Karst continued to be resolutely rebuffed.

Memories of The Spring

Beneath the surface, there was a vibrancy about Prague, not so much in the contrived atmosphere of tourist traps like U Fleků, with its long wooden tables and exuberant gangs of beer-swilling tourists, ours included, but in the underground cellar bars frequented by the locals, shelter and escape from the daily grind and reality of life in a system most believed they shouldn't be part of. Perhaps unsurprisingly given the geographical proximity to the West, here more than anywhere else behind the Curtain there was a sense of a people who felt it belonged to the other camp, and who strained with every fibre of its being to be there. Did I realise that before the war, Czechoslovakia was the ninth largest industrialised nation in the world? How often was this fact eagerly inserted into the opening exchanges of often drunken conversations with a new-found friend, a would-be entrepreneur whose brainwaves could not, for now, see the light of day, in some ancient, dimly lit subterranean haven. In the constant pall of lung-devastating smoke, we would choke our way through jokes and stories, the new-found friend gleefully trotting out a succession of political jibes and snipes aimed at oppressors at home and further east.

The simmering resistance in Prague was indeed under-ground, both physically and metaphorically, and was gaining momentum during 1989 as the Czechoslovak government, unlike their neighbours in Hungary and Poland, steadfastly refused to change tack and embrace reforms. Over twenty years had passed since the Prague Spring of 1968, twenty years in which Dubček's brave endeavours to bring about fresh freedoms, freedom of speech, of the press, his attempts to instigate new forms of governance and a less centralised economy had gradually dissipated into treasured memories. When half a million Warsaw Pact troops invaded the country in August 1968 and the Soviet leadership installed an old-style authoritarian communist, Gustav Husák, in his place, the fleeting flowering of hope had come to an abrupt end. In January the following year, the student Jan Palach set himself on fire on the steps of the National Museum, in the most prominent of locations at the top of Wenceslas Square, and died from his eighty-five per cent burns three

Phil Caldwell

days later, a lone and desperate protest against what was happening in his country.

On the anniversary of Palach's death, on January 19th, 1989, over five thousand attended a memorial rally at the spot where he had sacrificed himself twenty years earlier. It was not only a tribute to a national hero who had made the ultimate sacrifice but also a pushing at the edges, a recognition that the people of Prague were aware of what was happening across the borders, that they could see the shackles being loosened elsewhere, and were determined not to be overlooked.

At the other end of Wenceslas Square stands the Hotel Ambassador, its art nouveau façade a hint of a more glorious past. By the late eighties, its rooms and interior were a testament to years of neglect and underinvestment, and yet they still offered enough in terms of location, relative comfort and old-world charm to make it just about acceptable to accommodate our groups.

It was Wednesday, October 4th, 1989. After an early meeting with Marie, my counterpart at the local ČEDOK office, I'd spent most of the day wandering around the Mala Strana (Lesser Town) district, quite the essence of the old city with its narrow, cobbled inclines and its normally seductive tranquillity, a place where immersion in unspoilt history was a regular delight when time allowed. How many ways were there to reach the castle and the complex of grand buildings which lay behind it, the timeless squares, their palaces adorned with sgraffito? The whole stone paradise wooed the explorer in search of urban escape, even more so if one strayed back towards the river and ventured into the labyrinth of the Kampa district.

But today it was different. Jaw-droppingly different.

The West German embassy, housed in the stunning eighteenth-century Lobkovicz Palace in Vlašská Street, was under siege both inside and out, and had been for weeks. This wasn't from malicious forces, nor anyone who wanted to do it or its occupants any harm; but from people whom it claimed as its own, a claim made all the more real by the West German constitution, which had always maintained that it represented all Germans, including citizens of the GDR. The embassy grounds were full of thousands of GDR citizens who had taken matters into their own hands and climbed over the wall to get in, causing the embassy to close to the public. Outside were the thousands more who hadn't made it in: families camped in makeshift abodes, crude tents and cardboard shacks, staking out pavement plots as close to the embassy as possible, and to the protection and ultimate sanctuary it afforded them, and willing its perimeter to extend out into the neighbouring streets, oblivious to the bare rock mattress beneath their weakened bodies. It was a scene of hope, and of misery. Even by the standards of a normal Prague in early October, it was decidedly chilly. The West German Red Cross was in attendance, busily handing out blankets and medication to the needy, to mothers stressing over fading children, to exhausted elderly relatives. There were fears that some sort of epidemic would break out.

Local police officers patrolled up and down the street, surveying the scene of human defiance with a mixture of suspicion and disdain, an unconvincing show of power, power they saw evaporating before their eyes in the legions of the bedraggled strewn along Vlašská and beyond. Unable to fully comprehend the magnitude of what I was witnessing, I veered off down the narrow sidestreets leading up to Nerudova and Úvoz. What could be accessed by car had been accessed, sometimes blocked from further access, without fear of fines. Every potential place to park, or more correctly ditch a car, had been taken, for streets and streets around. A metal mass of diminutive Wartburgs, Polski Fiats and Trabants had been wedged up hard against the timeworn stones of formidable walls and tilted up on pavements at careless angles. Cars in their regulation pale blues, mustards and whites, whose owners would never drive them again. Keys were still in ignitions, back seats and ledges served as the final resting places of drawing books, schoolbooks and favourite toys. These had been jettisoned as non-essential, surplus impediments on the hoped-for journey to come, a journey to a place where the education system would be different anyway.

Perhaps this was the main source for the booming market years later in the Czech Republic in cheap, second-hand Trabis, often sprayed in multiple garish colours and handed over as wedding presents, or to mark some other big, celebratory occasion. If so, the lucky recipients could scarcely have imagined the emotions going through the minds of the former owners, on that brisk autumn day back in 1989, as they slammed the doors shut on the family car for the last time.

*

That evening, the hundreds, possibly thousands, who had gathered in the Lesser Town Square and the entrance to Karmelitská craned their necks in the direction of Tržiště where the forwardmost couple of a fleet of coaches, their interiors in subdued light, were just about visible. Between the crowd and the coaches, two rows of helmeted police spanned out, one positioned in front of the stationary convoy, the other, expressionless, motionless, menacing and solid, keeping the multitude of onlookers at a distance. In between lay a physical void, waiting in hope to be filled and for history to take its course.

The crowd, mainly locals with a thin smattering of curious foreigners like me, was utterly gripped by the scene it was witnessing: hushed, expectant, protesting just by being there to pursue the outcome, yet unconvinced that the impending exodus would have any direct bearing on its own fortunes.

I'd inadvertently been rubbing shoulders with a guy of similar age to me for the past twenty minutes. I turned to him and asked:

'Can you see this happening here too?'

'No, this will not happen here in Czechoslovakia, not yet. You know, I am very happy for these people, that they can escape, but here we must wait longer.'

In reality, it wasn't at this stage a given that the people on the coaches would escape. Weeks earlier on September 10th, the Hungarians had gone a step further from the 'picnic' event and completely opened their border with Austria, allowing the movement of the disaffected from east to west to gather pace. On September 30th the West German Foreign Minister, Hans-Dietrich Genscher, had proclaimed to the mass of humanity gathered with their meagre belongings in and around his Prague embassy that their departure to West Germany had been approved. Some were allowed to leave that same day, others the following day, but the Czechoslovak government – including many hardliners who were dead set against the reforms sweeping parts of the bloc, let alone letting their own people travel to the West – had grown increasingly alarmed at the speed of developments. When the East German regime announced, on October 3rd, that its citizens would no longer be permitted to enter Czechoslovakia with a simple ID card, as had been the case for years, but would henceforth require passports and visas, it looked like both governments were in cahoots in a last-ditch effort to stem the tide. The Prague government was in an extremely difficult position: it was in sync with the East Germans in opposing the exodus but worried that if it didn't facilitate the transportation of those camped out at the embassy its own citizens would join the protest movements. And where might that lead?

So the crowd quite literally held its breath as behind the scenes, in the corridors of rapidly dwindling power, decisions were being taken which would inevitably determine the direction of the nascent revolution in Eastern Europe. Would it be stopped in its tracks, or would the Czechoslovak government allow the coaches to make the short journey to the main station to unload their drained but euphoric occupants onto trains, trains which would follow tracks north to Dresden and onto the town of Hof in West Germany, and to freedom?

There was an interminable wait. Some of the throng departed, muttering or exclaiming to those around them in resigned tones: it wasn't going to happen tonight, probably never again; or words to that effect, I conjectured.

But then it did happen. Quite suddenly, as if someone somewhere had barked an order that must not, under any circumstances, be disobeyed. The cordon of police in front of the coaches split at its centre into two arms, now providing a funnel through which the coaches spluttered laboriously forward with their joyful payload, black clouds of toxic fumes puffing outwards and into the faces of the policemen, a parting insult to the captors of moments earlier. We burst into rapturous applause, applause sweetened by the feeling of doing something radical, illegal. The repressed gave voice and vent to passions too long pent-up. Hands clapped above heads as we caught glimpses of the faces of those on board the coaches: families, children, wet-eyed, scarcely able to believe their luck, noses pressed against windows, frantically waving at us as if to say 'goodbye, goodbye, we made it, you too can have hope now!'

Some of us scuttled back onto Charles Bridge to watch the distant convoy making its almost stately progress over a bridge and along the east bank of the Vltava, the silhouettes inside now calmer and more sedentary in the weak light inside the coaches. It had been a moment of pure euphoria, pure happiness, and at the same time a moment of pride and privilege at being present to watch one of the most notable events in German history playing out and, weirdly, playing out beyond Germany's own borders. And it was notable not only in German history: I had borne witness to one of the defining episodes in the history of twentieth-century Europe.

Hours later, transiting through Dresden station, those same fortunate refugees would have looked out from the safety of their compartments onto scenes of chaos, as security forces scuffled with locals desperately trying to board the train. Observing that their journey to freedom was not yet open to all in their country, the fortunate ones might have felt doubly lucky, maybe even slightly guilty, but above all they must have felt elation at the prospect of the new life to come, a life they had given up everything to attain.

*

In the end their compatriots didn't have much longer to wait, and any sense of guilt among the fortunate would soon be banished. The mere fact that the GDR authorities had allowed the exodus from Prague via its own territory to happen at all meant there could no longer be any justification for the existence of the Berlin Wall.

Late evening on November 9th, the Wall border crossings were opened. In the ensuing days, weeks and months, the massive slabs of concrete that had kept Berliners apart for twenty-eight long years were voraciously eradicated by a thousand chisels and mallets; any tool, in fact, that could make an impact and detach a small lump for posterity, to resell, or to show generations of children and grandchildren to come a fragment representing the agony of enforced separation.

*

The young guy I'd rubbed shoulders with on that memorable night in the Lesser Town Square didn't have long to wait either. November 17th, 1989, was the fiftieth anniversary of the killing of nine students in Prague by Nazi forces, and it was students who now descended on Wenceslas Square to demand change. At first, soldiers meted out beatings to some and arrested others, but the die had been cast; the numbers became overwhelming and by the 20th half a million protesters were crammed into the square and surrounding streets. And the soldiers stood back. The weight of people power and the inevitability of where this was leading made further intervention futile. The revolution passed off peacefully, it was 'velvet', and by the end of the year Czechoslovakia had a coalition of opposition parties – the Civic Forum – led by a former dissident imprisoned by the regime years earlier, one Václav Havel, and was on the way to having an elected president for the first time since the communists had taken over the country in 1948.

*

With all this seismic geopolitical activity putting the cities of Eastern Europe well and truly on the tourism map, bookings for our winter 1989/90 tours of Vienna, Prague and Budapest were showing a healthy upward trend. If people had been uncertain about where Prague was and hadn't known it had a large square named after a tenth-century saint whom they'd sung about for years at Christmas time, they were learning quickly now.

Brochures need photos, preferably good-quality ones so – without any foresight of the momentous events to come – I'd been persuaded to take the new company photographer on a mission earlier in the year to get some fresh angles of the city and the Hotel Ambassador. In reality there wasn't really an old, or previous, company photographer, but rather a series of them. These had been selected haphazardly from anyone who happened to wander into the office at the right moment and succeeded in persuading our marketing people that they knew the basics of operating a camera, and were prepared to do so for very low recompense (caveat, for reasons of accuracy and future family cohesion: with the notable exception of my dear brother Mike, who went on to become one of Britain's leading photographers). While keeping the marketing budget virtually unscathed, it predictably resulted in stylistic inconsistency and some truly shocking pictures.

Going out on a contracting mission with a photographer in tow was almost as distressing as being told at the last minute that you were to be accompanied by one of the magazine editors. Both required an acceptance of certain incompatibility. The nature of the brochure photographer's work is to spend protracted periods waiting for the perfect composition to take shape: the right light (for brochure purposes, preferably the sunny type of light) and the right balance of people, with a sufficient number of them looking happy with their lot, which in the Eastern Europe of the eighties presented a distinct challenge. In contrast, the contractor normally has to inspect as many hotels, restaurants, attractions and other points of interest as possible, and attend as many meetings as possible too, during waking hours. He or she must cover a lot of ground and be nimble, while the photographer is often rooted to the same spot for interminable lengths of time. After a relatively short period together, one will drive the other to distraction.

On this particular trip, and to make an already undesirable situation even worse, the 'new' photographer clearly had some issues. David was the boyfriend of one of the Reservations Girls, who had put him forward in good faith, and presumably because he was finding it tough to source work elsewhere. And this was his first ever photographic assignment. Anywhere. On the flight to Prague he was extremely talkative, possibly through nerves, and spent much of the journey revealing details of a visual impairment that made it difficult for him to focus on objects for more than a split second, and over which his optician was still puzzling.

Once in Prague, matters quickly came to a head during a shoot of interiors at the Ambassador. There was an especially ornate banqueting room we used for the clients' welcome drinks after check-in, which merited inclusion in the brochure. I left David alone for a few minutes to set up his equipment, and returned to find him taking shots of the room directly into a large, golden-framed, floor-to-ceiling mirror at the end of the room. I delicately pointed out to him that while I couldn't confess to being any sort of expert, a picture of himself stooped over his tripod was unlikely to make it into the brochure, and was there perhaps some other way of capturing the unique grandeur of the room which excluded an image of him and his camera?

The next morning, I issued David with a map of the city and instructions on what and where the most iconic buildings were, and from where the best cityscapes could be viewed. Meanwhile I hotfooted it to the ČEDOK office to meet up with Marie and her bosses, relieved to have found a way to extricate myself from David and the particular demands of his work. I'd given him the name and address of a restaurant where we should meet up for lunch at twelve-thirty, and circled its location on the map.

I had my meetings, got in a taxi and arrived at the restaurant shortly before the agreed time. Twelve-thirty came and went, and David didn't appear. I waited for an hour, and there was still no sign of him. These days we often tell our children how we managed to communicate quite adequately before mobile phones were invented, but this was one case where that was patently untrue. I had to leave at just before two o'clock to start the afternoon's agenda, and I was worried that something bad might have befallen him. Or had he simply got carried away by the excitement of his first ever mission as a professional photographer?

I returned to the Ambassador later that afternoon and hoped I might find him there, or at least a message. But there was neither. I called his room – no answer. No one at reception had seen him either. I began to fear the worst, that he might unwittingly have committed some act against the State and been spirited away for questioning and possible incarceration. I decided to order dinner in the hotel restaurant, guessing he might check for me there if he came back.

At around eight-thirty David staggered into the restaurant, spotted me, then tacked uncertainly across the room towards my table and piled himself onto the chair opposite me. He was sweating profusely and stank of booze. He grabbed the bottle of water on the table and proceeded to empty it in a series of unfeasibly long gulps.

'Where on earth have you been, David?' I enquired, trying to suppress my all-too-obvious irritation. 'We were supposed to meet at that restaurant near the castle at twelve-thirty.'

'Got lost,' blurted David. 'Got lost in them small streets.

Didn't know where I was. Couldn't find them famous buildings you told me about.'

'OK, fair enough, but that was eight hours ago. What have you been doing since then?' I continued, trying not to sound too inquisitorial. 'I was worried,' I added as an afterthought, an unconvincing gloss of empathy an attempt to conceal my mounting frustration.

'Yeah, well I found a bar and this bloke bought me a few drinks, then he took me to another place too, and we had a few glasses of this becher-something. Then we went to a bar in a cellar. No, wait, we went to the cellar first, then this other bar. I think...'

'It's called becherovka, and it's strong stuff,' I assisted. 'I'm amazed you found your way back here. Did you manage to get any good snaps?'

'God knows,' he spluttered, before resting his forehead on the table, and falling asleep.

Chapter Eight

COME THE REVOLUTION

In early 1989 I was promoted to running the Aviation department, where my duties were largely centred around contracting airline tickets for our groups. It was a step up the ladder but wasn't entirely what I'd had in mind as my next career move, and I took the job on the understanding that I could retain some operational responsibilities, namely the Eastern Europe portfolio and a new venture, South-East Asia, which I'd started to work on the previous year. The fact that the Aviation brief would involve a good chunk of high-level negotiating was appealing, but that alone wouldn't compensate for the loss of the planning, travelling and cut and thrust of my previous role, so Eastern Europe and Asia were added to the job spec to seal the deal.

An early attempt to combine all of these strands into one groundbreaking project met with complete failure, though it did give me a chance to immerse myself in my new Asian patch, and get some welcome winter warmth.

My contact, Radu, at TAROM called me one day to make an offer that he was sure I, on behalf of Page and Moy, couldn't and wouldn't refuse: a return fare on London–Bangkok of £190. This, he claimed, was now the cheapest way to get to the Orient, even cheaper than using Aeroflot, and he was certain this would provide the basis for an inconceivably cheap product to dangle temptingly before potential clients.

The catch was, of course, that it involved flying via Bucharest, and a seven-hour wait there for the connecting flight. In both directions. Nevertheless I, or rather we – the managers who cocooned themselves in the boardroom every Tuesday morning to plan the empire's expansion – felt that this was an opportunity too good to pass up, and that I should be the one to test whether a lengthy layover in Otopeni airport and twelve hours on an ancient 727 were things that we ought or ought not to be putting people through in pursuit of commercial gain. So off I went.

Two weeks later I reported back on the mission, still groggy and generally out of sorts from a distinct lack of sleep and a blend of jetlag and something I thought was probably dysentery. On the upside, I said, the flights had been practically empty, so there was plenty of the decidedly average food to go around and the ordeal of trying to sleep on bone-hard seats was made marginally more bearable. Each of the intrepid passengers had had an entire row of seats to stretch out over, so conditions on the flight were definitely not cramped. On the way out I'd spent several hours playing cards and drinking warm beer with three attractive, though clearly bored and rather unsmiling stewardesses, which had helped pass the time.

The layover in Otopeni airport had been challenging, I reported further. Fortunately, a couple of my contacts at ONT had come to see me and taken me for dinner in the airport restaurant, and that had killed a couple of hours. However, there was virtually no lighting in the airport, it was cold, there was nothing to buy or do, and the steak I was served was inedible. Airport layovers are generally bad enough, but this was in a different league; we would have to not only recommend but insist that customers take books in their hand luggage, or games or puzzles – anything which might go some way to alleviate the stark bleakness of their situation – plus a thick coat, despite going on holiday to the tropics.

The vote was unanimous. The stunningly low air fare meant we could take the market by the throat, and we might even break into the backpacker fraternity. It opened up that part of the world to a new audience. We would also give a choice of carriers, with the more recognised ones available at a hefty supplement so as to further emphasise what an astonishing deal this was.

A few weeks after the brochures had been neatly stacked on travel agents' racks, the full extent of our miscalculation became evident. There wasn't a single taker for the TAROM option. There was a smattering of bookings across some of the more expensive, less physically inconvenient routes, but it was almost as if the 'too good to be true' attention-grabber had put purchasers off. Or had TAROM, along with other Eastern European carriers, developed such an uninspiring reputation that no amount of cheapness would entice people to spend the best part of two days in their care?

Whatever the underlying cause or causes, that was our first and last foray into combining the European East with the Far East, and from there on we stuck to more established, less demanding ways of transporting our customers to paradise.

The Downfall

Not surprisingly, the fall of the Berlin Wall was an event unreported by the Romanian state media, though no doubt news of it percolated through to at least some of Ceauşescu's citizens. Few of these could have dared dream that in a matter of weeks they too would be in the throes of a revolution, albeit one far bloodier: far bloodier indeed than any which accompanied the collapse of the communist edifice in Eastern Europe.

Even allowing for what had happened that year in other parts of the bloc, the speed at which both events unfolded showed how terminally unstable the foundations of the edifice had become: it was on the point of near-certain collapse even before the bulldozer of People Power moved in to administer the final toppling. The Romanian Revolution took somewhat longer to run its course than the Wall took to be breached, but it could convincingly be argued that it lasted just six days, from December 16th, with the first protests in the western city of Timişoara, to the 22nd, when Nicolae and Elena Ceauşescu's attempt to flee was thwarted when they were captured at Târgovişte, some eighty kilometres northwest of Bucharest. At most, it was over by the time the couple were summarily executed by firing squad on Christmas Day after a short, hastily convened trial with a, by then, very predictable outcome.

It was predictable because in its final months the regime had plumbed the true depths of its depravity and brutality, and a population exhausted by crushing austerity, lacking everything from basic foodstuffs to basic human rights, could take no more. It was said that one quarter of that population consisted of Securitate members, while its leader was pushing forward relentlessly with his programme of destroying villages, forcibly moving their occupants into soulless 'agro-industrial' complexes, and squeezing every last drop out of the nation to pay off his crippling foreign debts.

It was perhaps predictable too that the first stirrings of revolt should happen in Timişoara, a Hungarian ethnic cradle and home to a people so long demonised by Ceauşescu, in response to the attempted removal of their pastor, László Tőkés, from his lodgings for speaking out against the repressive policies of the regime. The locals rallied round, the protests gathered pace and assumed a wider context beyond the plight of Tőkés; cries of 'liberty' were heard. The army started shooting, and protesters died. Yet more joined their ranks, even the thousands of supposed loyalists transported into the city, who changed sides when they realised they'd been duped into believing that troublemaking Hungarians were the cause of the civil unrest; and the protests spread to other cities, ethnic divisions being suspended for the greater good. The rising crescendo of dissent against the stranglehold of oppression, which had touched every group for far too long, now united them.

On December 20th, Ceauşescu returned from a short state visit to Iran. Parts of his country were in open rebellion, and he needed to re-stamp his authority on the nation before the situation worsened. But a re-stamping would not be enough: a last-gasp attempt at re-branding was needed. And in one of the most memorable, most geopolitically theatrical moments many will have witnessed in their lifetimes, he contrived to do both – though not through calculated planning but out of sheer, unforeseen expediency.

At home in Leicester, I sat glued to the TV footage coming in from Romania, a country that rarely made it into our news but was now taking centre stage, catapulted unasked into the headline spot. It was the good fortune of everybody who took an interest in what was happening there that Ceaușescu wanted his speech to be given and broadcast live from the lofty position of the balcony of the Central Committee headquarters in Bucharest. Viewers were therefore able to witness the extraordinary, breath-robbing moment when he became aware that this was not the usual pliant audience: that his subjects were actually heckling him, shouting abuse, invoking the massacre in Timișoara, and that there was genuine commotion on the fringes of the one hundred thousand or so souls crammed into what was then known as Palace Square. His expression, changing from uncertainty to incredulity and bewilderment as the realisation dawned that the game was up, even after a desperate, unseemly last-ditch go at salvaging the situation by announcing increases in wages and child support, will remain forever etched on the minds of those who saw it. It was not only the defining moment in the fall of Ceaușescu and his ghastly regime, but also the toppling of the last domino in the game that played out in Eastern Europe in the latter part of 1989.

At that moment, however, the game, and the drama on our screens, was not entirely over. Not by a long way. The following day the Ceaușescus only just managed to escape the clutches of the protesters who'd broken into the headquarters, and were spirited off the roof by a waiting helicopter. By now, the balance of power had shifted even further away from them, with the army having switched allegiance and sided with the revolutionaries. A senior military leader, Vasile Milea, had reportedly committed suicide earlier that morning, but rumours circulated that his death had been ordered from on high, and his army colleagues were incensed. But where was the helicopter heading, and had the couple fled the country?

In the office, we tried in vain to make contact with our colleagues at ONT. As full-scale rioting broke out, it became patently clear that even though the Ceauşescus had gone and the army had turned, there were vast numbers of Securitate, and others who were invested in the regime's survival, who were not going to give up status, privilege and quite possibly their lives without putting up a serious fight. A new National Democracy Committee was set up in the immediate aftermath of the Ceauşescus' rapid departure, and Gorbachev, believing that the couple had been arrested, signed off on a message of support to be sent from the Soviet government to the interim administration.

Hours of confusion followed before it was finally confirmed that the Ceauşescus had been arrested and were in custody: the helicopter pilot had feigned engine trouble and landed, and by the afternoon the couple were under lock and key. As word and relief spread, the fighting intensified.

The ONT office, which I'd visited so often, was close to some of the main flashpoints – the Hilton Hotel and the Athaeneum – and I wondered how my contacts there were faring. The reports became more and more alarming: Securitate groups and snipers were firing at will on protestors, now celebrators, scarcely able to believe that this Christmas would be different from all those past and they would be sniffing festive freedom for the first time.

And the frequent, almost frenetic calls and faxes to our contacts, enquiring how they were and about their safety, continued to go unanswered: the usual faraway, faint purring of the dialling tone seemed, if anything, even more distant than normal.

Christmas Day came and went. We saw the grainy images of the Ceauşescus' trial, with the two defiant yet visibly scared as they were harangued in the makeshift courtroom, charged amongst other things with genocide in Timişoara and siphoning off vast amounts from the state coffers. Then came the images of their crumpled bodies lying at the foot of the wall against which, only seconds earlier, they'd stood awaiting execution. Elena was alleged to have said to one of the soldiers leading her out to her death: 'I was like a mother to you', to which the soldier replied: 'how can you have been a mother to us when you killed our mothers?'

The fighting continued for two more days and then, with over 1,100 dead, mainly students and the young, it stopped.

*

The queue stretched up the hill and into the distance, then disappeared around a corner from where, as I later saw, it continued along another entire section of the palace boundary. My ONT escort insisted we go directly to the main gate where the front few were already filing through, frigid from the freezing air of a Bucharest March morning, having almost certainly waited several hours, perhaps all night. They were shivering, purple-faced and expectant – and no doubt filled with apprehension about what they were shortly to see.

I felt deeply uneasy about such blatant queue-barging and suggested we might be better advised to join the line at its end. I was rebuffed, however, and told that it could take hours and that it was very cold, which I knew. I stuck close as my companion strode forward with an air of purpose and flashed papers in front of a man on the gate, interrupting the flow of the queue. There was an objection from the next in line, from the man behind him, and then from several others: murmurs of discontent became shouts, fingers pointed in my direction, complaints made to authority in this new world order over why a foreigner, a westerner, was being given preferential treatment. I could just about follow the discourse:

'Why should he be allowed in before us, without waiting?'

'Because he is from England and he is only here for a short time.'

'Yes, but we are from Romania, we fought in the revolution, and we have waited hours to get in!'

'Yes, but this man is important, he brings tourists to our country, he brings us money.'

I was ushered through the gates, with memories of Omsk airport reverberating around my head and painfully aware that the discontented from the queue would probably be close to us during what I expected would be a regimented tour of the palace. I looked bashful and shrugged my shoulders as if this was nothing to do with me and I was just following orders, and they knew all about that, didn't they? I even tried uttering a weak '*Îmi pare rău*' ('I'm sorry') so as to appear more sympathetic and gain some brownie points via a couple of words of Romanian. But it cut no ice, and only succeeded in arousing more scowls and disdainful looks.

As this was the first day Ceauşescu's monstrous palace was open to the public, I was – according to my ONT guide – the first westerner to enter it since the revolution, though I have no hard evidence to support that. All I really knew about it beforehand was that it was said to be the second largest building in the world after the Pentagon, and I'd heard that a great many construction workers had died while labouring on it in dreadful conditions, and that it hadn't been finished. This massive loss of life (estimated at around 3,000 dead), combined with the perverted opulence of what we saw inside, explained why the mood of so many of the visitors that day shifted from a sort of fleeting awe and deference, on entering, to anger and often tears, as we processed through umpteen chandelier-dominated and walnut-panelled rooms and along endless corridors of polished marble. In all, the tour took us to only a fraction of the 1,100 rooms, and not to the nuclear bunker on the lowest, eighth, subterranean tier, though we did venture down to whichever level the theatre was on when we persuaded one of the guides to take us 'off limits', which she was only too eager to do.

The lavishness of the rooms was sickening, even for someone who hadn't suffered under the regime. The finest materials had been used, not only walnut for the panelling and wainscotting but sweet cherry, oak, sycamore, maple and elm. Curtains of velvet, tassels and braids of silver and gold, and the finest woollen carpets, adorned many of the rooms and those unfathomably long corridors. 3,500 tons of crystal had been used, much of it to create the 480 chandeliers. The irony of where the various materials came from was equally sickening: Romanian products channelled exclusively into Ceaușescu's self-glorification, whilst practically everything else in the country of quality and worth was sold abroad for hard currency.

As we filed into Nicolae and Elena's sumptuous offices, the epicentre of the appalling disaster that had befallen the Romanian people, there was a palpable sense that just three short months ago simply being here would have been inconceivable.

It was almost as if we were in a dream, not a dream that would take a sudden turn for the worse, a grotesque, unanticipated twist rapidly metamorphosing into a gruesome nightmare. For the demons were dead and buried in an unmarked grave.

The demons were dead, the nightmare over. This was a dream that was showing early signs of shaping up well, and had a good chance of ending happily.

Chapter Nine

NEW BEGINNINGS

That perishingly cold morning in early March of 1990 would turn out to be my penultimate day of overseas travel with Page and Moy. Six weeks later, my wife Moya and I left the company in search of a new challenge. We'd got married the previous year; Moya was an executive in my Aviation department, and was far better at dealing with airline reps than I was. Initially, the new challenge took the form of resurrecting the dormant UK office of a large French tour operator, but it soon became apparent that they were in financial difficulty, and it wasn't long before the company collapsed. While the writing was manifesting itself ever bolder on the wall, we decided the time was right to start our own show, and the idea of creating an inbound tour operation catering for groups coming to the UK from the brand new Eastern European market was born. It seemed like a logical move: not only were the political structures underpinning the system across the entire region in a state of total upheaval and transformation, but so were the formerly centralised economies, now rapidly giving way to a blossoming of private enterprise. People were defecting from the vast old state travel companies in their droves and starting up their own businesses wherever they could, even in kitchens and living rooms where the nearest means of communication was often the public phone down the road.

Moya and I, along with two friends who were our business partners for the first year, were sitting in toasty conviviality around the fire at The Old Barn at Glooston, our local rural hideaway of choice, debating possible names for the new company as we sipped our beers and ciders. In the end, Moya's suggestion – Go West – won the day.

It fitted the bill perfectly. It was easy for non-English speakers to understand (at this time, the second language of most East Europeans, especially amongst the middle and upper age ranges, was Russian), described the direction of travel from east to west in two short words, and was snappy and easy to fit into or around a logo. Now we just had to work out how to tap into a fledgling and disorganised market, though we had the helpful head start of a wealth of contacts from my previous life. There was a huge demand, but unsurprisingly a decided lack of the amounts of disposable income required to finance a cherished trip to Britain, or elsewhere in the West. Hungarian and Czechoslovak coaches were already reported to be clogging up any available parking space in Paris's Pigalle, with their occupants sleeping in the coaches as hotel prices were beyond their reach. The early omens were not good.

*

The days following our exit from Page and Moy had been troubled. One evening, I'd developed acute abdominal pain and taken to writhing around theatrically on the lounge floor, before Moya decided the situation might be serious enough to warrant calling 999. An interminable hour later, an ambulance arrived and whisked me off to hospital, still writhing and loudly insisting that the paramedics reverse their decision not to give me any pain relief before I'd been examined by a doctor. The diagnosis was a kidney stone ('the male equivalent of childbirth', as one of the nurses kept gloatingly reminding me as I sat on the edge of my bed, downing pint after pint of water in an attempt to flush the thing out, and prevent the medics having to get it out by other, far less appealing means), and I was in hospital for three days.

On the second day, Moya marched on to the ward and up to my bed, her expression best described as menacing. We'd only been married a few months, but I'd known Moya since my first day at Page and Moy and knew that something was gravely amiss. She was sorely displeased, almost certainly with me.

'Some mail came for you this morning, forwarded on from Aviation,' she said threateningly. 'How do you explain this? Mind telling me what's been going on?'

She threw a postcard onto my blanketed lap. I looked down to see a line of folk dancers, arms linked, all sporting an identical forced, synthetic smile, each with one leg raised high off the parched grass of the field in which they danced, wooden huts behind them. The quality of the photo was extremely poor, the colours garish.

I flipped the card over. On the back was written the office address and:

ROMANIA IS FREE!
WE WON THE REVOLUTION!
I LOVE YOU!!

It was signed with the name 'Antonia'.

This was tricky. Lying in a hospital bed, still in pain – and bloated, having spent nearly two days guzzling vast quantities of overchlorinated water in an attempt to rid myself of something that turned out to be almost microscopic in size – was one thing; having the added pressure of facing a charge of disloyalty so early in the marriage made the whole ordeal considerably worse.

I did my stammering best to convince a stern-faced Moya that Antonia's words were no more than an exuberant extrapolation of the unbounded joy she and countless others would be experiencing after ridding themselves of their oppressors, and that nothing had gone on between us. Understandably, however, this was not going to be an instant fix, and efforts continued unabated over the ensuing weeks to convince her of my innocence, with each plea probably sounding more desperate than the last.

*

My story ends on August 22nd, 1990.

This is a day I'll always remember, because it was the day we welcomed our first guests from Eastern Europe: five ladies from Romania accompanied by their organiser, Paul Zamfirescu, whose start-up travel agency in Bucharest we'd been liaising with for several torturous weeks as we tried to get our first Go West tour off the ground.

Moya and I waited apprehensively in the arrivals hall at Heathrow's Terminal 2, wondering whether the group would make it through customs and passport control, and whether Paul would bring the required amount of cash to pay us for the tour. They did, and he did, but in US dollars, and not enough to cover our costs, let alone any profit. But the loss was small, and manageable, and secondary to the fact that we were up and running and part of something much bigger, doing something which a few months ago would have been unthinkable. It was an emotional moment, and over thirty years later that moment still resonates. Moya and I gave each lady a rose as they came up to us, all five looking totally bewildered amidst the glaring lights and hubbub of the packed terminal.

We escorted our small band of wide-eyed visitors to the multi-storey car park, split them between our two cars, and headed off to one of England's most classic picture-postcard villages, Woodstock. We'd planned a pub lunch, but Paul insisted they would cater for themselves to keep costs to a minimum. So our guided walk around Woodstock was punctuated with impromptu and regular incursions into shops, most memorably into a fruit shop, with each guest emerging minutes later gleefully clutching a large bunch of bananas; Paul said that it was still difficult to find fresh fruit back home in Romania.

Then we headed to Oxford for another walking tour, into Christ Church College and the Bodleian Library, before driving to the Midlands and on to the north, and a week touring the best England had to offer. Halfway through the tour, one of the ladies disappeared and we never saw her again: Paul said this was no surprise, as even though Romania was emerging from the darkness, many had decided it offered no future and preferred to give up everything in pursuit of an assumed better life in the West.

In September we received our second group, this time from what was still Czechoslovakia: a 'proper' group of thirty-five people who arrived in London by coach, a mixture of young and old. Once again, I did the guiding. It was a fun week: everyone wanted to party and the nights were long, with my enthusiastic daytime commentary usually delivered to a comatose audience. Throughout that autumn and winter we had a steady stream, now from Hungary and Russia too. Many more Romanians came, and many disappeared into the shadows.

EPILOGUE

When I first had the idea of writing about this period of my life, my eldest daughter told me: 'Just start writing and see where it all leads, and don't worry too much about structure.' And that's very much the advice I've followed, with the result, I suspect, being three themes, each very different, yet all interwoven.

One theme is autobiographical: an account of fourteen unforgettable years during which I developed a fascination, maybe even a love, for Eastern Europe, and a deep engagement with what was happening there at that time in its history.

The second is about the travel industry, another of my life's passions, and how working and growing up within it in the Eastern Europe of the eighties presented unique challenges, frequent frustrations and regular lessons in acceptance and compromise.

The third theme is not so much theme as narrative, as I'm aware that for many who weren't born then or didn't live in the countries in which these events took place, Eastern Europe before the collapse of communism may largely be a closed book, and it doesn't seem to appear in many school curricula either. Hence, I've tried to interject some historical context, although – with no pretence to being a historian – this is fairly general and sketchy.

Predictably, given the nature of some of those events and what I witnessed and experienced at first hand, remaining impartial and non-judgemental has proved difficult, despite my best efforts. The book is not intended to be political, though it unavoidably ties in with the national, regional and global politics of the day. Nor is it intended to elevate one political ideology above another: I believe that the various manifestations of socialism as practised across the Eastern bloc before the system collapsed in the late eighties had some laudable aims and principles. Across the years, I became used to hearing members of the older generation speak in sentimental tones of the security, low crime rates, guaranteed employment and free healthcare they enjoyed, drawing contrast with what they increasingly saw happening around them: unemployment, insecurity, decadence and social mayhem.

The problem was that socialism ignored man's fundamental instinct for self-betterment, not least materially, and the universal need for basic freedoms. What's more, the presence of a self-interested, often barbaric elite, more obsessed with totalitarian, repressive rule than the system's sworn aims, meant that socialism – in the forms it presented itself – would be tarnished forever, both in the Eastern European countries in which it was practised and to the outside world at large.

The more enlightened socialist leaders realised that some concessions had to be made, and some opportunities for self-betterment created, if the system was to stand any chance of long-term survival. But it was the Oppression (I capitalise the O deliberately here) which sounded the death knell, particularly when in the eighties contact with the western world through media and the spread of tourism (socialist nations needed the hard currency reserves generated through tourism) brought the contrast between East and West in living standards and personal liberty into ever starker relief, and more visible to the average citizen of Eastern Europe.

If there is a moral to the story it is that we should never take our liberty for granted. As we look around the world and see, whether on Al Jazeera, the BBC or through any other form of media, the sheer number of societies that continue to suffer oppression, many run by governments that have absolutely nothing to do with socialism, we are justified in feeling deeply depressed and distressed. As I write, Russian troops are penetrating the free, independent nation of Ukraine, seeking to deprive it of its freedom and independence. As Margaret Thatcher memorably said in her speech at London's Guildhall just days after the fall of the Berlin Wall: 'When people have the freedom to choose, they choose freedom.' But there are still too many people who do not have that choice.

This is why I firmly believe tourism can be a driver and force for change and for good, in its own modest way, and where my themes come together. Of course, it would be over-exaggerated, simplistic and plain wrong to state that East and West Europe finally united, and the Cold War petered out, because of tourism and personal connections between the peoples of both spheres. But I am convinced it played an important role, and can continue to play an important role throughout our world today.

One of my favourite sayings, one that has always stayed with me, comes from my school and university days studying German literature. It's from the great poet and playwright JW von Goethe, who wrote:

Die beste Bildung findet der gescheiter Mensch auf Reisen.

This, loosely translated, means: 'To the smart and open-minded, travel is the best education.' And I'm sure that by 'education' Goethe wasn't referring to the amassing of geographical facts and figures, and knowing one's way around various parts of the globe. He was far more likely telling us that travel is a means to learning about mankind in all its forms – its beliefs, its customs, its religions – and in doing so we become more tolerant, more empathetic and conclude that there's in fact little that divides us. The courtesy and good humour of the waiter who served us in that restaurant, that family from another country we got to know at the hotel pool, the welcoming smile of the lady in the souvenir shop: all are contacts and microcontacts bringing us closer, creating bonds between us and making an outbreak of enmity between us less likely.

Gorbachev himself had his eyes opened when he started to travel beyond the USSR's immediate sphere of influence, and was blessed with pacifist proclivities. He saw the ills of totalitarianism, and there have been others, such as FW de Klerk in South Africa, who recognised that oppression was no bedrock upon which to build a functioning, successful, happy society, and who duly raised their heads above the parapet and triggered wholesale change.

We must hope there will be more like them where they are needed.

POSTSCRIPT

November 13th, 2021

It's Saturday night in Vienna's 'Bermuda Triangle', its bars normally a hive of activity and an early point of convergence for the city's fun-seekers. Tonight, however, it's more sparsely populated and subdued as the latest lockdown takes its toll.

Barrie and I are sitting at a window table in the elegant but unstuffy Salzamt restaurant, with art deco chandeliers the nod to elegance and the rest wooden, natural, simple, cosy and authentic. It was the perfect venue for a reunion on a chilly November evening. And not far from our former workplace, the Danube.

We reckon we last saw each other in London in late 1982. Barrie had a flat in Phillimore Gardens, in London's Kensington, and we had met there and gone out for a drink, or maybe dinner: we can't really remember much about it now. It was thirty-nine years ago. And then we lost touch.

Barrie Mon Lloyd's life still revolves around the Danube. He's carved out a successful career in Vienna working for the cruise company Noble Caledonia, who operate far posher ships on the river than those we endured during our summer together.

We reminisce about games of football on Margaret Island and nights at the Hajó Disco; I tell him that I recently tracked down Almut, who's become a specialist in Polish mediaeval history, and he tells me he's still in touch with one of the Romanian cruise directors, Rodica.

I quiz him. 'There's something I've always been curious about. Who was officially top of the pecking order on board: the foreign or the Romanian cruise director?'

'Are you kidding me?!' he exclaimed, with an unmistakable air of being affronted. 'They may have thought they had overall control, but they were deluded. We ran the show, no question about that. The number of times I had to put them in their place, I can't tell you.' Barrie's Welsh lilt became ever more pronounced as he recalled bygone battles.

'And you know what, in 1984 the Romanians banned me from ever entering their country. I must have ruffled too many feathers I think.'

We reminisce about Agi, the elderly Hungarian guide, concluding that our decision to dispense with her services had, on balance, been the right call; we talk about life and conditions in a C deck cabin, with Barrie reminding me that for all the obvious drawbacks it had been a damn sight cooler down there than in the stifling heat of a swankier home on A deck.

We both knew what had become of the ships: *Oltenita* was destroyed by fire close to the Slovakian village of Sap in October 2005 as it cruised upstream to Vienna. Thirty French and forty-seven Norwegian passengers were rescued along with forty-two Romanian and two Serbian crew; but tragically the onboard singer, also from Serbia, perished. The cause of the fire was never determined.

MV *Carpati* had a less dramatic end and is spending her retirement in the nautical equivalent of the knacker's yard in

Giurgiu. We agree we should venture there soon to pay our final respects, before she meets her ultimate fate. If, that is, the Romanians relent and let Barrie in.

*

Two days earlier, I'd boarded a train at Budapest's Keleti station for the three-hour journey to Vienna, passing beneath the statues of my fellow countrymen James Watt and George Stephenson as I made my way through its imposing entrance, a jewel of Budapest's heritage, rising proudly above the faded tenements of Józsefváros to stare resolutely down Rákóczi Street to the Danube beyond.

I'd just spent a few days in our Budapest office with my team there, battered and bruised from eighteen months of pandemic salaries yet amazingly still brimming with belief and optimism for the future. It was the first time we'd been able to meet up in person since the virus took its crippling hold, and the five girls eagerly tapping away on their keyboards were practically all that remained of my shattered business. Susi had founded the Hungary office with me in 1997 and had been with us ever since, and Judit had joined a couple of years later. The two of them were able to tell the newer recruits about happier times: about the unforgettable parties we'd had over the years in a myriad of European cities. The last of those had been in July 2019, in Budapest itself, when we'd chartered a small craft for a dinner cruise and whiled away a perfect couple of hours drifting up and down the river in a haze of warm, dreamy evening sunlight and good wine. We'd spent the afternoon further upstream inside the ramparts of Visegrad Castle, dressed up as mediaeval knights and playing silly games with wooden swords and mini trebuchets, taking time out from the hilarity disguised as team building to gaze down on the sylvan beauty of the Danube Bend far below our ancient hilltop perch.

After the cruise and with spirits high, the twenty or so Poles, Slovaks, Hungarians and Brits who made up Go West piled into Budapest's bustling backstreets and the seemingly limitless selection of quirky bars and nightspots they concealed. No wonder the city had become the latest magnet for party people from all over Europe and beyond, with many determined to find out what the famous 'ruin pubs' were all about. From the tiny to the cavernous, these usually dark drinking dens created from some derelict building – perhaps abandoned and unloved since the days of '56 – complemented the cheerful, boundless, all-pervading hedonism gripping the city.

Over the years Susi, Judit and I have found ourselves flying the Go West flag in various corners of Eastern Europe, including all the Baltic States, Bulgaria, Poland, Slovenia and Croatia. Attending and exhibiting at travel shows has always been our tried and tested means of drumming up business, the simple theory being that the more time you spend digging for gold, the more chance you have of striking it, provided of course you're digging in broadly the right place. On occasions in the late noughties, this small-scale mining operation took place in Bucharest, in what became known after the revolution as 'The People's House', Ceaușescu's grotesque palace which I'd first visited on that raw and rather testing March day back in 1990.

By the time the National Association of Romanian Travel Agencies had hit upon the idea of taking over one of the palace's rooms to stage its annual trade fair, both houses of the state's parliament had been ensconced elsewhere in the building for some years. However, that still left tens of thousands of unoccupied and unutilised square metres to fill, and very few practical ideas on how to fill them. There was talk of developing the space into a vast retail and entertainment emporium, and of converting a small part of it into a hotel. As exhibitors, we felt dwarfed, almost cowed, by the dizzyingly high ceilings and opulent surroundings. In terms of proximity to our operational base, the conveniences were decidedly inconvenient, with access in times of need involving a lengthy expedition down a succession of very long corridors.

And yet, despite the incongruity of it all, I felt an inner contentment that at least some minuscule portion of this dreadful monument, which so many had made the ultimate sacrifice to construct, was now a place where dreams could be realised, where the generation following those that had suffered so egregiously could exercise a right and a freedom that their abused predecessors could never have envisaged.

This symbol, surely the most visible in Ceaușescu's Romania, of fear, repression and enslavement, was now being used for people to plan their holidays, their annual escape to foreign parts, and there was a great poetic justice in that.

*

The morning after my evening with Barrie, which culminated in cocktails at a trendy bar called Roberto, full of Vienna's hip and chic mostly thirty to forty years younger than us, I walked down Mariahilferstrasse to clear my head and seek out a very late breakfast. A crusty 'semmel' filled with a slice or two of salami or cheese, ideally both, accompanied by a powerful verlängerter coffee, preferably a double, would, I reasoned, appease a lingering headache and gnawing hunger.

I spotted some black graffiti scrawled on what appeared to be some sort of electrical junction box on the side of the pavement. It read:

Gorb sei dank

The word 'Gorb' had what looked to be a crude halo above it.

Now it's quite possible that 'Gorb' is someone, or something – maybe some Austrian underground cultural movement – of which I have no knowledge. And if that is the case, I apologise to all Gorb's followers for my ignorance. But I'd like to think that what is a corruption of the German exclamation *'Gott sei dank!'*, meaning 'Thank God!', has been thoughtfully amended to form a tribute to the 'Gorb' who was so instrumental in bringing about the events leading to the fall of the Berlin Wall, the overthrow of Ceauşescu, and the liberation of millions of Eastern Europeans from repressive regimes. Indeed, could the author of this pithy, if rather irreverent example of Viennese street art be a descendent of one of my former colleagues who jumped ship on a Saturday night back in 1982? And did things subsequently turn out so well that the family decided to deify Gorbachev this publicly and eloquently as homage and gratitude to him?

Who knows. In the story, I left Gorbachev in the very late eighties making waves at home and on the wider European stage, waves which rocked the ship carrying the nations of Eastern Europe until it eventually capsized. His willingness in the second half of 1989 to let events take their course was the ship's death knell. Yet at home in his Soviet Union, a union set to disintegrate within the next two years, his star was waning. Despite his election as President of the USSR in March 1990, the economy was in serious trouble, and even though incomes were on the rise there was a woeful lack of goods in the shops. The republics in the Union were increasingly keen to move towards greater autonomy, and protests were becoming more widespread on its fringes, in Lithuania and, more bloodily, in Azerbaijan. In Moscow and other Russian cities demonstrators were on the streets, pushing for still greater freedoms. Even the formal sanctity of the annual May Day parade in Red Square was violated by the angry shouts of thousands insisting on faster change. And while Gorbachev's star waned, that of his fiercest rival Yeltsin was in the ascendant. In the push for greater democracy, Yeltsin went boisterously about elevating his status as the people's champion, his penchant for drink seemingly only further endearing him to his growing fan base.

Control of the juggernaut Gorbachev had so dramatically set in motion years earlier was being fought for by aspiring drivers with different routes in mind. The hardliners, the communists, wanted the vehicle to turn back and return whence it came. The reformers, progressive forces and the Soviet's republics, wanted the accelerator pedal to be pushed to the floor. Gorbachev, the driver, prevaricated. And the juggernaut stalled.

As our starry-eyed Romanian ladies landed at Heathrow airport in late August 1990, Gorbachev was trying in vain to navigate a path between the two competing sides. He felt he might be getting on better with Yeltsin, but his optimism was premature. Caught between the two stools of radicalism and conservatism, any momentum he hoped to maintain petered out. Within a year, an unsuccessful coup attempt had been made against him. By the end of 1991, Gorbachev had resigned his presidency of the Soviet Union, and the Soviet Union was no more.

*

Back in my world, and by way of an upbeat footnote, here's a quick report on three of the *dramatis personae* in the story.

As the waters of the Black Sea lapped Mamaia's sun-kissed beaches, Jenni Brown was doing her best to fend off a sustained assault from a procession of irate holidaymakers recovering from unpleasant gastric ailments. Her solace was the shared siege mentality within the rep team and the companionship of the cat she'd secreted in her room. It was far from certain that Jenni would see out the summer, and I'd sent her what I hoped would be a few morale-boosting lines to give her what support I could.

Jenni did survive the summer of 1985 and went on to have a stellar career, resort-based and on the road, a career that – save for a pandemic-induced interlude – is still in full swing today. After Romania she was a regular fixture on Austrian and Swiss House Parties, before graduating to escorting tours all over Canada. She became our first employee at Go West, helping me and Moya to get the business up and running and taking charge of some of our early Romanian groups, before returning to guiding overseas.

Her work and travels have since taken her from Cairo to Cape Town, from China to the Caribbean, and many points in between. She is now married and living in Melbourne, Australia, where she conducts tours of her new home country, and accompanies followers of the annoyingly successful Australian cricket team to whichever unfortunate nation their bowlers and batsmen are set to inflict misery on next. Jenni is a great friend, and whenever she's back in town we enjoy nothing more than chatting about old times, triumphs and tribulations over a bhuna or vindaloo in one of Leicester's many fine curry houses.

And what of Paul Bowden, responsible for the early stages of my journey in the travel industry? Paul grew and prospered in the world of travel, eventually combining that with his other great love, football, consulting for a number of companies across both spheres. He came to specialise in working on major sporting events, most notably the London and Rio Olympics, the 2014 Football World Cup in Brazil and the 2016 European Football Championships in France. His strong involvement in sport made a transition to his latest role, as a football agent, both logical and straightforward.

What he would no doubt have given to be representing the late, great, real Bobby Moore.

Then there was the trading standards officer, Harry Whitehead, tasked with investigating precisely why so many visitors to the Romanian Black Sea coast had felt moved to alert him to those unpleasant gastric ailments, who'd made an unwelcome visit to our London Road offices in pursuit of justice and to take me to task.

Many years later I gave a job to a very talented girl called Rhian, and discovered soon after she'd taken up her position that Rhian was Harry's daughter. Before long, my path and Harry's had crossed again, this time in the mountains of Northern England, where both of us participated in charity walks with our families and friends. Our paths in fact not only crossed but joined, as we huffed and puffed our way up and down the Three Peaks and various Lakeland fells together.

More recently one of my three daughters, Mary-Jean, whose trade as a performer was interrupted by lockdown and the resulting closure of theatres, has been giving Harry's grandson Euan (Rhian's son) online singing lessons.

It's funny how things turn out.

SOCIALISM AND COMMUNISM
What's the difference?

In a book which doesn't pretend to be about either, these two words and concepts crop up in its pages with such regularity as to, quite possibly, give the impression that they are at its heart. And, like many before who have alluded to, for example, 'socialist systems' and 'communist regimes', or 'socialist regimes' and 'communist systems', there is a blurring of distinctions in my book too.

In an effort to give some clarity, what better place to start than pages 333 and 1569 of my trusty, voluminous *Chambers Dictionary*, which in truth has languished on the bottom shelf and not had a decent airing for some time, as the telltale thin layer of dust on its top edge testifies. The dictionary pronounces as follows:

Socialism: 'the theory, principle, or scheme of social organisation which places the means of production of wealth and the distribution of that wealth in the hands of the community.'

Communism: 'a social theory according to which society should be classless, private property should be abolished, and land, factories, etc collectively owned and controlled; a system of government adhering to these principles.'

I dig a bit further, and come across a website called *dictionary.com*. This states that:

'Socialism has three main meanings:

1. A theory or system of social organisation that advocates the vesting of the ownership and control of the means of production, or capital, land etc, in the community as a whole.

2. Procedure or practice in accordance with this theory.

3. (In Marxist theory) The stage following capitalism in the transition of a society to communism, characterised by the imperfect implementation of collectivist principles.

Socialism is a social theory; it theorises that a collective cooperation of citizens will make all governmental institutions public.

Communism is a branch of *socialism*. It's similar in that it's still founded on the idea of collective cooperation, but differs in that communists believe that cooperation should be run by a totalitarian government made up of one and *only one* government.

So, although *communism* is a form of *socialism* .... it's definitely the rotten egg of the two.'

By now working up a head of steam, and thirsty for further detail and definitions, and a more profound explanation of the differences, I stumble upon another website, this one called *diffen.com*.

Here I find the following:

'Communism is an extreme form of socialism. Socialism is sometimes used interchangeably with communism but the two philosophies have some stark differences. Most notably, while communism is a political system, socialism is primarily an economic system that can exist in various forms under a wide range of political systems.'

Diffen goes deeper, and some of its illuminating extracts include:

'A communist society is stateless, classless and governed directly by the people. This, however, has never been achieved. In practice, they have been totalitarian in nature, with a central party governing society. (In contrast) socialism can coexist with different political systems.

(Under communism) all people are the same and therefore classes make no sense. The government should own all means of production and land and also everything else. People should work for the government and the collective output should be redistributed equally.

(Under socialism) all individuals should have access to basic articles of consumption and public goods to allow for self-actualisation.

The philosophy behind communism: From each according to his ability, to each according to his needs.

The philosophy behind socialism: From each according to his ability, to each according to his contribution. In socialism, there is an emphasis on profit being distributed among society or workforce to complement individual wages/salaries.

On economic systems: (In communism) the means of production are held in common, negating the concept of ownership in capital goods. Production is organised to provide for human needs directly without any use for money. Communism is predicated upon a condition of material abundance.

(In socialism) the means of production are owned by public enterprises or cooperatives, and individuals are compensated based on the principle of individual contribution.'

And further on the *diffen* site:

'Theoretically in communism there is no state control, whereas in socialism there is usage of a government.'

In a section called 'Disadvantages', *diffen* says that:

'historically, communism has always fallen into single-party control over society. This can be due to its basic structure of consolidating all the power and resources, but then they are never relinquished to the people.' And on socialism, that: 'socialism has hardly ever been successfully demonstrated, and never on a large scale. Human nature tends away from egalitarian sharing and toward private ownership. This foible will never change.'

Quite apart from getting me off the hook for my less-than-concise use of the two terms, the sense of much of the above is of two systems, one intended to progressively morph into the other, and neither of which in reality succeeded in adhering to its stated aims or definitions in the Eastern Europe of the Cold War. Nor, arguably, anywhere else, for that matter.

ACKNOWLEDGEMENTS

A book is rarely, I suspect, the work of one person, and mine is no exception.

A noble band of family members and acquaintances from my past and present have been instrumental in providing me with facts long forgotten, nuggets of information, old photos, brochures, creative genius and feedback on early drafts of the book, and I sincerely hope I have successfully remembered them all in the following roll of honour:

Marie Broumova
Jenni Brown
Almut Bues
Laura Caldwell
Mike Caldwell
Scott Caldwell
Brigitte Herdin
Barrie Mon Lloyd
Peter Schroers
Paul Taylor
Mihai Voicu
Ian Williamson

To my wife Moya, a special word of thanks for enduring my own, frequent, self-imposed lockdown during lockdown.

To my publisher, Sarah Houldcroft at Goldcrest Books: thank you for all your guidance and expertise during my maiden voyage into a new world.

For those interested in accessing a far more comprehensive account of Gorbachev's life than that detailed in my own brief summaries, I would thoroughly recommend William Taubman's excellent *Gorbachev: His Life and Times*. It is compelling reading from start to finish, and I drew on some of Taubman's factual content in outlining some of the main events in the great man's life.

ABOUT THE AUTHOR

A long time ago, Phil Caldwell graduated from Leeds University with a Modern Languages degree and – the day after getting his results – embarked on a career in the travel industry, a career which continues to this day.

He combines his love of travel with a passion for sport and the outdoors, being both a keen runner and hillwalker.

His travels have taken him to all four corners of the globe, but he is happiest on the hills and beaches of Northumberland, in the mountains and valleys of the Lake District and Austria, or savouring the local fare in Prague, Vienna and Budapest, three places that came to play such a pivotal role in his life.

Printed in Great Britain
by Amazon